Alfred Thompson Denning was born on January 23, 1899. He was educated at Andover Grammar School and Magdalen College, Oxford. A brilliant student, Eldon Scholar and Prize Student of the Inns of Court, he was called to the Bar in 1923 and became a KC fifteen years later. In 1944 he was knighted and appointed a Judge of the High Court of Justice. He became a Lord Justice of Appeal and a Privy Councillor in 1948. Created a Life Peer in 1957, he took the title Baron Denning of Whitchurch. The same year he was also appointed a Lord of Appeal in Ordinary. Lord Denning has been Master of the Rolls since 1962.

'One of the great judges of modern times . . . gives an evocative account of his own life' – SUNDAY TELEGRAPH

'It would be an error of classification for *The Family Story* to be stacked among the law books . . . It is a simple but moving account of the writer's family and experiences' – SUNDAY TIMES

'Lord Denning is a true hero of our time . . . Among his many gifts is his capacity to tell a tale' – NEW SOCIETY

'We spend our years as a tale that is told.'

Psalm 90:9

Authorised Version (King James)

'This story shall the good man teach his son; . . . We few, we happy few, we band of brothers.'

Shakespeare, *Henry V*, Act IV, scene 3

The Rt Hon
LORD DENNING
Master of the Rolls

The Family Story

Hamlyn Paperbacks

THE FAMILY STORY
ISBN 0 600 20592 4

First published in Great Britain in 1981
by Butterworth& Co (Publishers) Ltd
Hamlyn Paperbacks edition 1982
Copyright © 1981 by The Rt Hon Lord Denning MR

Hamlyn Paperbacks are published by
The Hamlyn Publishing Group Ltd,
Astronaut House,
Feltham,
Middlesex, England

Printed and bound in Great Britain by
Cox & Wyman Ltd, Reading

Contents

Preface

Some time ago I promised myself to try and write the Family Story. Now I have done it. And I offer it for you to read. It is 'a tale that is told' by me.

I start of course with our parents. They made us what we are. Often I am asked: 'What were they like? Your father and mother, I mean. To have brought up such a family. One a General, another an Admiral, and you a Judge. What were they like?' To which I say: 'You forget. We were five brothers. Two were lost in the First World War. They were the best of us'. So I tell now of each of the five brothers. I tell of what they did in the two World Wars. I let each speak for himself – so far as I can – by giving extracts from letters or writings. I also tell of myself – far too much about myself – but only because there is more to tell: and because students ask me all sorts of questions about myself: 'What made you go in for law?' 'Why didn't you go in for politics?' And so forth. They seem to want to know about me.

In telling the story I have drawn upon Shakespeare:[1]

> All the world's a stage,
> And all the men and women merely players:
> They have their exits and their entrances;
> And one man in his time plays many parts,
> His acts being seven ages.

In the telling I find that it means weaving a kind of tapestry. So many things go to the making of the story – go to the making of a family.

Descent by blood counts a good deal. Heredity it is called. 'Saxon, Norman and Dane are we' as Tennyson sang. All come together in us. From the Saxon strain we have our regard for fair dealing. From the Viking, the hardihood to withstand the storm. From the Norman, the capacity to lead. All these strains

1 *As You Like It*, Act II, sc. 7.

combine to produce – as they have for the last 900 years – our native English race.

Surroundings play their part. In a countryside of beauty – with fields, hills, rivers and mills – going back for hundreds of years. In a town where everyone knows everyone else and no one will tolerate wrong-doing. In a large family – with its internal stresses and strains – but with a united front against all else.

Education too. School – for three of us an Elizabethan grammar school. What could you have better? University (only for me) – Oxford – spoken of lovingly as the 'home of lost causes'. The teachers who taught us. All go to the making of us.

Then as you start out in the world. The people you meet – their talk – their standards – have their impact. Especially when you are young. They influence you. And you them.

Religion – perhaps the chiefest influence of all. Not talked of much. Yet very present in our family. Faith in God handed down from generation to generation.

In weaving the tapestry I have used many colours. I have drawn many pictures. To keep your interest. I make occasional references to history, even though I am no historian. I quote from literature. So often that it is almost an anthology. I cite from law cases. Because truth is stranger than fiction. Debates in the Lords. They come in as well. I make passing allusions to persons. None, I hope, disparaging but if so, quite unintentional. I tell of peace and of war. I tell of failure and success. I tell of right-doing and wrong-doing. I tell it from a lifetime which spans the greater part of the 20th Century. I tell it for you and those who come after you – in case they should wish to know how we carried on – in our time.

Denning.

January, 1981

The Family

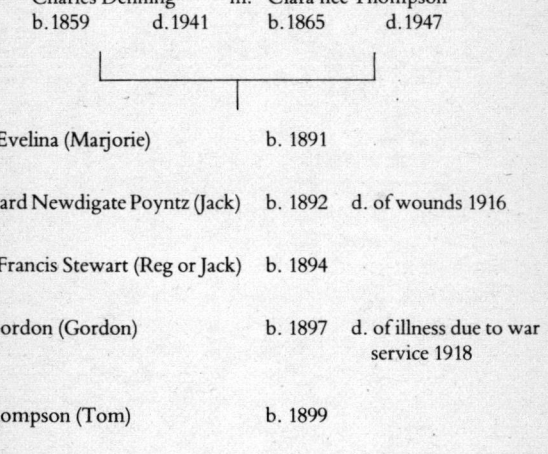

Charles Denning   m.   Clara née Thompson
b. 1859   d. 1941   b. 1865   d. 1947

Marjorie Evelina (Marjorie)   b. 1891

John Edward Newdigate Poyntz (Jack)   b. 1892   d. of wounds 1916

Reginald Francis Stewart (Reg or Jack)   b. 1894

Charles Gordon (Gordon)   b. 1897   d. of illness due to war
                                          service 1918

Alfred Thompson (Tom)   b. 1899

Norman Egbert (Norman or Ned)   b. 1904   d. 1979

Book One

Before the Wars

Section One

The Start

1 The background

Introduction

In this part I tell the story of our forefathers – so far as they are known. When you are young, you are not much interested in them. You are much more interested in yourself. But when you are old you want to know more about them. Many of my friends fill in their retirement by searching for their ancestors.

In some families this is unnecessary. They have records going back for years. They have their family trees with countless branches. They take great pride in them. Other families wish to do likewise. They employ genealogists. They scan the parish registers. They go through the wills. They look into holes and corners. They come up against a bastard. That brings them to a full-stop. Family trees only take root in a marriage bed. But when you do enough to become famous or notorious or well-known, everyone becomes interested in you. 'What strange mixture of blood produced him or her?' Take the Prime Minister, Margaret Thatcher. She is a grocer's daughter. Or even me. I am a draper's son. Whence came I?

1 The early story

i *The Danes*

The early story has proved difficult to trace. Some of it is lost. Other of it has been handed down by word of mouth. Father tells his son. Mother her daughter.

The first beginnings are myth – derived only from names. But they are worth telling – if only to remind you of a few pages of our island history – with a little law thrown in.

The very name Denning recalls the Danish invasions of the 9th century. DENNING means DANE-ING. 'Ing' means 'son of'.

So 'Denning' is just 'the son of the Dane'. The end syllable –
'ing' – shows it. It is what scholars call a patronymic. The
Shorter Oxford Dictionary tells us that 'the English patronymic
suffix, corresponding to the Danish *son*, is *ing*'.

Beyond doubt the race started in Somerset. Although the
Dennings are not a numerous race, there were and are far more
in Somerset than elsewhere. Go back then to the 9th century.
Somerset was peopled by the Saxons – the West Saxons. They
fed their animals. They cultivated their crops. Their peace was
broken by the invaders from the north lands. The Danish pirates
came in their long-boats. They landed in south Devon and
pushed their way inland as far as Somerset. Some of the Danes
settled and stayed. One of them took to himself a Saxon girl.
They had a son. The neighbours called him Dane-ing – the son
of the Dane. The mingling of Danish with Saxon produced
good progeny. The Danes were, of course, a branch of the
Vikings – warriors and seafarers. This is how G. M. Trevelyan
praised the combination:[1]

For the Vikings were of a stock kindred to the Saxon, but even more full of
energy, hardihood and independence of character, and with no less aptitude
for poetry and learning…. Had it not been for the Scandinavian blood infused
into our race by the catastrophes of the ninth century, less would have been
heard in days to come of British maritime and commercial enterprise.

Trevelyan tells us too of the influence of the Danes on the law,
from which we have inherited something:[1]

Law, like many other good things, received a stimulus from the coming of
the Danes. The very word 'law' is Danish, and has survived its rivals, the
Anglo-Saxon word 'doom' and the Latin word 'lex'. The Scandinavians,
when not on the Viking war-path, were a litigious people and loved to gather
in the 'thing'[2] to hear legal argument.

Perhaps that is why I like to hear legal argument now – before
coming to a decision – instead of having it all set down in
writing.

ii *The Saxons*

It is at this point of our story – derived from names – that I
come upon Alfred, called afterwards, the Great. I was named
after him. My first name is Alfred. My second is Thompson (my
mother's maiden name) from which I have always been called

1 *History of England.*
2 In Scandinavian countries, a public meeting or assembly; a court of law.

Tom. I was born in 1899, just one thousand years after King Alfred's death. He was being remembered here in Wessex. A fine statue was set up to his memory in Winchester. My father and mother decided that I should be christened 'Alfred'. Our connection with him is not proved. But he took shelter in Somerset where the Dennings were. I like to think that there the son of the Dane may have married into the family of Alfred the Great. It is from Somerset that we have our childhood story about the cakes. Alfred promised the housewife that he would turn the cakes: but, deep in thought, he forgot to do so. Even when they burnt, he did not smell them. They burnt to cinders. She scolded him. I have been guilty of like indiscretion myself – and have been likewise scolded – but it is no passport to greatness.

But, leaving fable on one side, Alfred was the first of our law-givers. He drew up a code saying: 'Those laws which seemed to be rightest, those I have gathered, and rejected the rest'. That is a point of view which appeals to me. He was also the first of our writers of English prose. He turned the Christian teachings of the Venerable Bede from Latin into English – so that they could be understood of the people; an example I have always followed – so to express myself as to be understood by ordinary folk. J. R. Green [1] tells us that, when nearing his end, Alfred wrote:

So long as I have lived, I have striven to live worthily. I long to leave to the men that come after a remembrance of me in good works.

Can I, his namesake, say the same?

iii *The Normans*

The next invasion was the Normans. 1066 and all that. The Normans were a remarkable race. Only a few thousands came over here. Yet they stamped an impress on England, on its law, its language and its people, which can never be rubbed out. Hilaire Belloc describes them as:[2]

Vivacious, and splendidly brave....

We know that they were a flash. They were not formed or definable at all before the year 1000; by the year 1200 they were gone. Some odd transitory phenomenon of cross-breeding, a very lucky freak in the history of the European family, produced the only body of men who all were lords and who in their collective action showed continually nothing but genius.

1 *A Short History of the English People.*
2 The Normans (*Hills and the Sea : Ely*).

They introduced the feudal system of tenure. They gave form to trial by jury. Their Norman-French was used in the Courts. Legal concepts were expressed in it. The Norman barons insisted on Magna Carta – with one Englishman, William Hardell, the Mayor of London.

From the Normans our family is descended by direct line through the noble family of Poyntz. Our branch is linked with another Norman family, Newdigate. Every eldest son for many generations has been christened 'Newdigate Poyntz' Denning. William the Conqueror gave the Poyntz family manors and lands. He made them tenants-in-chief of land in Gloucestershire under the feudal system. I always like the picture which Rudyard Kipling draws in *A School History of England* for which he got the material from a history don who was teaching at Magdalen when I went up there in 1919 and who was highly regarded by us all – C. R. L. Fletcher:

'My son', said the Norman Baron, 'I am dying, and you will be heir
To all the broad acres in England that William gave me for my share
When we conquered the Saxon at Hastings, and a nice little handful it is.
But before you go over to rule it I want you to understand this:–
The Saxon is not like us Normans. His manners are not so polite,
But he never means anything serious till he talks about justice and right;
When he stands like an ox in the furrow with his sullen set eyes on your own,
And grumbles, "This isn't fair dealing", my son, leave the Saxon alone'.

We have learned the lesson. In our time, at any rate, we, the Judges, have done all we can to ensure fair dealing. The rapid development of our system of administrative law has been based on the 'duty to act fairly'. If any tribunal or body has not given a person a 'fair deal', the Judges will set it aside.

iv *The Civil War*

It was the Newdigate Poyntz branch which was outstanding. In the Civil War of 1642–1646 the sons took opposite sides. Our direct ancestor, Sir Sydenham Poyntz, was for Parliament. His brother, Newdigate, was for the King. Newdigate was killed early on in the fighting at Gainsborough. But Sydenham became one of Cromwell's most famous generals. He held the most unusual of all military ranks – Colonel-General Poyntz. He commanded the Parliamentary forces at the Battle of Rowton Heath near Chester and defeated the forces of the King. 800 killed or wounded. 1500 taken prisoner. After the Civil War he went to the West Indies. He took his first wife Elizabeth and their children with him. He established himself at St. Kitts. He became Governor of Antigua. He retired to Virginia and died there. It is very probable that he was there with the first George Washington.

v *The elopement*

It was about 1720 that Sir Sydenham's granddaughter eloped with our great-grandfather's grandfather. That was the joinder of the Dennings with the Newdigate Poyntz branch. There was a dance in the great house. The Newdigate Poyntz daughter slipped out in her dance frock – with the lights shining into the night – and rode off with the Denning on his horse. Our great-grandfather – his name was Thomas Newdigate Poyntz Denning – told his children the story. It has come down in the family these nigh 300 years. I like to picture it in the words of Sir Walter Scott:[1]

> One touch to her hand, and one word in her ear,
> When they reached the hall-door, and the charger stood near;
> So light to the croup the fair lady he swung,
> So light to the saddle before her he sprung!
> 'She is won! we are gone, over bank, bush and scaur;
> They'll have fleet steeds that follow', quoth young Lochinvar
> > *(alias Denning)*
> So daring in love, and so dauntless in war
> Have ye e'er heard of gallant like young Lochinvar?

The union of the eloping couple is evidenced by the eldest son of each generation ever since being baptised 'Newdigate Poyntz' Denning. The Poyntz Dennings had their coat of arms enrolled in the College of Arms in 1806. The Poyntz is a simple shield with bands of gold and red. In heraldic terms *or* and *gules*. The Denning is the heads of three lions. These are combined into one coat.

vi *The estates are lost in Chancery*

What happened to the family estates? That question has been asked from generation to generation. One thing is clear. They got into Chancery. Our great-grandfather was left an orphan in 1807 when his father died. He was then only nine years old. His affairs were managed by the Court of Chancery under the guardianship of two uncles. In the end our great-grandfather succeeded to nothing – except the mind and character of his

1 *Marmion.*

9

forefathers. The estates suffered the same fate as those so vividly described by Charles Dickens in *Bleak House*:

This is the Court of Chancery; which has its decaying houses and its blighted lands in every shire; which has its worn-out lunatic in every madhouse, and its dead in every churchyard; which has its ruined suitor, with his slipshod heels and threadbare dress, borrowing and begging through the round of every man's acquaintance; which gives to monied might, the means abundantly of wearying out the right; which so exhausts finances, patience, courage, hope; so overthrows the brain and breaks the heart; that there is not an honorable man among its practitioners who would not give – who does not often give – the warning, 'Suffer any wrong that can be done you, rather than come here!'.

At the end the family asked the final question as put by Dickens:

'Excuse me, our time presses. Do I understand that the whole estate is found to have been absorbed in costs?'
'I believe so'.
'This will break Richard's heart'.

Richard was the name of the father of our great-grandfather.

Some branches of the Poyntz Dennings did well. One of them, Stephen, was a painter of miniatures. You can see in the Dulwich Art Gallery a delightful miniature of Queen Victoria when she was three years old. Another, William Denning of Bristol, was an astronomer and was awarded a Gold Medal for his discoveries.

vii *As poor as church mice*

But our branch had no money. As soon as the story becomes authenticated, they were as poor as church mice or, shall I say, as poor as the church organist – for that is what they were.

2 The authentic story

Introduction

Now I turn to facts which are authentic. They can be proved – from the records of births, deaths and marriages, from the census returns, and from our own knowledge. None of our forefathers kept a diary. At least none is extant. So details are lacking.

i *Great-grandfather plays the organ*

Our great-grandfather was born in 1798 at or near Frome in Somerset. When he was only a few weeks old, his father and mother took him up the forty miles to Dursley in Gloucestershire. We do not know why. There he was christened in the parish church. They named him – most exceptionally for those days – with three first names. Usually children were baptised with only one first name. This baby they named Thomas Newdigate Poyntz Denning.

Great-grandfather grew up in Dursley and married there in 1820. He was an organist and teacher of music and is so described in the census returns of 1851 and 1861. He had three sons and two daughters.

Our grandfather was the third son, William Denning. He moved to Leckhampton near Cheltenham and made his home there.

ii *Grandfather teaches music*

William Denning, our grandfather. We have a Victorian photograph of him. A tall, spare man – dressed in a surplice – ready to go to church. Like his father, he was an organist. He played in the church in Cheltenham. He taught the girls music at the Ladies' College, recently started by Miss Beale, of whom you will know the pupils' rhyme:

> Miss Buss and Miss Beale
> Cupid's dart do not feel
> How different from us
> Miss Beale and Miss Buss

He and his wife Anne – her maiden name was Browning – had the usual large family of the Victorians. Three sons and four daughters – Charles our father and our uncles and aunts – devoted one to another. A jolly happy family. Well-read and well-spoken – with a Gloucestershire accent.

iii *Father reads and sings*

Father especially was well-read. He could quote poetry and prose from authors, known and unknown, much to our delight. Without any recourse to such modern aids as the *Oxford Dictionary of Quotations*. We were astonished that he knew so much – Shakespeare, Byron, Scott, Wordsworth – he had them all at his command. But most prized of all was an early edition of John Bunyan's *Pilgrim's Progress*. We have it still. Published in 1824. Tattered with use. Well printed with etchings. We pored over the picture of Apollyon barring the way to Christian:

Then Apollyon straddled quite over the whole breadth of the way, and said, 'I am void of fear in this matter. Prepare thyself to die; for I swear by my infernal den that thou shalt go no further: here will I spill thy soul'.

And with that he threw a flaming dart at his breast; but Christian had a shield in his hand, with which he caught it, and so prevented the danger of that.

The etching shows the hideous Apollyon with his darts: and the bold Christian with his shield and his sword. Beneath is that threat, 'Here will I spill thy soul'.

Not only literature. But music too was our father's delight. He had a good bass voice: and never made a false note. He sang at our parties and at home. He sang for us those old Victorian favourites: 'There is a tavern in the town' and 'Little brown jug, how I love 'ee'.

iv *He is not a very good poet*

He liked to think of himself as a poet. He often tried his hand. He sent his poems to the *Andover Advertiser*. It published them. We have the copies now. One I remember was in gold lettering on a blue background – composed for the occasion of Queen Victoria's Golden Jubilee. But the one which touches me most is the poem he wrote 100 years ago. It was in 1880 when he was 21. It was set to music by a friend and was published as a piece of sheet music. He used his mother's surname as a nom-de-plume – C. Browning. It moves me greatly because it was written eight years before his marriage to our mother: and 36 years before the death of their son. It is almost as though he saw into the future all those years. It describes their own sorrow when their son Jack was killed in 1916 – at the age of 23. These are the words:

THEIR DEAD SOLDIER
Pathetic Song

There's none can comfort mother,
Now that her boy is dead.
Her hair has grown the whiter,
Since came the tidings dread;
But through the tear of sorrow,
She'll give a look of pride,
If you say how in battle
He like a soldier died.

And father feels it sorely,
Although he seldom speaks,

And silent in his sorrow
Pity from none he seeks;
But he looks up the prouder,
When folks talk of his son,
And say how nobly daring,
A Hero's death he won.

v *He is not a man of business*

So you see father was a dreamer, a singer and a poet, not a very good poet, but deep with feeling. Sensitive, good, kind and generous. Yet he was a draper in our little town of Whitchurch in Hampshire. He was not in the least suited for it. Not a man of business. Not hard enough. But he was, I think, happy in it. Because he knew and liked all his customers – and they knew and liked him. Nay – not customers – but friends. He shared their joys and their sorrows, their work and their play. Our Dolly, who still works for us, is now 84. She is still very active, coming each day – walking a mile – to help us. She remembers as a child coming with her mother to buy their Easter bonnets – made of straw and trimmed with flowers, daisies or buttercups – at 6½d each; and coming at Michaelmas to buy the family's shoes for the winter. Mother always brought in a tray with biscuits and wine. No wonder they all loved father – and mother.

vi *The Sheriff's trumpeter*

Mother came of Lincolnshire stock. Her grandfather was a sailor. Her father, John Thomas Thompson – our grandfather – lived in the Bail Gate at Lincoln itself, nearby the great cathedral. Its triple towers top the hill and command the wide levels for miles and miles. As a lad, he joined the Militia. He learned to play the bugle. He became a bandsman. He put his skill to good use afterwards. He used to blow the Sheriff's trumpet when the Judge of Assize came to Lincoln. He started work as a coal porter. He had a good head. He worked hard. He saved money. A strict moralist. He became a coal merchant in a good way of business. Very respected. He became a churchwarden. Six daughters and one son. He had them all well educated and brought up. Our mother was Clara, the eldest. She was a schoolteacher – each day going down and up 'Steep Hill'. It is steep indeed. You can only do it on foot. Then she went on a visit to friends at Whitchurch. It was the turning point of her life.

13

It led to her meeting our father – to her marriage – and to us, the outcome of it.

vii *'The law is a ass'*

How did this meeting come about? Indirectly, from the work-house system. In the middle of Whitchurch there was an old workhouse – dirty and insanitary – very much like that portrayed by Charles Dickens when Oliver Twist asked for more: and where the beadle Mr. Bumble made his celebrated comment on the law of coercion:

'The law supposes that your wife acts under your direction'.

'If the law supposes that', said Mr. Bumble, squeezing his hat emphatically in both hands, 'the law is a ass – a idiot. If that's the eye of the law, the law's a bachelor; and the worst I wish the law is, that his eye may be opened by experience – by experience'.

I may say that I agree with Mr. Bumble. In the judicial words of the junior in the Court of Appeal, 'I entirely agree and there is nothing I can usefully add'.

viii *The workhouse*

Now under the reforms of the Poor Law that old workhouse was replaced by a new building in a good situation just outside the town. The new workhouse master came from Lincoln. He and his wife had good accommodation and were highly esteemed. They were close friends of our grandfather and grandmother. Our mother, as a girl of 21, came to visit them. They had a party. Our father was invited to it. Often I have thought that the lives of all of us start from chance meetings. Shakespeare knew it as well as anyone:[1]

> Trip no further, pretty sweeting;
> Journeys end in lovers meeting
> Every wise man's son doth know.

Talking of workhouses, it recalls for me the plight of the poor and aged when I was a boy. The 'tramps' used to tramp the roads from one workhouse to another. A man in tatters would stop at a cottage and hold out a tin mug. All he asked for was 'hot water'. To ask for more was a criminal offence. It was begging – contrary to the Vagrancy Act. The goodnatured housewife took the mug – covertly put in tea and sugar – added a piece of her home-made cake. He went on his way to the next workhouse.

1 *Twelfth Night*, Act II, sc. 3.

ix *The wedding*

To return to father and mother. They were married at Lincoln on 17 October 1888. Father was 29. Mother 23. We have the wedding photos. Typical of the well-to-do Victorian family of the utmost respectability. The ladies in their high white hats and flowing white dresses. The men in their morning coats with white ties and waistcoats. Father's hair getting a little thin – even at age 29. It runs in the family. When I first married at 32, my hair was getting thin.

Grandfather Thompson at Lincoln did so well that he was able to provide for all his children. He provided for our mother by buying for her and father two old houses in Newbury Street (previously called Bere Hill Street) in Whitchurch. One of the houses was a chemist's shop. It had been there well over 100 years. The other was our father's shop.

x *Mother is the driving force*

Mother was a different temperament from father. She got it from her father. Like him, she was handsome with fine features. Very intelligent. Very hard-working. Determined to succeed in whatever she undertook. She was the driving force. Ambitious for her children. She would see that we worked to get on – as we did. Not sentimental. Not artistic. She was a foil to our father's fondness for music and poetry.

That is, I think, the explanation of the outcome. Each was the counterpart of the other. Each supplied what the other lacked. For over 52 years they were together till father died in 1941. But throughout all those years, not a thought, not a glance – for anyone else on either side. Trust and loyalty such as theirs – giving the children unshaken security – is what made us what we are. As the years passed, I often thought of their marriage surviving the passage of time as in Shakespeare's sonnet:

> Love's not Time's fool, though rosy lips and cheeks
> Within his bending sickle's compass come;
> Love alters not with his brief hours and weeks,
> But bears it out even to the edge of doom.
>   If this be error, and upon me prov'd,
>   I never writ, nor no man ever lov'd.

2 At home

Introduction

In this part I turn from our ancestry: and to the surroundings in which we were brought up. To our house – as children – in which we lived; the neighbours all about us; and what came after. There were six of us children. Marjorie was the eldest. Then came five boys – Jack, Reg, Gordon, myself (Tom) and Norman.

1 Our house

i *300 years old*

Our house was 300 or 400 years old – with stout oak beams, low ceilings, and narrow stairs, with cellar below and attics in the roof. It was just opposite our inn, the White Hart Hotel, which goes back to Tudor times. On 26 May 1863 Charles Kingsley, historian, man of letters and divine, while staying there wrote a letter – 'having been driven off the river by rain'. He described the chemist's shop next door to ours and identical with it:

Opposite me, again, across a street, rather wider than the room, is a Chemist shop, which is also a Post Office. The two stories are rather lower than one of an average London house, so that we will hope the folks inside are not tall. But there is a grand peaked roof, with dormers, in which, I suppose, servants are stuffed away; but I hold my nose at the thought. In the shop windows are a dozen bottles – some near a hundred years old, with drugs of ditto age. One hopes they are all labelled right; the only one I can answer for is of poppy heads; so I suppose toothaches are known here. There are two plaster of Paris horses, indicating that horseballs may be had within; a case of scents. In front, instead of pavement are great flints, and a row of posts, which prevent the carriages of Whitchurch from rushing into the house windows, and the drunken men thereof from losing their way home.

ii Unfit for human habitation

Although it looked attractive, our house would have been con-
demned today as totally unfit for human habitation. It had no
indoor sanitation. The WC – or, as people call it nowadays, the
toilet – was a deep pit covered by a seat. At the end of the garden
path – 25 yards from the house. No running water to flush it. It
stank in hot weather. Flies swarmed there. The night–cart came
every three or four weeks to clear it out. It was hidden from sight
by a corrugated iron fence. Next to the WC was the manure
dump and the rubbish heap. You would think it would harbour
diseases of all kinds. Yet we all kept in good health – except for
childhood complaints.

No water from the mains. No water at all except that which
we pumped up from a well just outside the back door beside the
drain. To fill the iron kettle to put on the kitchen range – to fill
the jugs with water to drink or to wash in – or to clean the
floors.

No electric light. No gas except in two of the downstairs
rooms a few flickering gas mantles which continually gave out.
A paraffin oil lamp as a stand-by. Only candles to take us up the
stairs and into bed.

No daylight in the kitchen. No light got into it at all except
through a glass panel in the door – or when the door was left
open. Mother had to cook the meals for us children in that dark
kitchen. It wore her out. Bath night was on Fridays. In a small
zinc bath. In front of the kitchen range.

No livingroom except a makeshift affair, a long narrow slit of
a room, with no window – only a skylight in the roof and a glass
door at the end. We boys sat on a long bench screwed on to the
wall – for our meals – and our homework. Mother sat there
every afternoon making up the books of the business.

iii Father goes on his 'journeys'

The front part of the house was the shop. One side was the
men's. The other was the ladies', where there was a girl
assistant. Father was in the shop in the morning, serving the few
customers, but in the afternoon he went on his 'journeys'. He
went with his horse and trap filled with parcels – for his
customers in the villages. The stable was at the end of the
garden, just beyond the WC. It was built of stout oak. It had two
stalls and a hay-loft above. It housed Sam, the big white cob, and

Queenie, the little brown mare. We bedded them down with straw at night. We cleaned out the dung in the morning. We took them to be shod. We harnessed them up into the trap. We got the lamps ready with the candles – on springs to keep them moving up. We boys went with father whenever we could. Off we would go with Sparkle, the rough-haired terrier, running beside the wheels. Father would go to different villages and hamlets every day – three, five or eight miles away – to call on the cottagers, and supply them with their needs. They were not able to come into the town. None of them had any transport except for 'Shanks's pony'. They were supposed to pay by instalments regularly when he called. Some were good. Others were not. He never pressed them for payment. He was too kind. No holidays except that the shop was closed on Wednesday afternoon and Sunday. On Sunday father put on his best clothes. He went to church and sang in the choir – for 50 years.

iv Gold sovereigns in the till

None of the complications of modern business. No telephone. No typewriter. No adding machine. No paper money. Only coins. 'Coppers' – pennies, halfpennies and farthings. 'Silver' – threepenny bits, sixpences, shillings, florins, half-crowns, and some crowns. 'Gold' – sovereigns and half-sovereigns. But not many of those in our till. (The father of our good Dolly was a head carter. His wages were 15 shillings a week – and he had to keep a wife and six children on it. He had also his Michaelmas money [£5].)

No motor-cars. Only horses and the railway. No wonder that we hardly ever went out of Whitchurch – except by train to school at Andover or with father on his 'journeys'. I did not go to London until I was 18 in the Army.

v Father goes to the Assizes

I doubt if father ever went to London in his life – except once or twice perhaps. He did go to Winchester – when he was summoned to serve on a jury – at the Assizes. He went every day for a week – at his own cost – which he could ill afford. He was much impressed by the Red Judge – 'Lord John Lawrence' – but I have heard since that he was nothing of a lawyer. You do not need to be a good lawyer to be a good judge. Father brought us back some chocolates covered with gold paper – to look like sovereigns. So do little things stick in children's minds.

vi '*I remember, I remember*'

So you see I can say with Thomas Hood:

> I remember, I remember
> The house where I was born,
> The little window where the sun
> Came peeping in at morn;
> He never came a wink too soon
> Nor brought too long a day.

I would not go on afterwards to be full of heaviness as Thomas Hood was. I would rather take joy in the happy memories that I recall from the time when I was a boy even until today.

2 Our neighbours

i *What is a mandamus?*

Our little community of Whitchurch was self-contained. Our friends were the tradesmen of the town. We children were brought up with their children. There was no need for anyone to go outside the town for anything.

Opposite us was John Roe, the brewer – with his brewery alongside his house. The men of Whitchurch drank much beer. There were 19 public-houses in the town. He was a big, fat man. Vigorously against the temperance movement. It was he who opposed the Salvation Army when they determined to play their band in the Square. There was a riot. Three of the Salvationists were sent to prison – and became the heroes of the place. The High Court issued a mandamus. My father asked John Roe what was a mandamus. 'A gurt big thing', he said, 'You couldn't get 'un through that door'. Now we use a mandamus often to command public officers to do their duty.

ii '*At first the infant*'

John Roe's wife was mother's greatest friend. When I was born – two months earlier than expected – I nearly died. Mrs. Roe hurried across the road, wrapped me in blankets, gave me brandy – and I lived. She knew what a hard time mother was having with the others all so young. She said as she wrapped me up, 'That's one we could have done without.' At any rate I had made the first of the seven ages of man:

> At first the infant,
> Mewling and puking in the nurse's arms.

19

I was so tiny and puny that I could be put in a pint pot. They called me Tom Thumb. Mother looked on me as the weakest – needing special care. Each morning, on my going off to school, she insisted that I had cod liver oil – raw – in an egg-cup of milk to take away the taste. When she wanted me to have a boiled egg, I exclaimed dramatically: 'Although I do not like it, I will eat it'. The others made fun of me for it – for years afterwards. They labelled me as 'Faddy' – not knowing that it was slang for fastidious. My wife tells me I am still fastidious – about my food. I dispute it. I just like simple food.

iii *A builder of character*

Equally great friends were the Geers – Charles Henry Geer, the schoolmaster, his wife, his daughters and one son. They ran a small private school in their own house beside the river. It was regarded as somewhat superior to the elementary school. The tradesmen and farmers sent their children there – paying as much as they could afford. Never more than 20 or 30 children all told. I often wonder how they kept going. My sister and two of my elder brothers, Jack and Reg, had their entire education there. It was quite the reverse of Dotheboys Hall so graphically described by Charles Dickens in *Nicholas Nickleby*. When I read it as a boy I did not appreciate the pun. I thought it was 'Doth' like 'moth'. It is, of course, 'Do-the-boys' – do down the boys! 'Cave' Geer was not Wackford Squeers. He had never taken a degree but he wore a scholar's gown – torn and tatty – to show his learning. The boys called him 'Cave' (pronounced Kay-vee), not knowing what it meant. I now know it is Latin for 'Beware'. But there was nothing in him to beware of – except wrong-going. His prime concern was to build character, and next to teach his pupils to write good English and to speak it. He always saw to their cricket, urging them in the game – as in life – to keep a straight bat. He played the organ, too, in church. His wife, lively and smiling, supported him. She taught music to the girls – and to a few of the boys. She taught me all I knew. I did my five-finger exercises: for we did have a piano at home. We all strummed upon it. I even tried to compose. I had blank sheets of music paper – and filled in the notes. At the age of 10 or 11, I suppose. But I had no ear for music. My elder brothers all sang in the choir in church. But I never did. I was given a try but the Vicar said I wasn't good enough.

iv *Happy families*

Then there were the other tradesmen – with their shops all round the market square. To name them is like the game of 'Happy Families'. Wallace Hutchins, the butcher; Harry Nichols, the baker; Sam Bennett, the grocer; Fred Hunt, the corn merchant; James Todd, the chemist; Fred Weeks, the builder; Llewellyn Lloyd, the miller; Jonathan Dance, the farmer. The professional men lived a little way up the street: Spencer Clarke, the solicitor (who was the Mayor for 50 years); Rustat Hemsted, the doctor; Carpenter Turner, the Vicar. With a great supporting team from all round – from the villages as well as the town – of carters, ploughmen, shepherds, carpenters, bricklayers, mill-workers. All their children went to the elementary school – where my brother Gordon and I went – till we went to the grammar school. We sat at our desks with them. We played with them. We had quarrels with them. A ploughman's son hit my head against a flint wall. I remember it to this day. I shot a little girl with a pea-shooter. She complained to my mother who sent her off, saying. 'Boys will be boys'. When my father had not got a new suit in time for a customer at St. Mary Bourne –four miles away – he drove over specially with a suit of one of us boys to use instead. I had forgotten these incidents but those concerned wrote and told me of them. They illustrate the characters. Father kind and thoughtful, beloved by all. Mother strong and determined, standing no nonsense.

v *'My garden top hat'*

Much above us in the social scale were Spencer Portal and his family. They lived at the top of the hill – Bere Hill – in a big house. His forebears had, as I shall mention later on, started papermaking here 200 years before. Every Sunday morning he walked down to church in his frock-coat and top hat – and read the lessons. Spencer Clarke, the solicitor, went to church too on Sunday mornings. I remember him coming back in a hurry exclaiming, 'I've got on my garden top hat.' He was going back for his best one.

3 After we left home

i *Writing home*

After we left home, each one of us wrote to father and mother every week. Father wrote to each every Sunday. Mother wrote

in the week. They continued with the shop and the journeys –
the pony and trap – all the time until the First World War.

ii *Tragedy*

The war brought tragedy. Blow after blow fell upon father and
mother as I will tell. Jack was killed. Reg was severely wounded.
Gordon was desperately ill. These blows hit so hard that they
could not carry on. They were shattered. No one to help them. I
was in France too. They had to give up the business.

After the war Reg bought a small house for father and mother
– not far from the church – called 'The Hermitage'.

iii *Move to the oldest house*

It is probably the oldest house in the place. It is very pretty. It is
built of oak timbers sloping upwards from ground level to the
roof. 14th Century. With later additions. And gabled roof.
Father and mother lived there – in peace after so much distress –
until father died in 1941 aged 81, and mother in 1947 aged 83.

iv *Marjorie*

Marjorie was fair, with blue eyes like her mother. Attractive and
gay, she made friends everywhere. She married into the Army –
John E. Haynes, affectionately called 'Johnnie'. They had four
daughters. To their regret, no sons. I venture to give his record:
for it is in keeping with the rest of us. At the outbreak of war in
August 1914 he joined the Royal Naval Air Service and was at
Antwerp in the defence of Belgium. On returning to England,
he specialised in mechanical transport. It was in the early days of
the petrol engine. He was in charge of convoys of lorries with
supplies for the troops. After the First World War, he joined the
Indian Army and they were in India for many years. 'Johnnie'
served in five frontier campaigns on the North-West Frontier. In
the Second World War he was in the campaigns in the Middle
East, in North Africa (with the 8th Army) and in Italy. Marjorie
was with him in India and everywhere – except when he was on
the campaigns.

On his retirement they returned to live at Whitchurch – at the
family home – 'The Hermitage'. There they won the respect
and affection of all – just as father and mother had done.

v *Remembrance Sunday*

'Johnnie' prepared the Roll of Honour of the men of Whitchurch who were killed in the two World Wars. He was a church-warden. Remembrance Sunday was his special care. (Armistice Sunday we used to call it – because of Armistice Day, 11 November 1918.) At the service, to this day I read out the names of the Fallen. Then we have the hymn which 'Johnnie' always wanted. Many do not like it. They think it too sentimental. But it always moves the veterans of war when they remember their comrades:

> O valiant hearts, who to your glory came
> Through dust of conflict and through battle flame;
> Tranquil you lie, your knightly virtue proved,
> Your memory hallowed in the Land you loved.

3 The environment

Introduction

Now I turn to what modernists call the 'environment'. All of us are influenced by the place in which we are brought up. The cockney in London is different from the geordie in Newcastle. The farm-hand in Hampshire is different from the textile-hand in Lancashire. Their speech is different. Their accent is different. Their outlook is different. So with us.

1 The country

i *A valley in the downs*

What brought my father to Whitchurch? To work for two ladies who had a small drapery shop in the middle of the town. He did not choose it for its situation. But the discerning know that it is situate in a exceedingly attractive countryside. Set in a valley of the North Hampshire downs – those great chalk hills which store the rain – and whence come the springs of living water, clear as crystal. William Cobbett rode these parts on his *Rural Rides* and was full of their praise:

There are not many finer spots in England; and, if I were to take in a circle of eight or ten miles of semi–diameter, I should say there is not one so fine. Here are hill, dell, water, meadow, woods, corn–fields, downs: and all of them very fine and very beautifully disposed.

ii *The white church is built*

Our Saxon forefathers built their township here – close to the stream, as they always did, so as to have the water at hand and its power to run their mills. There are three mills recorded in the Domesday Book of 1086 – still on the same sites today. They built their church – for they were Christians – and they built it before the year 800 with their own hands, using the chalk dug up from the ground. It showed up white, so they called it 'white-church' – Whitchurch. Still there is a Saxon stone found embedded in the wall – carved curiously showing Our Lord with his right hand raised in blessing and his left holding the Gospels. Our forefathers planted yew-trees in the churchyard – so that animals should not roam over it – for the yew is poisonous. A yew-tree is still there which must be 1000 years old. The picture drawn by Thomas Gray is appropriate for the churchyard where father and mother are buried:[1]

> Beneath those rugged elms, that yew-tree's shade,
> Where heaves the turf in many a mouldering heap,
> Each in his narrow cell for ever laid,
> The rude forefathers of the hamlet sleep.
> …
>
> Far from the madding crowd's ignoble strife,
> Their sober wishes never learn'd to stray;
> Along the cool sequester'd vale of life
> They kept the noiseless tenour of their way.

iii *The church bells are cast*

Long since the old chalk church has disappeared in one reconstruction after another, using flint stones which lie in strata in the chalk. In 1868 the Victorian restorers built a fine spire – with oak shingles – pointing high into the sky. But they did keep our Norman pillars – strong and round. They did keep our old tower and our oak stair turret leading to the bells. By tradition the oldest bells were cast in Whitchurch. The moulds were made of clay and cow-dung. The bell metal had a low melting point. The bells were cast nearby the church itself – to save a long carry. They have called the people of Whitchurch to pray – to rejoice and to mourn – to shut down at curfew – over the centuries. The heaviest, the tenor, tolled the knell for the departed. In my boyhood it was still tolled – one for a man, two for a woman, three for a child. We now have the full octave. They bear these dates: the first two were in 1448; the next were in 1611, 1612, 1724 and 1748; and the last two in 1919. I helped get the money for those last two which are in memory of Whitchurch men killed in the First World War.

1 *Elegy in a Country Churchyard.*

25

iv The great earthwork

If you go from the town up the hill to the north, you will soon see the lofty hill which dominates these parts. It is called Beacon Hill. There is a great earthwork encircling the top – a mile round. A fortress indeed. Two deep trenches and two high banks. It must have taken those Iron·Age men months and months to dig – even if there were hundreds of them. As children we used to be taken there for Sunday School treats. We climbed the steep – very steep – side, up the close-cropped turf, to reach the top. When it was clear, you could see Southampton Water 25 miles away – so my father told me – but I never saw it myself. But what struck my boyhood taste was the strong tea in the barn at the bottom of the hill. Strong tea – steeped with sugar – it made me feel sick. Ever since I have always had my tea weak – very weak, with lots of hot water – and no sugar. Our parish magazine of that time contains its own description of the outing:

The children vied with each other as to who could reach the crest of the hill quickest and, once on the top, the game seemed to be to rush down again.... Meanwhile, down at the farm, where tea was to be served, all was consternation because the van with the eatables obstinately refused to appear.... However, at last a prospecting party came along with the news that the cart was in sight....The children fell to with a vigour and enjoyment which did credit to the air of Beacon Hill.

v Sighting the Armada

Why is it called Beacon Hill? Need you ask. There are many beacon hills in England. They are the high hilltops along which the message ran – by fires of light – when the Spanish Armada was sighted, in the days of Queen Elizabeth the First. We flared them once again – in the days of Queen Elizabeth the Second – but this in time of peace – for her Silver Jubilee. All of us in England then recalled that night in 1588 as recounted by Lord Macaulay in his fragment:

> Such night in England ne'er had been, nor e'er again shall be...
> Far on the deep the Spaniard saw, along each southern shire,
> Cape beyond cape, in endless range, those twinkling points of fire... .

Then across Wessex:

> O'er Longleat's towers, o'er Cranbourne's oaks, the fiery herald flew:
> He roused the shepherds of Stonehenge, the rangers of Beaulieu... .

It was the beacon near the Stonehenge downs that passed the message on to our beacon. I suppose that Macaulay used

'Beaulieu' so as to rhyme with 'flew': but we in Hampshire never use the French pronunciation. We say 'Bewlee'. My brother Gordon and I, round about the age of 10, rode on our bicycles — 40 miles each way — to see the ruins of the abbey. We stopped in a glade in the New Forest — we ate the ripe tomatoes mother had given us. Another of the little things that stick in children's minds.

vi *The seven 'barrows'*

The south side of Beacon Hill – the lower slope – filled us boys with awe. There was once a great battle fought there – and many killed. It was long before history began. But it is shown by the seven round 'barrows' which were there. These are big mounds of earth. A 'barrow' is the old English word for a grave-mound. And there is a little hamlet nearby called 'Litchfield'. 'Lich' is the old English word for a corpse. Even now there is many a lychgate – where the corpse was halted. 'Field' is the old English word 'feld' for a piece of ground put to a particular use. So 'Litchfield' is 'the field of the dead'. When I was a boy we went up past these 'barrows' to see a venturesome flier – de Havilland – trying there to see if he could get his machine – a new invention – up into the air. He showed it to us. Back home, we little boys tried alike with paper and card – with no success. There are no longer seven 'barrows' there – but only three. The rest have been cut away – first, years ago, to make a railway, and later for a motorway. Desecration!

2 The town

i *The rotten borough*

To return to Whitchurch. It is a town – repeat *town*. The inhabitants dislike hearing it called a 'village'. That smacks too much of mediaeval 'vill' and of the people as 'villeins'. Since the early Middle Ages (1284), Whitchurch has had the standing of a borough. The land was held for centuries by a very ancient form of tenure called burgage tenure. Being a borough ever since Edward I's day, it had its mayor and burgesses and from 1586 used to send two burgesses to Parliament. It became a 'rotten' or 'pocket' borough – in the pocket of the landowner who nominated the members for Parliament. It remained so right until the Reform Act of 1832 abolished all rotten boroughs. Now it has little or no voice in selecting a Member of Parliament: it is swamped by the new town of Basingstoke. Often I have been asked: Why did you not ever stand for Parliament? I might have done so – in 1945 just as my contemporary Hartley Shawcross did and achieved fame – but I was appointed a Judge in March 1944. So I never turned to politics. I have never been a member of a political party. As a Judge I keep aloof.

ii *The King slept here*

Our old town has played little part in history. Except that we do know that in 1644 King Charles I slept two nights at the Manor House on his way to the second Battle of Newbury. The Manor House is now the Vicarage. The room he slept in is still known as King Charles's room. Another thing of which I tell my many friends in the United States – is that it was Richard Brooke who entertained King Charles at the Manor House in 1644. Robert, a younger brother, emigrated to America on 30 June 1650 – taking with him his family and 28 servants – and also his animals. It must have been a boat-load. He probably chartered a vessel: he settled in Maryland with a 'considerable plantation'. It was about the same time as my ancestor went to Virginia. That accounts for their good stock – of men and animals!

iii *Paper for the Bank of England*

The source of power in Whitchurch was the river which drove the mills. There were mills every half-mile down the river – as there had been ever since the Domesday Book: the town mill where they ground corn; the cloth mill where they made cloth; the fulling mill where they dressed it. A new mill, higher up, built in 1710 as a corn mill, became the paper mill. Henri Portal, a Huguenot, came over from France. He turned Bere Mill over to the making of paper. In 1724 the mill first made bank note paper for the Bank of England. This later came in for the scorn of William Cobbett – that radical economist and socialist. He thought the Bank of England, by issuing paper money, had changed the condition of mankind. He ridiculed our river Test. He described it as

the *river of Whitchurch*, which a man of threescore may jump across dry-shod.... This river, by merely turning a wheel, which wheel sets some rag-tearers and grinders and washers and recompressors in motion, has produced a greater effect on the condition of men, than all the other rivers in the world...

Oh! mighty rivulet of Whitchurch! All our properties, all our laws, all our manners, all our minds, you have changed!

This diatribe was misplaced. Portals' new mill at Overton, three miles away, makes bank note paper for most of the countries of the world.

3 The river

i *Tickling the trout*

The river still runs as smoothly as ever it did. The springs from the chalk feed it all the way – clear and pure. The watercress grows wild in it – but much is cultivated and sent up to London. So pure is the water that I have bathed in it ever since I was a boy. I still do. I swim in it – swallowing mouthfuls – and never come to any harm. I have leaned over the bank and 'tickled' the trout in it when I was very young. I do not fish it now. I like to see the trout lying just below the surface – to watch the river for the fly – sometimes to see the fish jump right out. There is always something to see by our river. The kingfisher darting bright blue – the heron standing dead still waiting to strike – the coots flurrying about – the flotilla of ducklings following their mother – the dabchicks or divedappers diving and coming up again – reminding me of Shakespeare:

> Like a didapper peering through a wave,
> Who, being looked on, ducks as quickly in.

ii *The 'fishing gents'*

The fishing was, and is, as good as can be found anywhere – with the dry fly. The 'fishing gents', as we boys called them, used always to stay at the White Hart Hotel. Each year they gave the Fishermen's Dinner to 'the aged poor of the parish'. It was at Christmas-time. The fare consisted of roast beef and mutton, rabbit pies, and plum pudding. On every occasion 'the Earl of Portsmouth kindly sent thirty rabbits'.

But long before my boyhood – in that same letter of 26 May 1863 already quoted, Charles Kingsley (having come for the May hatch of fly) described his days on the river:

First day: I took seven brace today, none very large, in three hours. Threw almost all in, for I had nought to do with them, which raised me infinitely in the keeper's eyes.

Next day: I have had a splendid day's fishing, and came home through the Park (the finest, I hold, in the south of England).

Oh! dear! I have had such a jolly day, and the lamb chops are so good, and there is such a sponge bath in my room.

iii *Capability Brown*

Notice that the Park was held by Charles Kingsley to be the finest in the south of England. When I was a boy, it was the estate of the Earl of Portsmouth. He used to let us wander in it to our heart's content. It is well wooded with the finest timber. It was laid out by 'Capability Brown' over 200 years ago. He was so called because when he was consulted on the landscaping of an estate, he would say: 'It has capabilities'. Now in these 200 years the young trees he planted have become great in size. They radiate in avenues from a monument in the centre. It is topped with the statue of a Roman soldier. Avenues of oak trees where we picked up the acorns, avenues of chestnut trees where we picked up the conkers, or the sweet chestnuts which we took home to roast. Often have I walked – boy and man – in this fine park. Then there was the cricket field in the Park where our Whitchurch team played against the neighbouring villages. It was a walk of over a mile, but we did not mind that – even at the age of five. There was a 9-hole golf course which the noble earl kept up – and on which he allowed us to play. Whilst I was at Oxford I studied hard in the vacations – so different from the youngsters nowadays – and my only recreation was to stride up to play each day – hitting hard and missing. I was never much good at it then – and I have gradually got worse.

iv *It goes on for ever*

The river is still my delight. I sit in my library within sight of it. I walk down to it. Tennyson's words are so appropriate:[1]

> I wind about, and in and out,
> With here a blossom sailing
> And here and there a lusty trout,
> And here and there a grayling....
>
> And draw them all along, and flow
> To join the brimming river,
> For men may come and men may go,
> But I go on for ever.

1 *The Brook.*

4 Education

Introduction

Some people think that education is all-important. But I would put it in second place. The home is by far more important. A broken home leaves an indelible mark – a dark, dark mark – on the character and temperament of the child. Education is important to equip the child for life – to read, to write and to think – to appreciate values – to give him the skills he needs. So it has a vital place.

1 School

i 'The whining schoolboy'

After the elementary school, the first step up the ladder – of education – for Gordon and me, and later for Norman, was to go to the grammar school (then in New Street) at Andover. It was Elizabethan in very truth. Founded in 1569. It had some free places – but most boys were paid for by their parents. My brother Gordon and I took the entrance examination. We were both awarded free places. But father had to pay for our season tickets on the railway. It was as much as he could afford.

Each morning we set off. Mother had put up our sandwiches. We had them in our satchels with our exercise books. We walked up the steep hill. It was half-a-mile to the station. The station staff were all our friends. We went up into the signalbox with the signalman. We went into the cab of the shunting engine. The driver used to boil his egg in water in his big shovel in the fire-hole. We got into the train. It had one stop – at Hurstbourne – two miles. The next stop was Andover Junction – another five miles. We made our way round the road by the river – dawdling by the stream – through the church-yard – till we reached the school. Always late by a quarter-of-an-hour. We had a good excuse. 'The train was late'. It was unanswerable. We had reached the second of the ages of man:

> And then the whining schoolboy, with his satchel,
> And shining morning face, creeping like snail
> Unwillingly to school.

But we did not whine.

ii *'The first room on the right'*

The school hall was of early date. At one end an old board commemorating the founder, John Hanson. His crest was a pun on his name. A red hand (Han) in a yellow sun (son). It was the school badge. Along the sides of the hall long seats on which successive generations of boys had carved their initials. In the middle a heating stove where we ate our sandwiches at the break. It was a small school. Only about 80 boys and five masters – the Latin master, the French master, the science master, the maths master – and of course the headmaster, R. O. Bishop, the 'old man' as we called him. We were frightened of him. He tormented us. He did not give us enough time to catch the train home. Only seven or eight minutes to go a mile. We ran our little hearts out. But he made us work. He taught us English. He stormed and shouted at us. His house was alongside the school. His room was along a passage. If we did anything wrong, we had to go to his room – 'the first room on the right' – where he inflicted the appropriate punishment. My brother Gordon braved his anger. He told him, 'I'll bet you a quid I did, sir'. In any scrape, Gordon always came to my aid.

iii *'I think I'll be a barrister'*

But I am unfair to the headmaster – as schoolboys often are to their masters. After all, it was his way of keeping discipline. Looking back on it now, we owe much to him. He was a first-class cricketer – a fast bowler – and encouraged us in our games. Only one afternoon a week – soccer in the winter, cricket in the summer and, of course, running in the school sports. Gordon did well. But I never won a single race – except the sack race – and the three-legged race – and they are not much commendation! In the classroom I was better. Every evening we worked at home at our homework. Once I looked up – when I was about 10 – and said to mother, 'I think I'll be a barrister', not knowing in the least what a barrister was. I read books – many books – quickly. I tried my hand at writing poetry – as youngsters do. I have the prizes which we were awarded. Bound in handsome calf and presented by local worthies. One of Gordon's prizes was for Science. It was the Revd. J. G. Wood's *The Brook and its banks* – very suitable for our river. Mine were year after year for English – 'The Great Authors', with descriptions of their lives and extracts from their writings; Macaulay's *Essays and Lays*; Carlyle's *French Revolution*; and Milton's *Poetical Works*. They have been of the greatest value to me. I have read them – and referred to them – a thousand times. Finally there was a book on Dynamics – bound in plain cloth, for it was wartime. I was working for a scholarship in Mathematics.

iv 'Was it rough in the Bay?'

Gordon was 20 months older than me. He was always keen to go to sea. It was in the blood. The only opening for him was in the Merchant Service. He wished to be trained to become a Master Mariner. At the age of 15 he was accepted by one of our oldest merchant fleets, the General Steam Navigation Company. He was appointed to the steamship *Stork*. She used to berth at the wharf just below Tower Bridge. She sailed with cargo to and from Genoa in Italy. 'Was it rough in the Bay of Biscay?' we used to ask. Gordon got a sextant. He brought it proudly home. He learned to navigate. He had started on his way.

v *Trying for Oxbridge*

At the outbreak of war in August 1914, I was still at school. Only 15. Not old enough to join up. So I stayed on. Most of the masters left to go to the war. Their places were taken by women. I wanted to get to the university. I studied hard – by myself – with no help from any teachers. None of them knew enough. I mastered books on Differential Calculus, Dynamics and Statics. I read the classics of English literature. I went to the Castle at Winchester for an examination – to qualify for the University College at Southampton. I did well. I came top in English and in Mathematics. The headmaster advised me to stay on and try for Oxford or Cambridge. I went up and sat their examination when I was 16. Only one college offered me anything. It was

Magdalen College, Oxford. They offered me an exhibition of £30 a year. It was not enough to live on. Father could not help. But I determined to accept it – and manage the best I could. Go without if need be. There were no grants in those days.

2 University

i *May morning*

It was in October 1916 that I first went up to Magdalen. I was 17¾ years of age. I could only stay nine months at the time. I had to join the Army at 18½.

I do not use the Latin, *Alma Mater*. I prefer the English, Fostering Mother. For Magdalen has been the College which has helped me to grow to what I am. It was founded by William of Waynflete over 500 years ago for just such as me – 'a home for poor scholars'. Its beautiful tower was completed in 1509. It was in building during the time that Thomas Wolsey (afterwards Cardinal) was Bursar of the College. Ever since that time, on May morning at break of day the scholars on the Foundation climb to the top – the 200 steps – and sing. At least, they did in my day. I went robed in a white surplice. It is not being done now. The tower is half down – under repair.

ii *The 'snob'*

The President was Sir Herbert Warren. He was decried by some as being a 'snob'. Under his influence, the highest in the land came to the College. The Prince of Wales (afterwards Edward VIII) had rooms in Cloisters. So did the Crown Prince of Japan. So did the sons of the noblest in the land. It became commonplace to be of 'Eton and Magdalen'. But I would refute this disparagement. The President was very good to me. He helped me at every turn. Owing to him my exhibition of £30 a year became a demyship of £80. (A demy is a scholar – a half-fellow.) He got the Goldsmiths' Company of London to grant me an exhibition of £30. So I was able to get through – but I had to watch every penny. I did not smoke or drink. And never have.

iii *A Clerk of Oxenford*

I was as poor and needy as that scholar described by Chaucer:[1]

1 *The Canterbury Tales*, Prologue.

> A Clerk ther was of Oxenford also,
> That un-to logik hadde longe y-go....
> For him was lever have at his beddes heed
> Twenty bokes, clad in blak or reed,
> Of Aristotle and his philosophye,
> Than robes riche, or fithele, or gay sautrye.
> But al be that he was a philosophre,
> Yet hadde he but litel gold in cofre;...
> Of studie took he most cure and most hede.
> Noght o word spak he more than was nede....
> Souninge in moral vertu was his speche,
> And gladly wolde he lerne, and gladly teche.

iv *A pail of cold water*

It was wartime that first year. The College was full of Army officers in training. Only a handful of us undergraduates. Some were medically unfit for service. Some were Rhodes scholars from the USA. One or two youngsters like me – under age – awaiting call-up. My rooms were up a stone staircase in Chaplain's Quad – on the first floor – right alongside the tower, whence chimes vibrated and sounded into the rooms every quarter of an hour. No running water. Each morning an old scout called Betnay ('scouts' are the manservants) came with a big pail of cold water and poured it into a round low hip-bath. I dashed in – and out – got quickly into shorts – ran up the High, along New College Lane, and into the Park – where we had to parade. There we drilled: and got the feel of military discipline – by which the lower ranks are brought into the habit of obedience – obeying commands without question. Tennyson put it in *The Charge of the Light Brigade*:

> Theirs not to make reply
> Theirs not to reason why,
> Theirs but to do and die.

There were others of age 18 with me on parade. A.B.C.D.: A for Armstrong (afterwards Sir Thomas Armstrong, Principal of the Royal Academy of Music); B for Bowra (afterwards Sir Maurice Bowra, great Oxford wit); C (I forget); D for me.

v *A lady makes advances*

In the afternoon, too, we did our military training. A route march over Boar's Hill: or night operation in Wytham Park. Much of our time was spent in uniform. But we did our studies too. I worked hard at my Mathematics. A. L. Pedder gave me tutorials – smoking his pipe – and throwing spent matches over his shoulder into the fireplace. I went to Chapel on Sundays. One of the demies is expected to read a lesson. I was taken unawares – in uniform – not with a surplice. I had not looked it up beforehand. I took the first reference that came in the lectionary. It was *Genesis* 39:7. I read it out, getting more and more embarrassed as it told how Potiphar's wife made advances to Joseph:

And Joseph was a goodly person, and well favoured. And it came to pass after these things, that his master's wife cast her eyes upon Joseph; and she said, Lie with me.

I went on reading:

…And she caught him by his garment, saying, Lie with me: and he left his garment in her hand, and fled, and got him out.

Our good Professor of Philosophy, Clement C. J. Webb – who was always kind to me – took me aside afterwards and consoled me. It was the first time I had ever had to read any passage aloud.

vi *Not a mechanic*

So that first year at Oxford passed, overshadowed by the war. In June 1917 I took Mathematics Moderation. I was given a First Class – undeserved. The examiner must have made allowance. Soon afterwards I was called up – but more of that later. I will go straight over to my return to Magdalen after the war. It was on Thursday 6 February 1919 that I was demobilised. I lost no time. I was determined to get on. On Monday 10 February 1919 I was back at Oxford. I had lodgings in the High Street opposite the College. I went up to the Physics laboratory that very afternoon. I was told to tie a piece of cotton on to a lead weight. It took me two hours before the demonstrator was satisfied. That decided me. Not Applied Mathematics for me. Only Pure Mathematics. That depends on reasoning, not on mechanical aptitude. I was never anything of a mechanic. If the car breaks down – even if a wheel has to be changed – I am no good at it.

vii *A girl paddles by*

That summer term of 1919 was one of the happiest of my life. One of the finest summers on record. Oxford at its best. Magdalen at its most beautiful. About 60 of us at the College back from the war. No examinations ahead for any of us. In the mornings, attend lectures or work. Afterwards take canoe or punt on the river, play tennis or cricket on the playing field. On Sundays, out for the day leisurely on the river with picnic lunch and tea. Magdalen the head of the river – with a crew of the very first quality – all blues.

I had rooms in Cloisters. On the next staircase was Edward Bridges, son of the Poet Laureate – a demy also – a First in Greats – and afterwards to become Head of the Civil Service. Each morning we used to run round 'Adders' – our short name for Addison's Walk – and plunge into our swimming pool. In the nude. One morning a girl student from St. Hilda's came round the corner in a canoe. We had to stay in the water – shivering – whilst she went paddling by – slowly – how slowly! At Parson's Pleasure, too, the men still bathe in the nude –whilst the ladies go round out of sight.

viii *'What school were you at?'*

Often freshmen ask one another, 'What school were you at?' Most men in my day were apt to name a famous public school. I turned the question on one side or prevaricated in one way or another. I felt ashamed at having been at a grammar school. But I need not have worried. Everyone was very understanding. And when I took a First Class in 1920, they were as proud of my achievement as I of theirs. Magdalen had the reputation of being a rich man's college – a college of all play and no work. The College had not had a single First for years. It is different now. It leads the field. My son is the Senior Dean of Arts.

3 What career to follow?

i *Teaching is not good enough*

Yes, I took a First Class in the Mathematical Final School. But then what was I to do? Mathematics did not lead into anything in those days – except to teach it. The headmaster of Winchester College offered me a post. I took it. It was near home. The salary was good for those days – £350 a year. I taught Mathematics all through the school. I taught Geology to the sixth book –reading it up the night before. But I did not like teaching. I did not like the prospect of teaching the same subject to young boys all my life. So I went back to Sir Herbert Warren in July 1921 and asked his advice. He said, 'I thought teaching was not good enough for you. Do you want to come back again?' By this time I had my sights set on the Law. Whilst at Winchester I had been one day to the Assizes at the Castle. I sat in the public gallery. I heard the argument in a civil case. I felt, 'That is what I should like to do. I would like to become a barrister as I told mother long ago'. I was ambitious too. I could see in the Law the way to succeed – how far I did not know – but to succeed – to achieve – to do something in the world. That is what I wanted to do.

ii *The tutor who knew no law*

Before I returned to Oxford my brother Reg and I had a holiday. At Chamonix in France – walking in the mountains, crossing the glaciers – coming down tired but happy to a good tea. I was set up for the next venture. I got law books and started on them. I went back again to Magdalen in October 1921. Sir Herbert Warren was again my supporter. He went to London and per-suaded the Trustees to award me the Eldon Scholarship. I had the necessary qualifications. I had obtained a First Class and was a communicant member of the Church of England.

I have never worked harder – or better – than I did that year. There was no room in College. I had lodgings in the Iffley road. My law tutor was Robert Segar – who had been an unsuccessful barrister on the Northern Circuit. He knew no law except on the Statute of Frauds – on which he had once had a case. I learned nothing from him. I went to lectures of other dons and took notes. When the questions were asked in the examination paper, I was able often to repeat the notes word for word. I had a good memory. At the *viva voce* a young don, Professor Cheshire, asked me about the new Law of Property Act. It had only just been passed – on 29 June 1922. I was prepared for it. I gave the right answers. I was awarded a First Class. Moral for the students – keep up to date.

iii *'Failed All Souls'*

I did not stay longer at Oxford. Some men stayed to take the BCL. But I was anxious to make my way at the Bar. So I joined Lincoln's Inn – for no particular reason. Except that the Under-Treasurer was Sir Reginald Rowe – who was a Magdalen man. I started in Chambers straightaway – that October 1922. But I went back to Oxford for a day or two to try for that most coveted of academic awards – a fellowship at All Souls. I could answer the legal questions all right, but we had to read Latin aloud. My pronunciation was mixed between the old and the new. That did not suit that stronghold of classicists. So I joined the distinguished company of 'Failed All Souls'! Like the more numerous company of 'Failed BA'.

The First World War

Introduction

War was declared on 4 August 1914. It was foreseen by many. Father told us: 'Coming events cast their shadows before'. I asked him where that came from. He knew at once, *Lochiel's warning* by Thomas Campbell. Such was his knowledge of poetry.

On the outbreak of war all the young men flocked to the colours. None stopped to inquire the need for it. Everyone accepted that we were right to go to war. We were to defend Belgium – whose neutrality we had guaranteed. We had given our promise – on 'a scrap of paper' – and must honour it. The Germans made scorn of it. Their despatch to our Foreign Office said:[1]

Just for a word – 'neutrality', a word which in wartime has so often been disregarded, just for a scrap of paper – Great Britain is going to make war.

There was no conscription at the beginning. Volunteers came forward in thousands. The girls used to sing:

> We don't want to lose you
> But we think you ought to go.

They gave white feathers to those who hesitated. They sang the recruiting song:

> On Saturday I'm willing
> If you'll only take the shilling
> To go out with any one of you.

A private's pay was a shilling a day. And his keep.

No need for any white feathers for us. I will tell of the four of us. Norman, of course, was too young.

---

1 To Sir Edward Goschen, 4 August 1914.

1 Jack the eldest son

1 Under training

i *Manning the guns*

Let me tell you first of Jack. He was the eldest son. He was given the full family name which included Newdigate Poyntz. He was christened John Edward Newdigate Poyntz. He was good-looking, with fine features like mother. Good at all games. Typically, at football he played centre-forward, leading the attack.

Jack had joined the Territorials nearly a year before war was declared. He was a gunner. On his afternoons off – and at weekends – he was under training. So when war was declared on 4 August 1914 Jack, at 21, was called on at once. He manned the guns at Calshot Castle guarding the entrance to Southampton Water. A few months later he was granted a commission in the 3rd Lincolnshire Regiment – because of his Grandfather Thompson's association with that county – and was under training there. He passed all his examinations success-fully. In May 1915 he wrote to the schoolmaster – Mr. Geer – at the small private school in Whitchurch:

I attribute it mainly to the fact that you taught me to use my 'common sense'. Altho' the exams appeared ridiculously easy, I think about 5% failed, several of whom I know boast of a public school education. Of course they were absolute duffers but that doesn't alter the case.

ii *Out to France*

Soon afterwards, he was posted to the regular battalion – the 1st Lincolnshire Regiment – and joined them in France. They were in and out of the line until the time came when they prepared for the attack on the Somme. Letters from his comrades speak of his courage in tackling the burning dugouts, when his coolness averted a catastrophe. He was known to them as 'Candy kid' because of his fondness for sweets.

2 In the fighting

i *His first wound*

Then came the fighting. Jack was twice wounded. The first time was a few days before the main attack on 1 July 1916. Everyone knew it was imminent. Our artillery bombarded the enemy position for seven days beforehand. The enemy artillery retaliated. Jack was wounded on 26 June 1916. This is the entry in the *War Diary*:

26 June: Third day of bombardment. The enemy artillery retaliated on our trenches at intervals during the day causing several casualties. The weather continued fine. Our machine guns were active all night to prevent the enemy from carrying out repairs to his wire or parapets. Enemy transport was heard to be in Fricourt at 10 p.m. and was dealt with by our artillery.

Casualties: Capt. A. E. O. Parish, 2nd Lt. W. E. Bartram and 2nd Lt. J. E. N. P. Denning wounded. Other ranks – 2 killed, 13 wounded.

Jack was hit by shrapnel in the head – but his tin hat (alias steel helmet – they had just been issued) saved him from the worst of it. His head was severely cut and he was sent back to the Casualty Clearing Station. He could have been sent down to the base or even to England. But he insisted on returning to the line – bandaged up as he was – so as to be with his comrades. He rejoined the regiment and helped to re-form it. A comrade wrote home saying, ' "Candy kid" was the best out of the remaining eight left on that day'.

ii *Enemy driven back 100 yards*

In the next seven weeks the battalion was in and out of reserve. Jack was made Acting Captain in command of 'C' Company. There is an entry in the *War Diary* of a successful attack by his Company. Successful – but it only advanced the line 100 yards. That is how every yard was fought over.

20 Sept. Attack by Battalion bombers and Company bombers of 'C' and 'D' Companies to clear Gas Alley up to a point within 50 yards of Gird Trench. Enemy driven back 100 yards and captured trench consolidated in whole attack.

3 The last days

i *His last letter*

Now I come to the last days:

23 Sept. At Fricourt camp. Notified that battalion was to be attached to the 64th Brigade and assist in attack to be launched in the region of Guedecourt.

On the next day, 24 September, orders were given for the attack to be made the next day, 25 September. Jack knew of this. He knew that he might be killed. He was in command of 'C' Company and had to lead the attack. In the morning of 24 September about 10.30 a.m., he wrote his last letter. They were to move forward up to the line in the dark and occupy switch trenches ready for the attack. They were to be the second wave. The first wave were expected to have attained their objective – and gone forward. He wrote in pencil a letter home and put it in his valise. It moves me to tears even now when I read it:

> Sept. 24th 16
> 10.30 a.m.

My own Dearest Mother & Dad,
  This may or may not be my last letter to you, as we are for it I think tomorrow. I sincerely hope it will be successful. At all events I am determined to go in and win as I know you would have me do. I know you may think this rather ridiculous especially if I come through alright.
  But you may rest assured that should I get pipped I shall have done my duty, and always remember it is far better to die with honour than to live in shame.
  This must be necessarily a short letter as we are moving shortly.
  The main object is that to please me, do not worry if I do get pipped.
  I was awfully pleased to hear Gordon had been recommended and his promotion. Please congratulate him for me if I don't have the opportunity.
  Well, darlings, best love to all I know. I am
                              Ever your loving Boy,
                                        Jack

ii *They spring over the parapets*

The *War Diary* gives a description of the next day. I hope you will forgive me if I set it out in full. It was written by the Battalion Commander. Rarely will you find any incident of the Battle of the Somme so well described.

24 Sept. To Pommiers Redoubt. Then to 64 Brigade HQ in Switch Trench. At 11.30 p.m. occupied trenches. 'A' and 'C' Companies in Gap Trench (supports). 'B' and 'D' Companies in Switch Trench (2nd supports).
25 Sept. Attack to commence at 12.35 p.m. Artillery of all calibres continued to bombard enemy's position during morning preparatory to the attack.

12.33 p.m. Battalion stood to, ready to go over the parapets. Bayonets were fixed and each man carried an extra bandolier and one Mills bomb in addition to the complement of bombs carried by the Battalion and Company bombers.

12.35 p.m. 'A' and 'C' Companies, under the commands of Capt. J. Edes and Capt. J. E. N. P. Denning respectively, sprang over the parapet of Gap Trench and advanced in quick line with a frontage of two platoons each Company, in two lines, the second line 50 yards behind the first line. 'A' Company were on the right and 'C' Company on the left.

iii *They come into barrage fire*

These two companies, after advancing about 50 yards, came into the enemy's barrage fire from the right and right front, but in spite of heavy losses, continued until the British front line was reached. Here it was found that the trench was still occupied by the two units which should have attained the first objective, and it became apparent that they had been unsuccessful and fallen back to their original position. Capt. J. E. N. P. Denning and the senior NCOs of 'C' Coy. had been wounded during the advance from Gap Trench and it was found necessary that this Company should reorganise in one front line.

'A' Company nonetheless advanced and 'B' and 'D' Companies moved from Switch Trench to join 'C' Company in the front trench.

'A' Company lost one officer wounded, 'B' Company lost one officer killed, 2 wounded. 'C' Company had lost the Company Commander (wounded) and 2 officers wounded. 'D' Company lost the Company Commander killed and 2 officers wounded. About 25% of other ranks had been killed or wounded.

At 1.37 p.m. the barrage began to lift but still heavy machine gun fire and impractical to advance to aid of 'A' Company.

On the 26th the Battalion withdrew to Bernafay Wood.

iv *Had someone blundered?*

There it is: the regiment lost two Company Commanders (one of them Jack), 8 officers, and 25% of other ranks. Nothing had been gained. The battalion had to withdraw. Had someone blundered? Nobody ever suggested it at the time. The men all trusted their commanders. Very few have known till this day the full story of the attack they made. It has never been set down till I write it now.

In 1854 – 72 years before – when the Light Brigade charged at Balaclava, there was a poet to describe it – a poet to ask, 'When can their glory fade?' But in our war in 1916 there was no one – from that time to this – and only now when the *War Diaries* have been released. But the courage of our men on the Somme should be remembered. At Agincourt it was all over in one day – with all the rushing of the Knights in armour and the steadfastness of the bowmen. At Waterloo – again over in one day – with the Guards in their red uniforms holding the square. At Balaclava – all over in an hour – with all the stirring of the blood by the sound of bugles, the galloping of horses and the waving of sabres. But on the Somme long hours in a trench – waiting for zero hour – waiting for our barrage to lift – then over the top – mown down like grass before a scythe – dead and wounded.

v *Fatally wounded*

Jack was one of those wounded – with a piece of shrapnel through his stomach – bleeding his life away. He lay there for about three hours. Then he was found. They carried him down on a stretcher a long way. To the Field Ambulance. Then by motor ambulance to the Casualty Clearing Station. They got him there by 10 p.m. As he was taken in he said to a comrade next him, 'I'm done for'. The nurses did all they could to relieve the pain. He was wandering all night, murmuring of home. He died in the morning of the 26th. The Chaplain wrote home to father and mother saying, 'I prayed with him....He was very grateful for my ministrations and died a good soldier of Jesus Christ.' They buried him in the war cemetery at Heilly-sur-Somme. They stamped out his name on a piece of tin and tacked it on to a rough wooden cross.

4 In remembrance

i *The telegram came*

Two days later, on 28 September, a telegram came. Mother opened it with trembling fingers. 'Deeply regret to inform you that Capt. J. E. N. P. Denning Lincolnshire Regt. died of wounds Sept. 26.' Mother swooned to the floor. I can see it now. Father stooped and took her in his arms. Tears in his eyes. It was thirty-six years after he wrote that poem, *Their Dead Soldier*. It had come true – of themselves.

ii *Two wild flowers*

Two years later, in 1918, I rode over to Heilly-sur-Somme on my horse – when we were out of the line for a rest. It was 20 miles from our camp. His was the only grave on which any flowers were growing. They were two wild flowers. One red and one purple. I picked them and sent them home to father and mother. In my letter I said: 'I thought you would treasure these flowers, which were the only ones growing there. It is all very peaceful there now'. They kept them in the folds of a book until they crumbled into dust. I got my sappers to make a new wooden cross – now since replaced in stone by the War Graves Commission. On it there are the words which he wrote in his last letter: 'You may rest assured that I shall have done my duty.'

iii *'Dulce et decorum est'*

In time his valise came back – with his few belongings. In his pocket he had carried a letter from me with quotations I had sent him. To you they will appear as schoolboy stuff: but to me, at the age of 17, they meant much. And Jack treasured them, I would like to set the letter out here – so that you can see the idealism which inspired us then:

August 14th (1916)

Here I am, close on post-time, trying to rush through something like a letter for you. I must try to write you bi-weekly.

Jack, in my diary I have made notes of the following quotations. I consider them good.

'I expect to pass through this world but once. Any goodness therefore that I can do or any kindness that I can show to any fellow-creature, let me do it now. Let me not defer it or neglect it for I shall not pass this way again.'

'The immediately possible is hardly worth living for. It is the ideal that kindles enthusiasm and gives inspiration and vigour to all human effort.'

> 'In the world's broad field of battle
> In the bivouac of life,
> Be not like dumb driven cattle
> Be a hero in the strife.'

Next time I will write one of my lately composed poems.

'*Dulce et decorum est pro patria mori*'. This is from Horace III. It means, 'It is sweet and honourable to die for one's country'.

When I wrote letters to my brothers, always I ended with that line of Horace. It finds an echo in Jack's last letter when he says it is better to 'die with honour'.

iv *'You'll be a Man, my son!'*

Amongst his belongings, too, was a small Bible given him by mother on his Confirmation, and a copy of Palgrave's *Golden Treasury* – the little green pocket edition of *The World's Classics*.

It did not contain Kipling's *If* – but he had written it out in pencil in full on the two pages of the flyleaf, ending as you know:

> If you can fill the unforgiving minute
> With sixty seconds' worth of distance run,
> Yours is the Earth and everything that's in it,
> And – which is more – you'll be a Man, my son!

v *'That is for ever England'*

I hope you will understand if I follow that with Rupert Brooke's poem, *The Soldier*. It fits Jack so exactly:

> If I should die, think only this of me:
> That there's some corner of a foreign field
> That is for ever England. There shall be
> In that rich earth a richer dust concealed;
> A dust whom England bore, shaped, made aware,
> Gave, once, her flowers to love, her ways to roam,
> A body of England's, breathing English air,
> Washed by the rivers, blest by suns of home,
> And think, this heart, all evil shed away,
> A pulse in the eternal mind, no less
> Gives somewhere back the thoughts by England given.
> Her sights and sounds; dreams happy as her day;
> And laughter, learnt of friends; and gentleness
> In hearts at peace, under an English heaven.

2 Reg the second son

1 In it from the beginning

i *A proud and gay heart*

Let me tell next of Reg. Equally as handsome as Jack. Still a most distinguished presence. Equally as good at games as Jack. Typically, at football he kept goal, maintaining the defence.

Very recently, he was asked by a professor doing research: 'What was the attitude of mind of those who fought in the First World War?' His answer was:

From the declaration of war in 1914 and until after I was wounded, it was with a proud and gay heart, because I considered myself privileged to be able to do something for the country in a time of dire need. The King and Parliament had declared that the country was in danger and that was quite sufficient for hundreds of thousands like myself. I was all eagerness to get to the Front. Even after being wounded, I retained a keen desire to return to the Front and to the fighting there....Convalescent at Hythe, I remember the wishfulness with which I saw ships leaving Folkestone with troops bound for the Front....

In 1918 I was gratified to be ordered to France where I arrived in time to meet the last big German offensive.

ii *Ypres – mud and lice*

Reg, at 19, was the earliest in the line of young men queueing up to enlist. He joined as a private in the Queen's Westminster Rifles. Proud to fight in the ranks, he scorned to apply for a commission – until Jack persuaded him to do so. He went out to France in the winter of 1914–1915 and was in the fighting in the Ypres salient – as hard as any that any troops have ever had to endure. Deep in mud, sludging along on duck-boards, up to the Front with heavy rifle and pack, constantly being shelled, crawling from one shell-hole to another, crouching in dugouts, standing in the trenches, looking out through a slit in the parapet wall – it meant death to look over the top in daytime. This is how he himself describes it:

....At Ypres we were in the trenches for six weeks at a stretch – before we were relieved. The trenches were full of water. The only dry place was the fire-step. We had to creep out at night and go back a mile to collect the rations. We slept in our greatcoats. We used to wake up with the rats crawling over our faces and biting at the collars of our coats. We were covered with lice. They were on our shirts and on every piece of our clothing. Even the cords of our identity discs. On being relieved, we went back to a rest camp and tried to get ourselves clean – in a big vat filled with hot water. Everyone accepted this without a murmur of complaint. It was part of the war we had to fight.

iii *Cutting through the wire*

Late in 1915 he was commissioned in the Bedfordshire Regiment. He then joined the 6th Battalion. They were in the front line for weeks. Often a raid in the night-time – seizing a prisoner – so as to get information – and then back. He says:

I was afraid of being afraid. So once I got out of the trench – and walked towards the enemy – to prove to myself that I was not afraid.

The *War Diary* for his Battalion is very disappointing. It is brief and uninformative. He has written down as much as he can remember – but it is very incomplete – owing to his severe head-wound.

2 The battle opens

i *The big offensive*

Some days before 1 July 1916, it was known by everyone that preparations were in hand for a big offensive. The men in the front line knew little of these preparations. They were only concerned with their own section. They were dug in – with the Germans only 100 yards away – across no-man's-land. Again, for a week, there was our bombardment of the enemy defences – going on for days, increasing in intensity all the time. Added to it, cylinders of lethal gas were brought up into the front line trenches – to be discharged at zero hour to cover the assault. Again there was retaliation by the Germans both with artillery and machine-guns. At dawn on 1 July the infantry went over the top but they were met by the terrific fire of the Germans. Nearly every man became a casualty. It was impossible to move forward.

ii *Dead British soldiers*

On 8 July the Battalion was moved to front line trenches further south. As they moved forward, Reg remembers:

We crossed the original line of trenches from which the initial attack was made. We had to pick our way through lines of the bodies of dead British soldiers. Each was facing the enemy. They had been mown down as they left their trenches.

During the next few days, whilst holding the line, the casualties, he says, were 'overwhelming'. The *War Diary* gives the numbers in the four days as 23 killed, 6 missing, 158 wounded. Reg's Company Commander was killed and he had to take over command. The battalion was then moved to a defence line further back. They thought they would have a 'little respite'. It was a very short-lived respite. On 13 July they moved to a new line.

3 Seriously wounded

i *'Gentlemen, we are to attack'*

Then on 15 July there was the attack in which Reg was wounded. The *War Diary* describes it in these few words:

15 July: Attack on Pozieres by 112th Brigade from trenches S. of Contalmaison. Battalion held up by hostile machine guns. Established itself about 100 ft. from the Lizière and dug in.

3 officers, 3 other ranks killed; 25 missing; 9 officers and 174 other ranks wounded.

Those terrible casualties tell their own tale: but even more is told by Reg's account of the action. He says, 'The Battalion was virtually wiped out'. The Divisional Headquarters must have made blunder after blunder. Remember his age. He was just 22. 'I was sleeping in a trench. (It had fallen in and buried me for a time.) At midnight an orderly arrived with the message, "Get ready to move. We are to move forward to start line at dawn". At first light we moved forward to an appointed meeting place. Enemy gas shells were falling all around. The Battalion Commander called the Company Commanders together. It was just below the brow of a hill and the enemy fire was intense. He said to us: "Gentlemen, I do not know the objective, nor does the Brigadier, but we are to attack the enemy holding Pozieres. The Loyal North Lancashire Regiment will be on our left". He then gave orders which were the vaguest of the vague because he had received few from the Brigadier'.

ii *A pole-axe blow*

'I rejoined my Company and gave orders as best I could. I led my men to the attack. It was 7 o'clock in the morning. "Come on the Bedfords", I shouted. We met a devastating fire. Many of my men fell. The Loyal North Lancashires should have been on our left – advancing with us. I saw some troops sheltering in a disused trench, about 50 yards away. I dashed over to them, stood on the top of the trench and shouted to them, "What are you doing? Who are you?" At that very moment I seem to remember a pole-axe blow on my head which felled me and toppled me into the trench'.

iii *Given up for dead*

The pole-axe was a bullet – right through his shoulder into the back of his head – from the neck to above the ear. He remembers nothing more. Those in the trench must have given him up for dead. Some troops from further back must have moved forward to attack, clambering over his body. After a while, he recovered consciousness a little. His clothing was soaked in blood. He managed to get out a flask of rum. It had been issued the night before. He had not drunk it then because 'I had always considered it weakness to summon up my courage by drinking alcohol'. He had a drink of the rum, but slipped into unconsciousness again. After some time he again recovered consciousness. Again some troops were clambering over him. 'Give the blighters one for me', he said, and slipped into unconsciousness again.

Hours passed. They had started at 7 a.m. It was late in the evening before someone discovered that he was alive. A corporal of his Company put him on his shoulder and carried him back. Stretcher bearers took him then to the Field Ambulance. He came to on the stretcher. 'I found myself being looked at by a doctor and a chaplain'.

4 Recovery

i *The surgeon saves his life*

They got him down to the Casualty Clearing Station. It was in a tent. He was lifted on to an operating table. The surgeon saved his life. He was taken in a cattle truck improvised as an ambulance train and on to a hospital ship. Later, in England, it was found that he had an 'aneurism of the occipital artery'. An operation was performed. A plate was put in his head and still remains there.

ii *Henceforth known as Jack*

Reg was in hospital at Tidworth on 28 September – when the news came through that Jack had been killed. Gordon happened to be at home at the time. He was on short leave from his ship. He and I went over to tell Reg. He was ill in bed. We told him that Jack had been killed. He turned over. He sobbed and sobbed. Jack was his beloved brother – his hero. Reg tried to take his place. In the Army henceforth he was always known as Jack.

iii *The wound takes its toll*

Reg recovered from his wound. To some extent. Such that the doctors passed him fit to go again to France. He went back early in 1918 and rejoined his Regiment – the 6th Bedfords – as a Company Commander. He was with them in time to meet the German offensive. But not for long. The wound had taken its toll. He struggled on and on until he collapsed in a trench. Exhausted. He was sent back to base. Once more he returned but this time – not to the front line – but to the staff of a Brigade and afterwards of the 3rd Army. By this time I was in the front line myself. He looked anxiously each day to see if I was in the casualty list. I was not.

3 Gordon the third son

1 The boy sailor

i *He was the sturdier*

Let me tell next of Gordon. Being so close in age (you will remember he was 20 months older than me) we did everything together. We went to the first school together. We went to the grammar school together. We were always in the same form together. We came out close together in the examinations. But he was always ahead of me. He was the sturdier of the two.

ii *His first letter home*

I have already told how Gordon started on his way in the Merchant Navy. It was in March 1913 that he became a cadet in the steamship *Stork* with pay of £1 a month. Our parents had to provide his outfit, including his cadet's uniform. This is his first letter home. It shows how he took to life at sea.

S/S *Stork*,
Genoa.
March 16th

....
We did not leave London till midnight and I turned in about 2 a.m. Seasickness started off Dover but I got over it before we reached the Bay, being sick for 2 days only. We had a good knocking about in the Bay and took several seas over. The Mate's and our cabins were flooded....We passed Gibraltar at 12.30 a.m. Wednesday 12th, and have had lovely weather ever since...

We are called at 5.30 every morning, start work at 6 and leave off at 5 p.m....

It is Easter next week, I wish I was going to Holy Communion with you; we don't work Good Friday and have Hot Cross Buns...

I like this life. The work is ... brasswork, painting, signalling, studying the stowage of cargo, helping the officers tallying cargo etc... I am not wasting my spare time, but I study.

iii *A first class certificate*

When war broke out in August 1914, Gordon was soon called on to serve in the Royal Navy. On 31 December (when he was 17½) he was appointed to be a midshipman in the Royal Naval Reserve. He was very pleased about this. At that time the usual way of becoming an officer in the Royal Navy was to go – at the age of 12 – to Dartmouth. But there was a recent Regulation which made it possible for an officer in the Royal Naval Reserve to be commissioned in the Royal Navy itself – if he greatly distinguished himself. That was Gordon's ambition. He was sent for training to Portsmouth – to the gunnery school on Whale Island – with its ship name of HMS *Excellent*. He worked hard and did well. Especially in Gunnery. It was to come in useful at Jutland. This is his letter home about it:

1 March 1915

I am glad to say I obtained a first class certificate, the only midshipman to get one. The Lieut.-Commander complimented me very nicely. I obtained 704 marks out of a possible 800 which is considered a very good percentage. The other midshipmen and nearly all the sub-lieutenants only obtained second class. In two subjects, Ammunition and Fire Control, I had full marks. In another 92 and 88. I will show you the certificate. I have not received an appointment yet. I hope it comes soon.

We are all very keen to get away to sea. There is plenty of work yet to be done there.

2 The midshipman

i *In the* Hampshire

On 13 March 1915 Gordon was appointed to one of the latest cruisers, HMS *Hampshire*. This pleased him because Hampshire is our county. There were eight midshipmen RNR who joined her on that day. Of those eight lads, six were lost when she hit a mine on 5 June 1916. The other two (one of them Gordon) would have been lost too except for being posted to other ships. But I would say a word about the *Hampshire*. Her loss – and that of his comrades – affected Gordon greatly. He often spoke of it.

ii *She strikes a mine*

At the beginning of the war, Lord Kitchener was the great military figure. He led the call for recruits to join the Services. I well remember the poster everywhere of the head of Lord

Kitchener with his finger pointing directly at you – 'Your country needs YOU'. His prestige was such that he was selected to lead a mission to Russia – to enlist her aid in the war. He and his party embarked in the *Hampshire* at Scapa Flow. She left at 4.45 p.m. on 5 June. Admiral Jellicoe decided that it was better for the *Hampshire* to follow a route along the west side of the Orkneys – because no minefield was thought to have been laid there. At about 7.40 p.m., whilst she was driving into the heavy seas, there was an explosion which seemed to tear the centre of the ship right out, and in a few minutes she went down with almost her entire company – of 800 – including Lord Kitchener and all. She had struck a mine. It had been laid by a German submarine a week before. It was one of 22 mines which had been specially laid – in the hope of interfering with a route used by warships. The *Hampshire* went down about 1½ miles from the shore – on one of the wildest parts of the coast. Fourteen men reached the shore on rafts, but two of them died before the rescue parties on the cliffs could reach them. Afterwards, when Gordon was ill and near to death, he spoke of his comrades in the *Hampshire*. Perhaps he would have preferred to have gone down with them rather than endure the long lingering illness.

3 In destroyers

i *HMS* Morris

Meanwhile – long before the *Hampshire* was lost – Gordon had been posted to destroyers. This was what he wanted. Service in destroyers carried with it high esteem throughout the Navy. It was arduous. It was dangerous. It was more likely to be engaged in action. It was so strenuous that usually an officer was appointed only for a few months before being posted elsewhere. But Gordon was the exception. His commanding officer assessed him as 'hard-working, promising'. He thought so well of him that he applied for his service to be continued. And Gordon applied for a transfer to the Royal Navy.

Gordon was appointed to the destroyer *Morris*. He joined her on 2 September 1915 when he was just 18: and served the rest of his time in her. She was part of the 10th Destroyer Flotilla – the Harwich Force – under the command of Commodore Tyrwhitt, one of the most intrepid naval officers of the war. The flotilla comprised some of the best and latest of our destroyers: the

Morris was one of them. Years later, the *Morris* was broken up. But we still have the ship's bell – a fine big brass bell – with *HMS Morris 1914* on it. We keep it bright and polished – as it was when she was in service.

ii *Escorting the transports*

When Gordon first joined the *Morris*, she was not actually based at Harwich. She was based – temporarily – at Portsmouth. She was escorting our troop transports across the English Channel. This was vital. The U-boats were a menace to our merchant ships. Even more to our troop transports. Then for a couple of months, December 1915 and January 1916, she was in the Irish Sea escorting mail steamers between Fishguard and Ireland. It was one of the most terrible winters for weather that has ever been known. Gordon experienced the heaviest of storms. He had to cling to the binnacle (which holds the compass) for hours – so as to save himself from being washed overboard – and no one could venture along the deck to relieve him.

iii *Attacking the Zeppelin base*

February 1916 saw the *Morris* back at Harwich – with the 10th Destroyer Flotilla. On 25 March 1916 she was engaged in the 'Hoyer Raid'. The Germans sent Zeppelins – great airships sailing in the sky – to spy on and raid England. They had a base at Hoyer on the Schleswig-Holstein peninsula near the boundary with Denmark. Commodore Tyrwhitt elaborated a plan to bomb that Zeppelin base – with seaplanes from a carrier. It was bitterly cold, with constant snow squalls. Seven seaplanes took off from our carrier. The destroyers circled around that carrier – protecting her – waiting for the return of the seaplanes. Only two returned. What had happened to the other five? The Commodore ordered his two flotilla leaders and eight destroyers to sweep the seas searching for them.

iv *Sinking two armed trawlers*

It was here that the *Morris* came into action. She did not find the missing seaplanes. But she came across two German armed trawlers. They showed fight, but they could not withstand our destroyers. They turned and fled. Our destroyers gave chase. The *Morris* sank them both. The *War Diary* says simply:

On 25 March 1916, with HMS *Lightfoot* and *Nimrod*, she sank two auxiliary trawlers in the North Sea.

The *Morris* and the other destroyers stopped to pick up survivors. Whilst they were doing this, German aeroplanes appeared and began to bomb them.

Soon afterwards strong enemy forces appeared. The Admiralty ordered Commodore Tyrwhitt back but, like his great predecessor, he turned a blind eye – or rather, took little heed of the wireless telegraphy. He went forward with the destroyers including the *Morris*. Meanwhile, our big ships were coming up. Sir Julian Corbett says:

For over three hours more the battle cruisers and light cruisers laboured through the mountainous seas towards their meeting-place, eager for the expected fight. Hardened by their continual activity in the past terrible winter, no weather could deter them.

But the enemy returned to port. So that was the end of the Hoyer Raid.

4 Jutland

i *Tyrwhitt misses Jutland*

Two months later, on 31 May 1916, came Jutland. Commodore Tyrwhitt, with most of the Harwich Force, missed the battle – to their intense disappointment. The Admiralty wanted to hold them in reserve – ready to come in at a crucial time and place. The Admiralty ordered the Commodore to be complete with fuel – ready to sail at a moment's notice. But no orders came. So Commodore Tyrwhitt proceeded to sea and told the Admiralty so. But with sinking heart he read his next instruction: 'Return at once and await orders'.

ii *The flagship* Lion *is hit*

Not so, however, with the *Morris* and three other destroyers of the 10th Flotilla. They had been detached from the Harwich Force and attached to the Battle Cruiser Fleet. This was under the command of Admiral Beatty in his flagship *Lion*. The *Morris* was one of the destroyers screening the battle cruisers – as they raced towards the battle cruisers of the enemy. Then there was the fierce engagement. One by one our great ships went up in flames. It was about 4 o'clock in the afternoon. Our ships were clearly defined against the bright western sky: whereas there was a 'vile background' obscuring the German ships. The German gunnery was extraordinarily accurate. The range was about

eight miles. The flagship *Lion* was first hit. A large shell pene-
trated her centre turret – the flames were about to spread rapidly.
They would have reached the magazine. But Major Harvey of
the Royal Marines (his legs had been blown off) ordered the
magazine doors to be closed and the magazine to be flooded.
That saved the ship. He died and was awarded the Victoria
Cross posthumously.

iii *The* Indefatigable *and* Queen Mary *go*

Next came the *Indefatigable*. The *Morris* was one of her six
destroyers detailed as a destroyer screen. So Gordon was there.
At 3.58 p.m. salvo after salvo hit her. She went up in a tre-
mendous cloud of black smoke. 57 officers and 960 men were
lost. So also with the *Queen Mary*. She was fighting hard and
well when a plunging salvo fell upon her deck forward. Her
bows went down. Her stern went up. Her propellers still
revolving high in the air. In a moment there was nothing left of
her but a dark pillar of smoke hundreds of feet high in the air. 57
officers and 1209 men went down with her. It was at this point
that Admiral Beatty made his remark to his Flag-Captain:

'There seems to be something wrong with our bloody ships today,' and he
altered course towards the enemy (a two-point turn to port at 4.30).

I have taken this account from Sir Julian Corbett's book
History of the Great War Naval Operations, Vol. III, and Arthur J.
Marder's *From the Dreadnought to Scapa Flow,* Vol. III. But I
repeat it here now because of the impact it made on the men in
the destroyer screen ahead of those battle cruisers. Gordon told
me of his feelings as they saw, one after another, those fine ships
going up. No thought of giving in. They were too heavily
engaged themselves. Simply the thought, 'We will fight on
ourselves. Come what may'.

iv *The destroyer action*

It was at this very moment that the destroyer flotilla took an
action which had a most important effect on the outcome of the
battle. Admiral Beatty ordered our flotilla to deliver a torpedo
attack on the enemy battle cruisers. At about the same time the
Germans decided to launch a torpedo attack on our battle
cruisers. So there were the two opposing destroyer flotillas
advancing. As our destroyers raced forward, they saw the German flotilla emerging from the smoke. This was, for Gordon

and all, the moment they had been waiting for – the moment of challenge – when they were to meet the enemy head-on. Either to destroy or be destroyed. The distance closed rapidly. The range was as low as 600 yards. No time and no need for any calculations. They were firing at low trajectories — almost point-blank – as the ships did at Trafalgar. They were launching torpedoes whenever there was an opening. It was the hottest fight of the whole Battle of Jutland. Sir Julian Corbett describes it:

It was a wild scene of groups of long low forms vomiting heavy trails of smoke and dashing hither and thither at thirty knots or more through the smother and splashes, and all in a rain of shell from the secondary armament of the German battle cruisers, as well as from the (German light cruiser) *Regensburg* and the destroyers, with the heavy shell of the contending squadrons screaming overhead. Gradually a pall of gun and funnel smoke almost hid the shell-tormented sea, and beyond the fact that the German torpedo attack was crushed, little could be told of what was happening, when, at 4.43, the *Lion* ran up the destroyers' recall.

v A matter-of-fact report

Those words describe the engagement far more graphically than the matter-of-fact report by Lieutenant-Commander E. S. Graham – the Commanding Officer of Gordon's ship, HMS *Morris*. His report dated the next day, 1 June 1916, simply says:

By the time I had drawn ahead to the beam of HMS *Lion*, I observed German destroyers making an attack on our battle cruisers. I turned to port and engaged those nearest me, one of which was sunk and two disabled. The enemy destroyers were driven off and did not get within torpedo range of our battle cruisers.

Shortly before the end of this destroyer action, I came within torpedo range of the enemy battle cruisers, but could not fire my torpedoes owing to my range being fouled by our own destroyers. I did not again get within torpedo range of the enemy.

vi The foremast 4 inch gun

Now I would give Gordon's part in the engagement. In each ship itself, the orders were by word of mouth or through speaking tubes. In the *Morris* the speaking tubes failed. They were the means by which the Lieutenant-Commander could control the fire of his guns. 'Primary control' it was called. The Lieutenant-Commander could give orders so as to train the guns on the target and to fire them in one salvo. But early on this 'primary control' broke down. No orders got through the speaking tubes to the guns. So each officer was left to himself. Gordon was in charge of the foremast 4 inch gun. A midshipman RNR just 19 years of age. Quick as lightning, he grasped the situation. He leapt into action. The gun-crew followed his lead. One man, Gordon told me, faltered. Gordon encouraged him – 'Come on. Get on with it'. He faltered no longer. Shells were falling all round. They were bursting close to the ship, scattering shrapnel all over. The enemy destroyers were so close that you could see the men in them. Gordon was sure they hit one of the enemy vessels and maybe two. The whole of the destroyers' action took about half-an-hour. From 4.15 to 4.43 p.m. Each side lost two destroyers but the English had succeeded in crushing the German attack.

vii *The* Invincible *goes too*

The *Morris*, together with the others, then formed a screen again around Admiral Beatty's battle cruisers. Beatty lured the enemy on towards the great battleships of the Grand Fleet led by Admiral Jellicoe in the *Iron Duke*. Beatty's battle cruisers were joined by Admiral Hood with his battle cruisers. Hood's flagship, the *Invincible*, led the fleet. In the *Invincible* was another young man from Whitchurch – from the top of the hill, 200 yards from us. Sub-Lieutenant Raymond Portal RN. Corbett and Marder tell the story. The *Invincible* took on the enemy battle cruiser *Derfflinger*. Admiral Hood spoke through a voice pipe to his gunnery officer: 'Your firing is very good. Keep at it as quickly as you can. Every shot is telling'. They were the last words he spoke. The enemy began rapid salvoes in reply. One after another they went home in the *Invincible*. Then a heavy shell struck the centre turret, pierced the roof, detonated inside and ignited the charges below. Several big explosions took place in rapid succession and there was a huge column of dark smoke. 'The mother of all battle cruisers had gone to join the other two that were no more…. her stem and stern rose apart high out of the troubled waters'.

So the courageous Admiral Hood met his end: and with him 1026 of our men. Among them Raymond Portal of Whitchurch.

viii *No victory. No defeat*

Night fell. Haze hid the ships one from another. The *Morris*, Gordon told me, lost contact with the other destroyers. His navigation came in useful. He helped to find the direction for the Firth of Forth. In the early morning they met with other stragglers and made for Rosyth. The Battle of Jutland was over. No victory. No defeat. But acts of gallantry rarely excelled in the history of war.

Individual acts of gallantry do not win battles. They are won or lost by the dispositions made by the High Command. It has often been said that Jellicoe was the only man who could have lost the war in a single day. But I would put it differently. He was also the only man who could have won the war in a single day. If the German High Seas Fleet had been destroyed, the enemy would have capitulated at once. There would not have been the Battle of the Somme – with the loss of the flower of our English youth. There would not have been the sinking of our merchant fleet by U-boats. No wonder that the fleet and the nation suffered a great disappointment.

ix *Poor Intelligence*

Why did Jellicoe fail? The reasons can now be told: It was largely because of faults in our Intelligence system. It was only in recent years that the files were released about Naval Intelligence in that war. Patrick Beesly has given an excellent account in the first chapter of his book *Very Special Intelligence*. There was Room 40 (Old Block) at the Admiralty which collected information about the movements of the German fleet: but there was no organisation for analysing that information and placing it into its context. Room 40 collected the pieces for the jigsaw, but there was no one to put them into place – so as to give the picture. In consequence, Admirals Jellicoe and Beatty were informed – four hours too late – that the German High Seas Fleet under Admiral Scheer had put to sea: and, at a later stage in the battle, when Jellicoe ought to have intercepted the High Seas Fleet, he was not given vital information. Room 40 knew that Admiral Scheer had planned an escape route – and what it was. But Jellicoe was ignorant of it. So the German fleet got back to its ports in safety. It was my brother Norman who afterwards made good the defects in our Intelligence system in that war. It was he who was responsible for the setting up – in the Second World War – of an 'Operational Intelligence Centre'. More of that hereafter.

x *And poor signalling*

Another contributory cause was the defects in our signalling system. You will notice that Corbett says that *Lion* 'ran up the destroyers' recall'. 'Ran up' – by hoisting flags with the message. That was the only way in which the flagship could signal to the ships under command. It was all so different from today. We are so used to radio telephones that we have forgotten the difficulties of communication in past days. But the only means from ship to ship was by hoisting flags with their code signals, 'Enemy in sight', and so forth; or by lamp and searchlight – giving the challenge – spelling out the words in Morse code 'dot-dot-dash'; or by wireless telegraphy. Our signalling system at Jutland was very poor compared with the Germans. Especially the system of 'challenge-by-flashing'. The Germans had given it up before the war. But we retained it. Marder tells us that when the destroyers challenged at night by flashing, the first flash (or certainly the second) told the Germans that the flashes were British and gave their exact position. It was said, 'On came the searchlights, off went the guns, and down went the destroyer'.

5 Trafalgar

i First-class Intelligence

Now compare the Battle of Jutland with Trafalgar in 1805. Lord Nelson was well supplied with Intelligence and his signalling system was first-class. Here are a few extracts from his diary:

Friday Octr. 18th: Fine weather, wind easterly. The combined fleets cannot have finer weather to put to sea.

Saturday Octr. 19th: The *Mars* being one of the look-out ships made the signal that the enemy were coming out of port....At 3 the *Colossus* made the signal that the enemy's fleet was at sea....At 5 telegraphed Capt. B^{d.} (Blackwood) that I rely'd upon his keeping sight of the enemy. At 5 o'clock *Naiad* made the signal for 31 sail of the enemy NNE. The frigates and look-out ships kept sight of the enemy most admirably all night and told me by signals which tack they were upon....

Monday Octr. 21st 1805: At daylight saw the enemy's combined fleet from East to ESE bore away. Made the signal for order of sailing and to prepare for battle. The enemy with their heads to the Southward. At 7 the enemy moving in succession....

October the twenty-first one thousand eight hundred and five: There is sight of the combined fleets of France and Spain distant about ten miles.

ii Nelson's prayer

Perhaps I may add that in addition to the good Intelligence that he received Lord Nelson put his faith in God. His diary goes on to record the prayer which he made before the battle started. It forms part of his will which was witnessed by Captains Blackwood and Hardy and as such it came into the custody of the Master of the Rolls. So I have a photograph of it. Few of you may have read it, so I reproduce it here.

May the great God whom I worship grant to my country and for the benefit of Europe in general a great and glorious victory, and may no misconduct in any one tarnish it, and may humanity after victory be the predominant feature in the British fleet. For myself individually I commit my life to Him who made me, and may his blessing light upon my endeavours for serving my country faithfully. To Him I resign myself and the just cause which is entrusted me to defend.

Amen, Amen, Amen.

iii *Nelson leaves a legacy*

....I leave Emma Lady Hamilton therefore a legacy to my King and country that they will give her an ample provision to maintain her rank in life. I also leave to the beneficence of my country my adopted daughter Horatia Nelson Thompson and I desire she will use in future the name of Nelson only. These are the only favors I ask of my King and country at this moment when I am going to fight their battle. May God bless my King and country and all those who I hold dear. My relations it is needless to mention they will of course be amply provided for.

Nelson & Bronte.

You will all know that he died in the battle and that the nation did not provide for Lady Hamilton.

6 The sub-lieutenant

i *Promoted at once*

To revert to Jutland. Gordon's part was recognised. He was promoted at once – almost on the field of battle. He was specially appointed to the Royal Navy as Sub-Lieutenant – without waiting for a formal decision by the Board of Admiralty. His promotion was announced in *The London Gazette* on 15 September 1916. It gives this recommendation:

Temporary Midshipman RNR Charles Gordon Denning.
  For the cool and skilful way in which he, as officer of the quarters, while continuously under heavy fire, controlled the foremast 4 inch gun, the primary control having broken down.

So he was a Sub-Lieutenant in the Royal Navy. We were all proud. He had achieved his ambition – an officer in the Royal Navy – without going through Dartmouth.

ii *A piece of shell*

We have at home a small piece of shell. It fell close to Gordon in the middle of the battle. It only just missed him. Afterwards he picked it up and brought it home to show us. We have it mounted on a piece of wood inscribed with these words:

> Battle of Jutland 1916
> Piece of German shell which
> fell on HMS *Morris* in which
> Sub-Lieutenant C. G. Denning RN
> was serving

After Jutland, the *Morris* remained under the command of Commodore Tyrwhitt. She was engaged in protecting the merchantmen moving during the night to and from Holland (a neutral country). On 23 July 1916, with another destroyer, she took on six German destroyers. There was a short engagement. It only ended because they were fast approaching a minefield off Zeebrugge.

7 The dread disease

i *He looks pale and thin*

That was the last engagement for Gordon. A blow was soon to fall heavily. The stress and strain of war had told upon him. The confined living quarters in the destroyer had undermined his health. He had no cabin: and no bunk to sleep in. He had to sling his hammock over the ward-room table – after the other officers had left. And it was a small ward-room in so small a ship. Often flooded with water. I remember him coming on leave in September 1916 when the news came that Jack had died of wounds. Gordon looked pale and thin then. He struggled on until he was taken to the Royal Naval Hospital at Chatham. In November 1916 tuberculosis was diagnosed. That was the dreaded disease – then called consumption – for which there was no cure. It consumed the life away. Captain Stephen Roskill RN wrote to me:

TB was terribly prevalent in those days in the Royal Navy – due of course to the very crowded conditions in which officers and men had to live. I know of several very good men who died of it during and after the First War.

So tragedy struck. Not only the disease itself. But the blows that followed it one after another. He loved the sea, his ship and his comrades. Yet here it was. He was discharged from HMS *Morris*. He was found unfit for further service. He was placed on the Retired List. At the age of 19.

ii *Only ill for 18 months*

He was only ill for 18 months. The one treatment known to the doctors was rest and fresh air. He was for a while in the King Edward VII Sanatorium at Midhurst. (Now a general hospital.) He had for a time a hut in the garden of Bere Hill House at Whitchurch – the home of the Portals – which was converted into a military hospital. He was nursed by the VADs including the kind and charming daughter of the house, Constance Portal. Two of her brothers had already been killed in the war. Oldric in the Life Guards and Raymond (as I have said) in the *Invincible*. Afterwards Gordon was in a nursing home at Boscombe.

iii *Sustained by his family*

He kept a diary during his illness. It tells much of his character. He records the progress of his illness, the letters he receives and sends, the kindness of those near and dear to him. Through it all runs his love of the sea. On the flyleaf he writes those lines of John Masefield which catch so well the feeling of the sailor for the sea:[1]

> I must go down to the seas again, to the lonely sea and the sky,
> And all I ask is a tall ship and a star to steer her by....
> And all I ask is a merry yarn from a laughing fellow-rover,
> And quiet sleep and a sweet dream when the long trick's over.

He records too an occasion when mother and I went to visit him at Boscombe – 16 March 1918. The entry says, 'Drive with Ma and Tom 11.15–12.30 along the front to Bournemouth.' The calm sea sparkling in the bright sunshine. He looked at it wistfully. His eyes filled with tears. He would never sail the seas again.

Also he tells in his diary how he is comforted and sustained by his faith in God. So also he told in his letters. He finds solace in Holy Communion. He writes in pencil on 23 February 1918:

Come unto Me, all ye that labour and are heavy laden, and I will give you rest.[2]

And on 27 April 1918:

1 *Sea Fever.*
2 *St. Matthew* 11:28.

Whoso eateth my flesh, and drinketh my blood, hath eternal life; and I will raise him up at the last day.[1]

Now I come to his 21st birthday. It was 18 May 1918. His entry reads, 'Received Holy Communion'. Then this passage:

I will lay me down in peace and take my rest: for it is thou, Lord, only that makest me dwell in safety.[2]

iv *At home to die*

You can tell from that last entry that he knew the end was not far off. But he wanted above all things to be at home to die. His determination gave him sufficient strength to do it. On Wednesday 22 May the last entry is, 'Ma and nurse arrived at 3.30. Packed'. They took him by ambulance home to Whitchurch. They put him to bed in the boys' room where he had slept as a boy. At last he was home. During the day the Vicar (the father of Mary, my future wife) caught a trout and sent it to him with a note, 'A fine fighter like yourself'. In the evening he asked mother to read the *23rd Psalm*. As she read it, he kept pace with his hand on the bedclothes.

The Lord is my shepherd. Therefore shall I lack nothing....His loving-kindness and mercy shall follow me all the days of my life: and I will dwell in the house of the Lord for ever.

He died the next morning.

v *His only sweetheart*

Reg and I were not there – as we were in France. I wrote and asked mother to tell me of his last hours – as I might myself not return from the war. She wrote in her firm bold hand on 10 June 1918:

You would like to know what dear Gordon had to say to me at the last. He asked me to sit by him and hold his hand. Then he said: 'Give my love to the boys, Marjorie, Johnnie. Give my love to Miss Portal, Mrs.Portal'. Then he said: 'Mother, I've got a little money for you and Dad. You have the model of the *Hampshire*. She was a fine ship. I had a nice time in her. My best shipmates went down in her'. After 'My love to Mrs. Portal,' he said: 'Sweethearts – no, I have no sweethearts. This is my sweetheart, the only sweetheart I have' and tapped my head. It was all so beautiful and he smiled all the time. His voice came back quite strong all the time he was saying this. That was in the middle of the night. He did not say much more. Only smiled each time any of us went in....In the middle of the morning he pushed me a little way off and waved such a sweet goodbye. I cannot write it as I could tell you.

1 *St. John* 6:54.
2 *Psalm* 4.

vi *'Home is the sailor'*

It must have been distressing for mother to write that letter to me. But she did it because I had asked to know. So Gordon died six days after his 21st birthday. At home as he wished. He was buried in our churchyard at Whitchurch. On his stone we have the words which fit him so well:

> Home is the sailor, home from sea.[1]

1 R. L. Stevenson, *Requiem.*

4 Tom the fourth son

1 Preparing for war

i *Too young at first*

Now let me tell of myself. None of us were allowed to serve in
the Forces until we reached the age of 18½. That was August
1917 for me – when the war had been on for three years. We
were not allowed to go to France until we were 19. But we were
all anxious to join as soon as we could. No hesitation – not even
on my part in spite of the grievous loss the family had already
borne. All the keener because of it. But quite unlike the soldier of
Shakespeare's time:

> Full of strange oaths, and bearded like the pard,
> Jealous in honour, sudden and quick in quarrel,
> Seeking the bubble reputation
> Even in the cannon's mouth.

That does not fit me at all. At 18½ I was fresh and boyish still –
with no need to shave as yet. Not bearded like the 'pard' – that is,
like a leopard – which has small tufts of hair. Not bearded at all. I
answered more to those other youngsters:[1]

> For who is he, whose chin is but enrich'd
> With one appearing hair, that will not follow
> These cull'd and choice-drawn cavaliers to France?

Nor was I 'full of strange oaths'. Our parents had forbidden
them. 'Damn' was a swear word – not to be used, profane,
irreligious – meaning 'condemn to hell'. 'Bloody' was worse –
why I know not. Even Brewer's *Dictionary* does not help much
except that it gives an illustration from Swift: 'It was bloody hot
walking today'. At any rate it was never to be used in our family.
In the Army I heard all kinds of 'strange oaths' – four-letter

---

1 *Shakespeare, Henry V*, Act III, sc. 1.

words and the rest – but I never copied them. I never put them into common use. So strict was my upbringing.

Nor did I seek the 'bubble reputation'. Military service was by my time compulsory. But I would of course have gone voluntarily anyway – like my elder brothers. When I was examined by the doctors – to see if I was fit to go to France – they rejected me – they said that there was a 'systolic murmur' in my heart – whatever that may mean. I appealed from their rejection. My appeal was allowed. I went to France. My heart has never failed me.

ii *The Royal Engineers*

I applied to join the Royal Engineers – because of my Mathematics. I thought it might be useful. It was at times. We had to make a deep dugout in France. It was behind the front line. We had to drive a tunnel from each end to meet in the middle. I worked out the directions. They did meet – exactly.

I went to the Officers' Training Corps near Newark. I was commissioned as a Second Lieutenant and was at the barracks at Aldershot. What I liked most was the horses. That war was fought with horses for transport. At any rate, for our Field Company. We had them to pull the wagons with our pontoons and bridging equipment. Each officer had his horse. Mine was once hit by a shell splinter – and survived. I said to myself Benjamin Franklin's maxim:

A little neglect may breed mischief, … for want of a nail, the shoe was lost; for want of a shoe the horse was lost; and for want of a horse the rider was lost.

Is there any parallel now for a car … for want of a spanner?

iii *Rushed out to France*

In March 1918 the Germans had advanced to within striking distance of Amiens and Paris. The situation was perilous. We youngsters of 19 were rushed out to hold the line. This was the order of Lord Haig to us on 12 April 1918:

Every position must be held to the last man: there must be no retirement. With our backs to the wall and believing in the justice of our cause, each one of us must fight on to the end.

We sailed from Southampton. We reached Rouen. Into the transit camp. We marched to the station. The band led us, playing the march *Colonel Bogey*; but left us at the yard gates. We clambered into the train with our equipment. A long slow ride till we heard the gunfire. Then I joined the Company with which I was to spend the remaining months of the war – the 151st Field Company of the Royal Engineers – attached to the 38th Welsh Division. I wore proudly the Red Dragon of Wales as an arm-flash. We were in the hot sector opposite Albert which was held by the Germans. There were long gaps in our line. We dug in – night after night – under continuous shellfire. Our Welsh regiments were the best of diggers – from the coal mines of Wales.

2 In the line

i *Night reconnaissance*

For the next three months we held the line. In trench and bivouacs. Never knowing where the next shell would fall. There was a cartoon by Bruce Bairnsfather which caught the mood exactly – the man looking over the top of a shell-hole, saying, 'If you knows of a better 'ole, go to it'. Night after night we made a reconnaissance – creeping close up to the enemy. It was a dangerous task. The river Ancre was flooded to a width of 200 to 300 yards and there were no bridges. The enemy held the other side in force. An entry in the *War Diary* for 15 August says baldly:

Lieut. Denning and 6 RE with light bridges got the infantry patrol across. The portable boat was quite useless. 25 men detailed for the purpose failed to get it along the main road.

I remember those 25 men. They were an American contingent – newly arrived. They had been attached to our Division for instruction in the line. They dropped the portable boat every time they heard a shell coming. Our own men would have got it there.

ii *Bridging the Ancre under fire*

In the next week we played our part in four most critical days —. 21 to 24 August 1918. The infantry made the crossing of the Ancre. They had to wade at night through water up to their chests under fire. We, the sappers, followed up making foot-bridges across the river and the swamps – and repairing them – under continuous rifle fire. Then there was the task of getting the wheeled transport across – the guns and ammunition wagons. Here is the one place where I am mentioned in the *History of the 38th Welsh Division*:

Meanwhile two battalions of the 115th Brigade had crossed the Ancre at Aveluy, over a bridge made by the 151st Field Company, RE, under the supervision of Lieuts. Denning and Butler, and formed up on a one battalion frontage....At 1 a.m. the attack was launched and the 114th Brigade stormed the heights and took Thiepval....By 4 p.m. the Division...had captured in this day's operations 634 prisoners and 143 machine guns.

iii *A direct hit*

I recall the occasion. We had to make a roadway across the marshes with logs and sleepers and anything we could lay hands on. We had to erect trestles and crossbeams and road-decks to get across the river itself. Shells were falling all the time. Whilst we were working an enemy aeroplane came over about 500 feet up, and going not more than 100 miles an hour – those were early days of aeroplanes. They signalled to their gunners where we were. They got a direct hit on the bridge and we had to start all over again. We did it in time. The guns and wagons went across it day and night. We maintained it. Two days and nights without sleep. I wrote a letter home. We were not allowed to say much because of the censorship. I know now that the Generals wrote descriptive letters and kept diaries – which have since been published. But not the likes of us. Mother kept my letter, written in blue pencil on thin paper. It says simply:

We have been very busy building a bridge – two days without sleep – and afterwards maintaining it.

Those of us there knew only what was happening in our little sector of the line. But Lord Haig described the operation of the Division from 21 to 24 August 1918 as 'a most brilliant operation alike in conception and execution which, with the days of heavy but successful fighting that followed it, was of very material assistance to our general advance'.

3 The final advance

i *'The gas is coming through my mask'*

After the river Ancre, there was the Canal du Nord. All the bridges across it had been destroyed, and the enemy were holding the further bank in strength. They smothered the canal valley with gas shells. Our task was to get the pontoons up and across the canal. We worked under shellfire and had to perform the whole operation in gas masks. At one point one of my men pulled off his mask and said, 'The gas is coming through my mask'. About half-a-dozen others pulled theirs off too. We went on without them – and completed the job.

There were other crossings made too – over the rivers Selle and Sambre – and there was heavy fighting all the way. I can still see the line of infantry advancing under heavy fire – first one falling and then another – with us following close behind them. I can still see the battlefield strewn with hundreds of our best officers and men – lying dead – shot down as they went forward. I can still see the dead horses lying in piles beside the roads; and dead Germans black in the face. Such is war.

ii *In hospital in Rouen*

At the time of the Armistice, I was ill with that evil type of influenza – which spread across the Continent – and destroyed more than the war itself had done. On 8 November 1918 I was taken in the ambulance train to the base hospital at Rouen. It was filled with sick men. So many that the nurses could not cope with the need. One after another died in our ward. The Armistice was at 11 a.m. on 11 November 1918. There was little rejoicing in our ward. Too many were ill. There was relief. That was all.

iii *Proud to have been there*

But now as I tell this story I feel proud to have been there, as were those at Agincourt near 600 years ago:[1]

> This story shall the good man teach his son;
> And Crispin Crispian shall ne'er go by,
> From this day to the ending of the world,
> But we in it shall be remembered;
> We few, we happy few, we band of brothers; ...
> And gentlemen in England, now a-bed
> Shall think themselves accurs'd they were not here,
> And hold their manhoods cheap whiles any speaks
> That fought with us upon Saint Crispin's day.

1 Shakespeare, *Henry V*, Act IV, sc. 3.

Section Three

Tom's next twenty years

Introduction

On returning from the war, the words of David Lloyd George rang out: 'What is our task? To make Britain a fit country for heroes to live in'. If that were the task set before the people, then it was never accomplished. Only too soon, the heroes were forgotten. There was the General Strike of 1926. I served as a Special Constable (I have my truncheon and arm-band still). We were on patrol outside the Lots Road power station. The soldiers were inside safe and sound. There was the unemployment, the dole queues, the distress of the 'thirties.

Nevertheless, for most of us life went on. Father and mother at home at Whitchurch. Marjorie married and away. Reg in the Army. Norman by this time had joined the Navy. And I was making my way at the Bar.

It is about myself that I speak in this section: because these 20 years from 1919 to 1939 were deep with emotion. In them I married and had a son. In them I got established at the Bar and took silk.

1 Marriage

1 Falling in love

i *A grain of truth*

Now I come to the age of man of which the melancholy Jaques makes such fun – as Shakespeare put it in these three lines:

> And then the lover,
> Sighing like furnace, with a woful ballad
> Made to his mistress' eyebrow.

The words have – for me – a grain of truth. I did sigh – but no puffing or blowing like a furnace. I did make a ballad – but not a woeful one. Nor was it to my sweetheart's eyebrow. Mine was more after the fashion of Shakespeare himself[1]:

> O mistress mine! where are you roaming?
> O! stay and hear; your true love's coming,
> That can sing both high and low.

ii *Shy glance*

Her name was Mary Harvey. She was the Vicar's daughter. The only girl with four brothers. I glanced shyly at her at our Confirmation. The girls in their white dresses on one side of the aisle. The boys in their best suits on the other. It was 25 October 1914. I was 15. She just 14. I know it was that day because we were confirmed by the Bishop of Winchester, Edward Talbot. He put his hands on our heads and blessed us. He stayed at the Vicarage that night. To mark the date, after supper he recited – by heart – these words of Henry V before Agincourt:[2]

> This day is called the feast of Crispian:
> He that outlives this day and comes safe home,
> Will stand a tip-toe when this day is nam'd.

1 *Twelfth Night*, Act II, sc. 3.
2 *Henry V*, Act IV, sc. 3.

80

The sidelong glance was often repeated later. Not really sidelong. Because our pew was a little forward from the Vicarage pew. So I glanced a little back as well as sidelong. Not thinking that anyone would notice. If I remember rightly, Samuel Pepys was guilty of like indiscretions; but then he ought not to have done it.

Shyly, yes. Because at that time there was some difference in our social standing. It spelt itself out in our education. Three of her brothers went to a great public school – Marlborough – and one to Sandhurst. We went to a grammar school. Her eldest brother, G. T. B. Harvey, had been at Marlborough when Geoffrey Fisher was an assistant master. Thirty years later when he was Bishop of London he appointed me Chancellor of the Diocese of London. When I spoke of Mary (then my wife) he remembered her brother, saying at once 'G. T. B.'. His memory was prodigious.

iii *The Vicar's daughter*

She came of clerical stock – on both sides. Not only was her father the Vicar of Whitchurch. But her grandfather (on her mother's side) was Canon Blackley. He achieved sufficient notice to be included in *The Dictionary of National Biography* – as a pioneer of temperance and national insurance. Her great god-father was John Keble. She loved his hymns in *The Christian Year*. She put her Christianity into practice:

> The trivial round, the common task,
> Will furnish all we need to ask;
> Room to deny ourselves; a road
> To bring us, daily, nearer God.

iv *Rose-coloured spectacles*

What was she like? I cannot put it into words. She was not pretty. She was not fair. But she was good by nature and good to look at. The first glance showed her bright dark brown eyes, sparkling with intelligence. Next, her well-shaped mouth and chin, ready to break into the most welcoming of smiles at the least provocation. Her nose was fine and straight; not broad and snubbed like mine. Her complexion was clear – not pale or blotchy – but glowing with good health – in those days. Overtopping all was her long black hair, falling a little over her wide open forehead. Never cut short. Always tied at the back of her head. In all —

> A countenance in which did meet
> Sweet records, promises as sweet.[1]

But there — you will see from the description how beautiful I thought her. I told her so – times out of number – but she would not have it so. 'You look at me through rose-coloured spectacles,' she said. 'Do not put me on a pedestal. I am not worth it.'

2 Disappointment

i *Broken-hearted*

Yet I was too shy for too long. During the war I hardly ever saw her. On my short leaves she was away at school and afterwards at Reading University, doing Agriculture. It was only when I was back at Oxford that we met: and then only during vacations. I was deeply in love with her. When I did at last venture to tell her, there was another before me. I did not know him. All she told me was that her parents were against it. He was so much older than her. Years later, she changed her mind. After we were married, she said to me' 'What a silly billy I was'.

I was broken-hearted. But I still hoped to win her one day. you may think me absurdly sentimental, but I had ever in my mind those words of Tennyson.[2] I knew them by heart:

> To love one maiden only, cleave to her,
> And worship her by years of noble deeds,
> Until they won her; for indeed I know
> Of no more subtle master under heaven
> Than is the maiden passion for a maid,
> Not only to keep down the base in man,
> But teach high thought and amiable words
> And courtliness, and the desire of fame,
> And love of truth, and all that makes a man.

ii *Trysting-place*

She told me tenderly – in words – that she did not love me. But in all other ways she did. She used to milk the cows each morning. She got up very early – before the household was

1 Wordsworth, *She was a Phantom of Delight*.
2 *Guinevere*.

awake. So did I. I would wait for her at our trysting-place. Whilst waiting, I would say to myself the words of Tennyson:[1]

> The red rose cries, 'She is near, she is near';
> And the white rose weeps, 'She is late';
> The larkspur listens, 'I hear, I hear';
> And the lily whispers, 'I wait'.
>
> She is coming, my own, my sweet;
> Were it ever so airy a tread,
> My heart would hear her and beat, ...
> Had I lain for a century dead

So we met as lovers do. We talked as lovers do. We did things together. We played tennis. We picked the apples. We stored them together. I mowed the lawn. We rolled it together. We rode out on our bicycles. On all of these, loving incidents flash into my mind.

iii *Eights Week*

Just once she came to Oxford for Eights Week – with her friend Kathleen. I took them in a punt on the river to see the races. It was a glorious day. But they were not wearing their pretty summer dresses. They came in coats and skirts. It had been raining before they left Reading. Such a disappointment for a lovesick swain!

I gave her, as a present, on her birthday and at Christmas, a little book. I have some of them beside me now. One of them is Ruskin's *Sesame and Lilies*. 'To Mary from Tom, 24 September 1920'. That was her birthday. Another is *The Oxford Book of English Verse*. 'To Mary from Tom, Christmas 1922'.

Once I bought for her a brooch. It was only a little one. I could not afford more. It had a thin silver bar with a stone of amethyst. After we had been together to a party, I was seeing her home. We stepped into the church porch. I gave her the brooch. 'It is beautiful', she murmured, 'but I cannot accept it'. She ran off down the Vicarage path.

All this was when we were at home in Whitchurch at the same time – during the holidays. But when parted, we wrote letters to each other every day – also as lovers do.

iv *Solace in work*

But then in 1923 her father left the Vicarage at Whitchurch and

[1] *Maud.*

became Rector of Fawley. So I did not see her on holidays any more. Gradually we ceased to write to one another. I turned for solace to my work. I was called to the Bar and worked as hard as anyone ever has done. Not forgetting Mary. She was still my sweetheart.

In London I was seen as a coming young barrister. I was invited to dances in the large London houses. In those days in their big drawing-rooms. Glittering with youth and beauty and wealth. I went for weekends to country houses. I met the fairest in the land. But I never lost my heart to any. I had already given it away — beyond recall.

Over these years of waiting Mary was at home with her father and mother. Fawley is now a great oil terminal. But then it was the loveliest of villages – on the edge of the New Forest – near the sea – on the corner between the Solent and Southampton Water. Mary helped with the work in the parish. She played her violin in the Musical Society. She kept half-a-dozen cows in the Glebe. She milked them and looked after them. They were stricken with foot-and-mouth disease and had to be slaughtered. She was distressed beyond measure.

3 Engaged to be married

i *St. Paul's Day*

Six years passed. At length Mary changed her mind. She wrote inviting me for the Spinsters' Ball at Brockenhurst. I stayed in the Rectory at Fawley. I told her that I loved her still. This time she no longer rejected my suit. She wrote as soon as I had left. I replied at once. The very next Saturday, she met me at Southampton station. We went to the jewellers together. We chose her engagement ring – gold set with five small diamonds. She bought me a little gold pencil. She told me how to remember the day. It was St. Paul's Day, 25 January 1930. She knew the Saints' Days. I did not. Her father wrote a little line of congratulation on 'winning the girl you have so long loved'. We were very happy. All the sighs of the past forgotten – in the joy of the present.

Sometimes I wonder what might have happened if Mary had accepted my suit all those years before when I was 21 and she was 20. We could not have married then. I was not earning enough money. Perhaps by some strange twist of fate – or of Providence – all was for the best. For it took me all of six or seven years to get established at the Bar. By the time that Mary did change her mind, I was in a position to get married. I was earning £1,000 a year.

i *A marriage is arranged*

At that time in 1930 I was getting very busy at the Bar. But every weekend I went down to Fawley. The living was one of the best in the diocese. The Rectory was a large rambling house of the period of Queen Anne. No modern conveniences. Oil lamps in the living-room. Candles up to bed. Two or three maids in the kitchen. A spacious drawing-room opening up by three large French windows on to a wide expanse of lawn – and beyond, the flower-garden and the kitchen-garden. It was there that Mary and I happily planned our future together. We would be married in August – during the long vacation.

ii *Mary becomes ill*

It was in June that Mary fell ill. She had pains in her shoulder. The doctor did not know what it was. Perhaps it was rheumatism. She started to run a temperature. The good kind doctor had her taken to a nursing home in Southampton. Then she was taken up to London to Guy's Hospital to see a specialist. It was when I was on circuit at Exeter – with a brief of some kind. I was not staying at the Bar hotel – The Royal Clarence. That would be expensive. Mary had arranged for me to stay with her cousin – Dr. Blackley and his dear wife Mary – in their lovely house and garden high on the hill.

Then in the evening there was a ring on the telephone. It was for me – from Mary's mother. 'It is worse than we thought. The doctors have diagnosed it as TB'. I fell to the floor in a faint – for the first time in my life. It was the shock. I knew what it meant. I remembered my brother Gordon. When I came to, the doctor and his wife were there. They helped me upstairs. I did not sleep much. But next morning I went down to the Castle and did my case.

iii *Love is never shaken*

As soon as I could, I went to see Mary. I bought some grapes in Southampton and took them to her. She was in bed in the nursing home. With tears in her eyes she said, 'I do not think I should hold you now'. I pressed her hand. I kissed her brow.

'We will go through with it together'. She sobbed with gratitude. I kissed her brow again. I did not kiss her lips – for fear of infection – not from that time onwards. She knew that. And so did I.

To Shakespeare again:[1]

> Love is not love
> Which alters when it alteration finds,
> Or bends with the remover to remove:
> O, no! it is an ever-fixed mark,
> That looks on tempests and is never shaken;
> It is the star to every wandering bark,
> Whose worth's unknown, although his height be taken.

v *The wedding is postponed*

The wedding was only six weeks away. It had to be put off. The invitations had to be cancelled. Some day, we hoped, we would get married. But how long? No one could tell. Mary was under the care of Dr. Geoffrey Marshall (afterwards Sir Geoffrey Marshall, Royal Physician) of Guy's Hospital. He became a close friend of ours. We trusted him completely. He recommended that she go to a sanatorium at Mundesley in Norfolk. She was there for several weeks. A strict routine, keeping to a rigid timetable.

Then she was back at home at Fawley. She had a hut in the garden. Set in the middle of the lovely lawn. She had her bed there. We took her out her meals. Whilst there she went to London every three weeks or so for treatment. Dr. Marshall could see by screening which was the bad part of the lung. Then he would collapse that bad part by pumping in air through a needle. So putting the bad part out of action. This treatment succeeded to a degree. But it was long-drawn-out. She filled in the time by reading and knitting and doing jigsaw puzzles. She was very good at them. I tried but could never find the right pieces. I went every weekend and sat with her. She had a dear little Scotch terrier called Meg.

4 Happiness at last

i *Mary recovers*

So the days passed. The weeks passed. The months passed

---

1 Sonnet, *Let me not to the marriage of true minds*.

Gradually Mary got better. We were able to go for lovely walks together – in the park – through the village – or by the shore. We sat by moonlight watching the great ships sail out, blazing with lights. So well did she get that the disease was not only arrested. It was cured – so we believed. It had taken two years and a half.

So at last the time came when the doctors thought we could get married. They advised us not to have children as yet. This we accepted. But what happiness at last! That we could get married. And where should we live? To be near my work. Could she live in London? We asked Dr. Marshall. He came to see the flat. It was the top floor of No. 1 Brick Court. Light airy rooms overlooking the Middle Temple Hall. Dr. Marshall said we could live there. I took the lease. We got the furniture for it. All was arranged.

ii *The wedding*

Our wedding-day was 28 December 1932. We were married in the little Norman church at Fawley. (Since hit by enemy bombs and much damaged.) The Bishop of Southampton (Dr. Boutflower), an old family friend, married us. Mary was in her lovely bridal frock of cream satin and had a ringlet of orange-blossom – with the family veil. The orange is to signify the hope of fruitfulness. The white blossom is the sign of innocence. We had three little bridesmaids in green. We sang the hymn which is very well known but especially appropriate for us:

> Praise, my soul, the King of heaven,
> To his feet thy tribute bring;
> Ransomed, healed, restored, forgiven,
> Evermore his praises sing.

iii *Flat in the Temple*

Our wedding night at Salisbury. On to Torquay for a fortnight. How happy we were! Back to London to the flat. Just opposite my chambers at No. 4 Brick Court in the Temple. So I could look in very often. In those days, no heating except by coal – carried up to the bin outside the front door. No refrigerator. Only a safe on the north wall. No lift – but sixty stairs to climb. None of those things worried us. Mary did her cooking in a gas stove. Once a cake came out as black as a bowler hat!

iv *Guy's Hospital*

To live in London was a mistake. It was before the use of

smokeless fuel. It was before Central London became a smoke-less zone. It was in the days when coal was the principal source of heat. Grime and soot came in by the windows and covered everything each day. Dust came in when the workmen scraped the brickwork outside. It was too much for Mary's health. After eight or nine months her lungs broke down again. She went this time to Guy's Hospital. A new treatment was tried. It was called the 'gold treatment' – by medicines and drugs. This was very distressing. Her lovely skin became covered with whitish scabs. She was there for Christmas. The doctors and nurses were very good to her – and to me. We got to know some of the other patients too. One was Laurence Binyon who wrote those words *For the Fallen* in the First World War:

> They shall grow not old, as we that are left grow old:
> Age shall not weary them, nor the years condemn.
> At the going down of the sun and in the morning
> We will remember them.

Looking back, they are appropriate for her and me.

That treatment did not succeed. The one lung became so bad that surgery was the only remedy. This time in the Brompton Hospital. All the ribs on one side were removed – so as to collapse that lung completely, leaving her with one good lung. The wound went septic. She had intense pain. A long stay in the hospital. But the surgery did succeed. We had to give up the flat in the Temple. Mary went to stay with her father and mother. He had retired from Fawley and they were living in a small house in Southampton. Near the cricket ground – for he had once played for Hampshire. I went down there every weekend.

5 Much much better

i *A house of our own*

To our joy she got better. So much better that at last we were able – after two years – to look for a house of our own. Not in London. But some place where she could be in the country and I could go up and down by train every day. We found it in Sussex. At Cuckfield. A small house near the road halfway to Haywards Heath.

This was in 1935. And then for four or five years we were able to live a normal life. Everyone was very welcoming. We made many friends. I walked to the station – 1½ miles – in the

morning: and back by bus. It cost one penny (old coinage).
Mary helped with all sorts of good works. One was Braille for
the Blind. We had our good Rose to help in the house. (She came
from Wales at the age of 15 and was our real friend.) We went on
holiday together. We did everything together.

ii *A son*

Two years later, in 1937, Mary was so well recovered that Dr.
Marshall said she might have a baby. What a joy it was! The year
1938 was the happiest of years for us. On April Fools' Day (1
April) I took silk. On 3 August our son Robert was born. It was
in Nuffield House in Guy's Hospital. Both mother and baby did
well. We went home – with a nurse for the baby for three weeks.
And then Mary managed herself – with Rose to help.

This blissful time was all too short. On 3 September 1939 the
Second World War broke out. We were in church when there
was an alert. It was a warning of enemy aircraft. Robert was in
his pram. Just one year old. We rushed home to see if he was
safe. He was. The alert was a false alarm.

6 The impact of war

i *In 'bomb alley'*

At first the war made little impact. It was a 'phoney war'. We
changed house. Only a quarter of a mile. We bought a lovely
house in Copyhold Lane and moved there early in 1940.

Then the war started in earnest. We were in 'bomb alley'. The
enemy aircraft – carrying their bombs to drop on London –
crossed over us each night. If they had not been able to use them
all, they dropped them on us. We were all 'blacked out'. But
troops billeted near us were careless. They used to leave the door
open – so that their light shone out. The enemy dropped their
bombs wherever they saw a light. So they dropped them near
us. We used to take shelter under the stairs – not that it would do
any good. One bomb dropped so close that our front door was
forced open by the blast: but no other damage done. Mary and
the baby – and Rose – were often there alone. I had to be away at
Leeds – detaining 'fifth-columnists' – or in London unable to get
home owing to an air attack.

ii *I get meningitis*

1941 was the worst of years. Rose left to join the Women's Royal Naval Air Service. So we were without help. I contracted meningitis. Due to the travelling to and from Leeds -- in the crowded dirty trains – slow, slow journeys owing to bombs. I came home one day desperately ill. So ill that I would have died – except that a doctor from Brighton prescribed a new drug called M & B. I was taken to hospital. I recovered. But Mary had the strain of my illness.

iii *Mary's last illness*

Soon afterwards she fell ill again. This time the doctors diagnosed gallstones. They advised their removal. Mary went to the Brompton Hospital for the operation. It appeared to be successful. At home Mary's old Nanny came to look after our baby Robert. She had been Nanny to Mary and her brothers when they were babies. Those Nannies were a wonderful race. Devoted to the bringing up of children, they brought up one generation after another. So in our hour of need, she came to help us. We still managed to keep the garden going – with a gardener whose name was Parker. I say this because I would like to tell you of the letters which Mary wrote from hospital to Robert – when he was just three years old. They tell so much of us.

16 September 1941

My dearest little son,

It seems a long time since I saw my Robert and I expect he is getting very big. You will have to ask Daddy to see how tall you are by the door in the sitting-room, when Daddy is home next Sunday.

And one written on her 41st birthday:

24 September 1941

My dearest little son,

Thank you ever so much for the nice birthday present you bought for me and which Daddy brought me. The tape measure is just what I wanted – to measure and see if I have knitted enough for your suit! and I love the nice card you chose, with the doggie in it. I am afraid I shall have to wait for my birthday party until I come home again and I hope that won't be long.

I have nearly finished your green suit and then I will start on the one with the nice wool you and Nanny bought the other day.

I hope you are helping Nanny and Parker and Mrs. Parker all you can.

Please will you give Nan the letter inside yours.

X X X X X X for Robert

O O O O O O for Daddy

Lots of love from Mummie.

7 The end

She did get well enough to come home. Just for three or four weeks. But then one evening – after she had gone upstairs – and I was working in the room below – I heard her knock on the ceiling. I rushed up. She said, 'I've had a haemorrhage'. She had coughed up blood. It was the beginning of the end. The doctors did all they could. Cylinders of oxygen were brought every day. Dr. Geoffrey Marshall came down himself to see her. He said, 'There is just a hope if we can get her to Brompton Hospital'. The ambulance took a long time coming. At last it came. I went with her. I stayed in the hospital. She was distressed all night. Early in the morning, I was beside her. I held her hand. She spoke so low that I could hardly hear. Just 'Goodbye, my beloved'. I kissed her goodbye. She passed peacefully away. Our romance was ended. 22 November 1941. Nearly 40 years ago now. But to me it is but as yesterday.

We buried her in the churchyard at Cuckfield. Each Sunday I took Robert to the children's service. We walked across the fields to the church. Each Sunday we tended her grave. The daffodils we planted still come up each spring. In remembrance.

2 At the Bar

1 Getting a start

i *Good credentials*

In 1922 the start was the same for me as it is now. The fledgling barrister must get a seat in chambers. As a pupil to begin with. In the hope that he may stay on permanently. But how is he to get a seat? He must be introduced to a promising junior – only juniors can take pupils – who has a vacancy for a pupil and persuade him to accept him. For this purpose he must present his credentials. It is a help to have a good degree. But better to have a good personality. This you will have begun to develop – for better or for worse – by the time you are called to the Bar. But it can be cultivated. Not cocksure. Rather diffident. Those who know least often assume to know most. Not taking the initiative at your age. Rather wait until your views are sought. Not making an outward show of your merits. Let them be drawn out of you. But nevertheless do not be tongue-tied. It is by your answers that your worth will be assessed. They will show whether you have good sense or not: or whether you have a pleasing manner or not. It is on these two – good sense and a pleasing manner – that the result depends. Not only in being accepted as a pupil. But throughout your career at the Bar.

I did not know anyone. But my Army brother Reg had known a KC during the war. Mr. Merriman KC (afterwards Solicitor-General and President of the Probate, Divorce and Admiralty Division). He suggested that I should seek pupillage with Henry O'Hagan – a junior with a good commercial practice. He agreed to take me. So I started at 4 Brick Court, off Middle Temple Lane. It was in September 1922. I was there for the next 22 years – until I became a judge.

ii *No. 4 Brick Court*

Barristers' chambers were very different from now. It was a small set. In No. 4 Brick Court, Temple. There was no silk. Only two juniors — Henry O'Hagan and Stephen Henn Collins. Each with a fine large room overlooking Brick Court. Each with his own complete library. The only other room was the small dark pupil room jutting over Middle Temple Lane. Two or three pupils there. And there was a tiny room – a cubby-hole – for the clerks. A senior clerk and a young lad working his way up. And a typist.

But it was a good place to learn the trade. O'Hagan did commercial work and some libel. Henn Collins did railway work and copyright. Each instructed by leading solicitors. The pupils saw all the paper work of both: but did not attend the conferences with solicitors – except when specially invited.

iii *Being a pupil*

Now I did something unusual. I started pupillage – too early – before I had taken the final Bar examination: but I wanted to get going. I started pupillage in September 1922. The Bar final was in June 1923. It was vital that I should do well: because I had no money except the Eldon Scholarship. So I wanted to get the Prize Studentship of the Bar. This meant that I was – at one and the same time – studying in Lincoln's Inn and reading in chambers. But it had this advantage: The reading of books in libraries – or the attending of lectures by professors – gives you only a blurred and incomplete picture. In order to understand what the law is all about, you must see it working in practice. You must see what a writ looks like; what the pleadings look like; in what way counsel gives his opinion; and how he conducts a case in Court. That is learnt by pupillage. It stood me in good stead when I took the Bar examination in June 1923. I came out top and was awarded the Prize Studentship. It was 100 guineas a year for three years. It enabled me to carry on. Even more important, I was given a seat in chambers. My name was painted on the door.

iv *Being a 'devil'*

In those days it was usual for the young barrister in chambers to spend the first few years 'briefless'. Many gave up and turned to other occupations: but, even then, the experience in chambers stood them in good stead. I, too, was briefless for a time. I used to 'devil' for the busy juniors – in our chambers and outside. That is, I used to look up cases, to draft pleadings or opinions – all without payment. Save that Mr. D. N. Pritt did give me a most welcome cheque sometimes. He had one of the biggest commercial practices of the day: and also in the Privy Council. He helped me much. When he was a silk he gave me my 'red bag.' A new barrister has only a blue bag. If he does well in a particular case, the silk may give him a red bag. By and large, however, in those days 'devilling' was not paid. Like others, I did it in the hope that my work would be approved: that my name would be mentioned to the solicitors as a 'good young man in these chambers.' Better still, that the chambers should think well of me. It was on their assessment that the future of the young man depended. It is the same today. The barrister's clerk says to the solicitor's clerk (now the legal executive): 'Mr. X is too busy. But we have a good young man available. He has already done a lot of work on these papers. Give him a try'.

v *Writing a text-book*

Another way to get started was to write a text-book of some kind or other. Some take a new statute. They write a commentary on it. They are reputed to have knowledge on it. And are briefed on it. I did differently. A new edition was required of *Smith's Leading Cases*. It was in 1837 that John William Smith collected together the leading cases of his time – with his commentary on them. The Bar used to take his two volumes round the circuit with them. They had been brought up to date by eminent editors (some of the most learned in the law) over the last 90 years. Sir Thomas Willes Chitty was to edit a new edition – the 13th. He asked two of us young men – Cyril Harvey and me – we had each taken Firsts at Oxford – to help him. It was an immense task – involving much research. But it taught me most of the law I ever knew. I was bold enough to be drastic in some of my notes – rewriting them and suggesting new principles – especially those in the leading cases of *Lampleigh v Braithwaite, Cutter v Powell* and *Taylor v Caldwell*. Years later these notes of mine came to be accepted by the judges – without any recognition of their origin. Our edition was the last. Later, when I was a judge, the publishers asked me to edit another. I did not have time. Nor has anyone else had time.

vi *Discovering 'The Reasonable Man'*

Throughout all this time, I discovered the character who dominates all our Common Law. He is 'The Reasonable Man'. He was drawn with characteristic fun by A. P. Herbert. He made a pun on *Smith's Leading Cases* when he used a title, *Misleading Cases*. In an Introduction Lord Buckmaster said: 'Mr. Herbert's misleading cases will be turned to with relief by many who find Smith's leading cases a little dull'. A. P. Herbert had been called to the Bar and with gentle irony exposed the law's uncertainties – to the delight of us all of his generation. Here is a typical illustration. He called it the case of *Fardell v Potts The Reasonable Man* and gave this as the judgment of the Master of the Rolls:

… The Common Law of England has been laboriously built about a mythical figure – the figure of 'The Reasonable Man'. He is an ideal, a standard, the embodiment of all those qualities which we demand of the good citizen. No matter what may be the particular department of human life which falls to be considered in these Courts, sooner or later we have to face the question: Was this or was it not the conduct of a reasonable man? …

It is impossible to travel anywhere or to travel for long in that confusing forest of learned judgments which constitutes the Common Law of England without encountering the Reasonable Man. He is at every turn, an ever-present help in time of trouble, and his apparitions mark the road to equity and right. There has never been a problem, however difficult, which His Majesty's judges have not in the end been able to resolve by asking themselves the simple question, 'Was this or was it not the conduct of a reasonable man?' and leaving that question to be answered by the jury.

…The Reasonable Man is always thinking of others: prudence is his guide, and 'Safety First', if I may borrow a contemporary catchword, is his rule of life. All solid virtues are his, save only that peculiar quality by which the affection of other men is won….Though any given example of his behaviour must command our admiration, when taken in the mass his acts create a very different set of impressions. He is one who invariably looks where he is going, and is careful to examine the immediate foreground before he executes a leap or bound….Devoid, in short, of any human weakness, with not one single saving vice, *sans* prejudice, procrastination, ill-nature, avarice, and absence of mind, as careful for his own safety as he is for that of others, this excellent but odious character stands like a monument in our Courts of Justice, vainly appealing to his fellow-citizens to order their lives after his own example….

vii *No reasonable woman*

To return, however, as every judge must ultimately return, to the case which is before us – it has been urged by the appellant, and my own researches incline me to agree, that in all that mass of authorities which bears upon this branch of the law *there is no single mention of a reasonable woman*. It was ably insisted before us that such an omission, extending over a century and more of judicial pronouncements, must be something more than a coincidence; that among the innumerable tributes to the reasonable man there might be expected at least some passing reference to a reasonable person of the opposite sex; that no such reference is found, for the simple reason that no such being is contemplated by the law; that legally at least there *is* no reasonable woman....

I find that at Common Law a reasonable woman does not exist.

2 Work of my own

i *In Hampshire*

Whilst working on *Smith's Leading Cases*, I began to get work. First, in my own Courts in Hampshire. I had a little influence. Mary – my sweetheart – had an uncle, T. H. Woodham. He was a solicitor and the Clerk of the Peace for the City of Winchester. He had little work but he gave me a start by small briefs for the prosecution: for a fee of £2. 4s. 6d. I attended quarter sessions and got the occasional dock brief of £1. 3s. 6d. This led to more and more work on circuit. I went regularly to the Assizes at Winchester and Exeter. It was still the time of the Grand Jury. The Bar were excluded from the Court whilst the Commission was read. The Judge was to hear and determine the causes 'doing therein what to justice shall appertain'. The foreman of the Grand Jury took the oath in words which Lord Goddard regarded as most impressive:

I swear by Almighty God that I, as foreman of this grand inquest for our Sovereign Lord the King and the body of this County of Southampton will diligently inquire and true presentment make of all such matters, offences and things as shall be given me in charge or shall otherwise come to my knowledge touching this present service. The King's counsel, my fellows' and my own I will observe and keep secret. I will present no person out of envy, hatred or malice, neither will I leave anyone unpresented through fear, affection, gain, reward or the hope or promise thereof, but I will present all things truly and indifferently as they come to my knowledge according to the best of my skill and understanding.

Afterwards, the Bar were called into the Court. The Judge took the pleas. Every few minutes the Grand Jury came back into an upstairs gallery. They sent down a piece of paper in a fish-net at the end of a long pole. The Clerk said, 'You find a true bill against John Roe'. And so forth.

ii *In London*

I also got small work in London. Before magistrates or in county courts. The breakthrough came when Stephen Henn Collins mentioned my name to the solicitors for the Southern Railway Company. I went all round the Southern Region doing their small work. I went often before the magistrates, prosecuting persons who travelled with intent to avoid payment of fare. I wrote a railway police manual giving guidance to the police. I redrafted the railway by-laws. I went to county courts on claims for possession. I got to know the Rent Acts backward. In short, I got going in the same way as young barristers have done in the past – and still do – by satisfying the solicitors and getting known.

In time I was entrusted by the Railway Company with the bigger work. In personal injury cases – assessing compensation. In cases where they relied on exempting conditions on tickets. Also by other firms in commercial cases of all kinds. I had taken the Sale of Goods and Charterparties as special subjects in the Bar examination and knew *Chalmers and Scrutton* nearly by heart. In libel cases for *The Times* and *The Tatler*. I covered the whole range of common law. With an occasional appearance in Chancery too. I had three or four pupils. They saw my papers, but I had little time to teach them. They played 'shove-halfpenny' in the pupil room. I looked in for tea.

iii *The Double-First and the Old Hand*

As I worked in the Middle Temple – and hoped to take over the tenancy there, I was called *ad eundem* to the Middle Temple. It cost then £25. It costs now £200. I lunched daily in the hall. Often at the same table as Theobald Mathew. 'The O'. Mathew was the best of raconteurs. He could make lightning sketches. He wrote the humorous classic *Forensic Fables*. In one of them he portrayed – with some exaggeration – a contest in which I was opposed to Martin O'Connor – who had a big running-down practice. Mathew entitled it *The Double-First and the Old Hand*. (I was the Double-First and Martin O'Connor was the Old Hand.)

A Double-First, whose Epigrams were Quoted in Every Common-Room of the University, became Weary of Tuition and went to the Bar. His Friends were Satisfied that he was Bound to become in the Near Future either Prime Minister or Lord Chancellor. They Doubted, however, whether Either of these Jobs Afforded Sufficient Scope for his Splendid Abilities. Shortly after his Call, a Near Relative Provided him with a Brief. He was to Appear for a Public Authority which Owned a Tram-Car. The Plaintiff was a Young

Lady who had Sustained Injuries while being Carried Thereon from her Place of Residence to her Place of Business. Her Story, as Set Forth in the Statement of Claim, was that the Conductor, without Any or Alternatively Sufficient Warning, had Rung the Bell whilst she was Stepping off the Vehicle, and that by Reason of his Said Negligence she had Fallen Heavily in the Road, Abraded her Shin-Bone, and Suffered from Shock and Other Discomforts. Her Claim (including Extra Nourishment and Various Items of Special Damage) Totalled £583. 4s. 9d. The Double-First had Little Doubt that the Claim was Grossly Exaggerated, if not Actually Dishonest. He was Confident of Victory. When he Got into Court the Double-First found himself Opposed by an Old Hand of Unrivalled Experience in that Class of Action. He Looked Harmless Enough, and the Double-First Felt no Alarm. But Strange Things Soon Happened. The Old Hand Conducted the Case for the Plaintiff in a Manner which Shocked the Double-First Exceedingly. After the Jury had been Sworn he Informed his Solicitor-Client in a Whisper which could be Heard in the Central Hall that he would not Settle for Less than Five Hundred, and he Asked the Double-First in Stentorian Tones, with Reference to the Plan, whether he would Agree (1) the Exact Spot where the Pool of Blood was Found, and (2) the Precise Locality where the Conductor had Admitted to the Policeman that he had Done the Same Thing on Another Occasion. When the Double-First Cross-Examined the Plaintiff, the Old Hand Asked the Judge to Protect his Client from Insult; and when he Addressed the Jury the Old Hand Repeatedly Begged that he would not Deliberately Misrepresent the Evidence. The Double-First Struggled against these Tactics in Vain. In his Final Speech, the Old Hand Reminded the Jury of the Possibility that Tetanus or Paralysis might Hereafter Supervene, and the Certainty that a Disfigured Tibia would Seriously Impair the Plaintiff's Matrimonial Prospects. Apart from his Successful Application for a Stay of Execution on the Ground that the Damages (£1,000) were Excessive, the Double-First had a Disastrous Day.

Moral – *Despise not Your Enemy*.

iv *My name in the* Law Reports

After about seven years, my name used to appear in the *Law Reports* or occasionally in *The Times*. That was the only legitimate form of advertising allowed to a member of the Bar. Anything in the nature of 'touting' was prohibited absolutely. No barrister was allowed to do anything which suggested that he was seeking to curry favour with solicitors. If I was out on a case with a solicitor's clerk, I must not pay for his lunch. The Inns of Court would not allow solicitors to dine in their halls. The barrister had to rely solely on his own reputation – on the personal recommendation of others. This is still the basic rule.

I will not recount here the various cases in which I was engaged. That is the bane of legal biographies. But I would like to tell of two of them – when I was a junior.

3 Cases to remember

i *The automatic machine*

The first is *L'Estrange v Graucob*.[1] There was a lady in North Wales with a little tobacconist's shop. A salesman came and sold her an automatic machine, payable by instalments. He said to her (I remember now the long brown form) – he said: 'Sign here'. So she signed there. The machine was delivered, but it didn't work. They sent the mechanic down three times. Still it wouldn't work. So she didn't pay the instalments. The Company took her to the County Court. When she said it wouldn't work, they said: 'Look at the clause'. There in very small print, if you could read it:

Any condition or warranty, expressed or implied, by statute or by common law, is hereby excluded.

The County Court Judge managed to get round that clause somehow. The lady took the case to the Court of Appeal. I was there instructed for the Company. I said to Lord Justice Scrutton: 'But look, she's signed it. Even though she couldn't – and didn't – read it, in the absence of fraud she's bound'. Lord Justice Scrutton said: 'Yes, yes, in the absence of fraud, or, I would add, misrepresentation,' he said, 'she's bound'. So we, the Company, were victorious in the Court of Appeal. In those days I wasn't concerned so much with the rightness of the cause. I was concerned only, as a member of the Bar, to win it if I could. But, the reporter was wise. He didn't think much of it. He didn't record it in the Law Reports. But my Company had it privately printed: and I went round the County Courts of England winning case after case most unrighteously for this Company. That was my first contact with exception clauses. We have done a lot more since. We invented the doctrine of fundamental breach. We got rid of those exception clauses altogether until the House of Lords in the *Suisse Atlantique*[2] case said we were wrong. But we've been getting round that case ever since!

ii *The gallant Major*

The second case of which I would tell you is *Beresford v Royal Insurance*.[3] This is a dramatic story.

1 [1934] 2 KB 394.
2 [1967] 1 AC 361.
3 [1938] AC 586.

There was a Major Rowlandson once who insured his life for £80,000. The insurance was due to come to an end at three o'clock on a June afternoon. If he couldn't find the premium, it would lapse. If he died before three, all the money would come in. If he died after three, there would be no money at all. That afternoon, at half-past two, he went to his solicitor in Chancery Lane. At a quarter-to-three he came out and called a taxi. He said to the taxi-driver: 'Drive me to my flat in Albemarle Street'; and added: 'As you pass St. James's Palace clock, look at the time and note it'. The taxi-driver went along Fleet Street and the Strand. He went along the Mall. As he passed St. James's Palace clock, there it was. Three minutes to three. Up St. James's Street. The taxi-driver heard a bang, stopped the taxi, got out. There in the cab was Mayor Rowlandson – dead! Two minutes to three – just in time!

We were instructed for the personal representatives.

We claimed against the Insurance Company for the money. They said No. It was a crime: and we couldn't get it, although the contract said we could. We said that Major Rowlandson was *non compos mentis*. It was tried before Mr. Justice Swift with a special jury. I was led by Sir William Jowitt. He put the case dramatically to the jury. 'Three minutes to three,' he said, 'two minutes to three'. The Judge, as I have said, was Mr. Justice Swift. He went out to lunch. He always had a good lunch, did Mr. Justice Swift! He liked one or two tots of whisky. In the afternoon he came back. In summing up to the jury, he said: 'Wasn't this the act of a gallant English gentleman, killing himself for the sake of his creditors?' The jury found him of sound mind. The Court of Appeal said that, as a result, we could not claim the money. We went to the House of Lords. Sir William Jowitt led me. He had to leave early and turned to me; and, referring to the suicide of Ophelia, said 'Give then all that'. I gave it to them. It didn't do any good. The House of Lords said that suicide, *felo de se*, was the most heinous crime known to our English law. A man rushing into the presence of his maker unasked. So we lost.

Now let me tell the sequel. In the House of Lords afterwards we had a Bill, now an Act of Parliament.[1] Suicide is no longer a crime. Attempted suicide is no longer a crime. We should have won that case now. More of this Bill later.

---

1 Suicide Act 1961.

4 Taking silk

So much for life as a junior. I did it for 15 years. Then came the time when I was so busy that I applied for silk. In those days a junior was very cautious before applying for silk. He had to notify all those on the circuit senior to him. The word got round to solicitors. They would cease to instruct him. If he were refused, it was a bad mark against him. So applications were restricted to those who had a good claim. The number of successful juniors was so small that anyone acquainted with the profession knew them. So I wrote a short letter of application to the Lord Chancellor – without giving any references. I was granted it.

It is very different today. Nowadays applications run to as many as 150 a year. Each has to fill in a form giving particulars of his earnings. Very few get it on first application. Only about one-quarter of the applications are granted. The rest are refused.

So I took silk on 1 April 1938. There were only 15 then. Now there are 40 or 50 each year. We were sworn in before the Lord Chancellor. Then Lord Maugham. He was very clever. He had a sarcastic and supercilious manner – which made every advocate feel small. He was only there for one year. We made our way to the Courts in the Strand and took our seats within the Bar – in the accustomed way. No longer able to draw pleadings – or to appear in Court without a junior. A silk's work is confined to appearing in Court as an advocate – and to writing opinions. At first I was short of silk's work. I wrote an article or two for *The Law Quarterly Review*. But next year the war came. It altered everything.

The Second World War

Introduction

The war started on 3 September 1939. It had been brewing for some time. Hitler had come to the top in Germany. Hitler, the demagogue who could sway thousands by his strident speeches. Hitler, who proclaimed the Germans as the Master Race. Hitler, who hated the Jews. So much so that many scientists and lawyers took refuge in England – and enriched us by their skill and knowledge. Hitler, who established the Nazi regime with its hated gestapo and police state. Hitler, who marched by force into the Sudetenland. Hitler, who deceived Neville Chamberlain with the Munich Agreement so completely that he told this country: 'I believe it is peace for our time....Peace with honour'. Hitler, who in 1939 invaded Poland and precipitated the Second World War.

In this war two of the brothers were regular officers. Reg in the Army. Norman in the Navy. They brought their intelligence and ability to help in the fighting. I will start with Norman. I will tell of his life. He died at the end of 1979. Only Marjorie and two of us boys left now.

1 Norman the fifth son

1 In peacetime

i *The Paymaster cadet*

Norman was the youngest of us. At the end of the First World War in November 1918, he was only just 14 years of age. He went daily to the grammar school at Andover, like Gordon and me. He was devoted to his brothers. When Jack came in May 1916 on his last leave – and was going back to France – Norman, at 11½, cycled the seven miles from school at Andover to see him off at Whitchurch station. When Gordon was ill at Bere Hill in 1917, Norman went every morning to see him – on his way to school. I remember that when Norman left school in 1921, we considered what he should do. Unlike the rest of us, he had bad eyesight. But there was a possibility that he might be eligible for the Paymaster Branch of the Royal Navy. He took the examination and was accepted. He became a Paymaster cadet. At that time the Paymaster Branch was rather looked down upon by the Executive Branch – they had been to Dartmouth. But this disparagement was redressed in later years – largely, I like to think, by the distinction which Norman brought to the Paymaster Branch. The Paymasters were in charge of all the stores and supplies for the victualling of the Navy. They were secretaries to the Admiralty. They were the brains behind the administrative side.

ii *A really strong breeze*

Norman climbed up the naval ladder. He sailed in ships all the world over. Some might think that, being in the Paymaster Branch, he was not a real sailor. But a letter to me shows how well he could handle a boat – and how well he could describe it. The sailors among you will understand the nautical language.

HMS *Capetown*
North America and West Indies,
Bermuda.
2 June 1927

Dear Tom,

....Yesterday I had one of the most thrilling experiences of my life, but not a word to Mother or Dad, in case they accuse me of foolhardiness. I attempted a feat I have always longed to do; previously I have taken a 16 ft skiff out sailing alone in a light breeze and I had always longed to take her out by myself in a really strong breeze. Yesterday was my opportunity. I wanted to test myself and also the skiff in a very strong wind, without taking a reef in the sail. I got my office messenger to rig the boat, in order to save time, and I started off from the ship to the cheers of my brother officers on the quarter-deck. All went well until I got out of the harbour and then because of the wind I got into a very loppy sea. However, I had her well in hand. I noticed that the *Calcutta*, which had been out for exercises, was just entering harbour, but I was well clear of her. I should have been perfectly all right but unfortunately my messenger had forgotten to bowse the sheets. First of all the fore-sheet carried away. I immediately rushed forward and lowered foresail and attempted to sail clear with the mainsail only. Unfortunately the main-sheet carried away immediately after. There was only one thing for me to do, which I did, and that was to brail up. After a minute or two I managed to make fast the mainsail and set it. I had no time to make fast the fore-sheet as I was being rapidly carried by the wind into the *Calcutta*, as during the operation of fixing the main-sheet the boat had drifted on to the other tack which was carrying me straight into the *Calcutta* which was under way; with only a mainsail set and the sea being so loppy, I couldn't get the boat to go about on the other tack. There was only one thing to do and that was to get an oar out and pull her round, which I managed to do just in time and sailed down the *Calcutta*'s side at about ten yards distant, gazed upon by the Chief of Staff and senior officers. When I finally got clear I hove to and made all shipshape again and sailed on, meaning to get the mastery of the boat, which I did, and only then did I return to calmer waters and take in a reef, but even then I found it very thrilling. It is a sensation, or whatever one likes to term it, to live for, alone in a boat, with half-a-dozen ropes to handle, all struggling for mad, and realising that one mistake will mean the capsizing and sinking of the boat; not only has one to watch the wind for squalls but also the state of the sea, in case a breaker might swamp her, but on returning to harbour safe and sound one feels that glorious, uplifted feeling that you have achieved and mastered something.

Today my hands are sore and blistered, pieces of skin have actually been worn off to the flesh by the rubbing of the sheets in my hand, and I have the quiet conviction that not everybody in the world (although more experienced than me in boat-sailing) would have taken the boat out lone-handed in a wind of that force....

Norman

2 A genius for Intelligence

i *Norman the expert*

Norman was promoted to the various posts open to the Pay-master Branch. He was secretary to Admirals. He was in charge of supplies to great ships of war. But his genius was for Intelligence – with a capital 'I'. With a small 'i', intelligence only means information or news. With a capital 'I', Intelligence means the agency for obtaining and handling secret information.

Wellington once said:

All the business of war, and indeed all the business of life, is an endeavour to find out what you don't know by what you do; that's what I called 'guessing what was at the other side of the hill'.[1]

In that process of 'guessing what was at the other side of the hill', my brother Norman proved himself the most expert of experts. Until very recently I never knew what was the nature of Norman's work. It was highly secret. He told no one. All I knew was that during the war he spent days and nights in the Citadel – the fortress built next the Admiralty building in Whitehall, with one day's rest a week – if things were quiet. Some of his work has now been disclosed: because of the '30-year rule'. The general rule now is that, as soon as the records are 30 years old, government departments should send them to the Public Record Office – where they can be inspected by any member of the public. But there are exceptions to that rule – in the interests of national security or for other reasons. In the case of the records of Naval Intelligence during the Second World War, a good deal was disclosed in 1975 (30 years after the war ended). But much of that which was most secret was not disclosed. Norman told me so. So the story is incomplete even today.

ii *Two books*

Two books have told of the work which Norman did in Intelligence. They are both by men who worked with him in Intelligence during the war. Donald McLachlan, who became editor of *The Sunday Telegraph* (he has since died), and Patrick Beesly. They describe Norman's work. They call him Ned as he was always called in the Navy – from his initials N(orman) E(gbert) D(enning). They also describe the work of Rodger

1 *Croker Papers* (1885), vol. iii, p. 276.

Winn. He was at the Bar. He had a distinguished career in the law. He became in due course Treasury Devil, High Court Judge, and a Lord Justice of Appeal. A dear colleague of mine of great ability. During the war he worked in the Admiralty with Norman. He did great work in tracking down the German submarines. This is how Patrick Beesly puts it:[1]

An immense debt was owed to these two men. Many well-earned tributes have been paid to Rodger Winn – fewer to Ned Denning: but the latter's contribution, both in respect of pre-war planning and wartime control of surface ship intelligence, was of no less importance than Winn's great work against the U-boats. Denning, throughout the whole war, spent six days and nights a week in the Admiralty. He was almost continuously on call.... Denning, the professional, was the better administrator and, in some ways, the easier man to work for; Winn, the amateur, was possibly the more skilful advocate with the flair for what would now be called 'public relations'; both of them were, in the words of Clayton's deputy, Captain Colpoys, 'the intelligence officers de luxe of all time'.

The first of the books is *Room 39* by Donald McLachlan. I have the copy before me which was given to me by Rodger Winn. He writes on the flyleaf: 'Tom. With all good wishes to the Brother of the Hero of the Book. Rodger Winn. 2/5/68'. The second of the books is *Very Special Intelligence* by Patrick Beesly. He had access to far more information than Donald McLachlan. He writes on the flyleaf of the copy before me: 'To Ned. With many thanks for all your invaluable help. I only hope that I have done you and the subject justice. Pat. February 1977'. These books describe Norman's work so well that you might think it unnecessary for me to add more: but he himself, not long before his death, wrote a paper in which he describes many incidents and which fill in the picture, so I hope you will understand if I quote considerably from it.

iii *Norman warns about Singapore*

In the early 'thirties, Norman was stationed for two years in Singapore – which was our great base in the Far East. It was there he first showed his flair for Intelligence. His office overlooked that part of Singapore harbour reserved for coastal shipping. He became interested in the large number of Japanese fishing vessels. He noticed that they were supported by three, four or five Japanese fishery research vessels, equipped with all the modern navigational aids. Norman was suspicious. He

1 *Very Special Intelligence*, p. 253.

knew that the whole defence of Singapore was based on the assumption that, in the event of a war with Japan, the Japanese would mount a frontal assault on Singapore Island from *seaward*. Norman, from his investigations, thought that that assumption was wrong; and that the Japanese might land an assault force far up on the east coast and advance down the peninsula for an assault from *landward*. Norman prepared a report for submission to the Director of Naval Intelligence. He did not know what had happened to it until he made inquiries six years later. He then found that it had been dismissed with the comment:

This young officer is over-exercising his imagination. The Japanese have no seaborne assault force. It is ridiculous to imagine an army advancing hundreds of miles through jungle territory.

Norman in his paper makes this comment:

Just three years later (December 1941) the Japanese invaded Malaya, their first landing being at Kota Bharu on the border with Thailand and began their advance down the peninsula which culminated in the fall of Singapore. Wishing to vindicate myself I again asked the Far East desk to see my report, but it had disappeared....With hindsight, I know that I should have prevailed upon my Captain to bring my report to the attention of local military authorities, including the Governor and General Officer Commanding, rather than leave it to someone to consign it to stagnate in the archives of the Admiralty.

iv He is the 'astute man'

In 1937, Norman had been called back to the Admiralty for a new task. It was in Naval Intelligence. Admiral James had recommended that a centre should be built up to assess the value of information received. In a minute he wrote:

If astute men are put on to this work, there is no doubt in my mind that very soon a valuable form of Operational Intelligence will be built up.

They did find an 'astute man'. He was Paymaster Lieutenant-Commander Norman Denning. He started work in the summer of 1937. It was he who built up the Operational Intelligence Centre (OIC). It is not possible here to set out all that he did but I will pick out some incidents of especial interest — in his own words — from his paper.

v He finds a treasure

Before starting work in the Naval Intelligence Division (NID) I had spent three or four weeks with the Secret Service organisation and the Government Code and Cypher School (at Bletchley). On returning to the Admiralty, I was handed a key which I was told was the key to a certain room in the attics of the Admiralty building and which was believed to contain some old NID records. One day I decided to investigate. The only light filtered in through a cobweb-covered window but a naked electric bulb revealed racks filled with files of papers covered with layers of dust and grime and apparently not touched for years. On examination of some of the files it soon became clear that they were the records of Room 40 OB (Old Block) comprising all the intercepted German original messages of World War I and their decrypts. Despite the dust, dirt and cobwebs it was to me treasure trove. For days whenever I had spare time I went through some of the records.

vi *A signal not passed*

I found the original of the signal made by Admiral Scheer requesting a dawn reconnaissance by Zeppelin of the Horns Rift. This signal, if it had been passed to Admiral Jellicoe, would have enabled him to deduce the actual channel by which the German High Seas Fleet would return to the safety of German waters. Instead, the actual course which Jellicoe selected took him farther away from Scheer and enabled the latter to slip behind the Grand Fleet during the night and thus escape.

vii *Titbits*

The most important find was some papers which had been written after the war by one or two unknown members of the staff of Room 40 OB and which contained constructive criticism of the work of that Room and how it could have been used more effectively in influencing the conduct of operations at sea. It became my bible in planning an organisation which I hoped would be effective and avoid the faults and errors in the organisation of Operational Intelligence in World War I.

Amongst the papers was one which was more or less a philosophical essay on Intelligence. One sentence stuck in my mind and I quote: 'Information is not Intelligence until it has been refined in the crucibles of intellect, experience and common-sense'. There was good cause to remember this later on in World War II when we found that someone was feeding the Prime Minister with titbits or snippets of raw intercepted messages upon which he was drawing his own somewhat imaginative conclusions and discreet steps had to be taken to see that in future he was supplied only with evaluated information.

3 The first breakthrough

i *'I am Winston Churchill'*

Munich was the turning-point and stirred the apathy of the politicians who at last acknowledged that the nation might become engaged in war.

Politically Winston Churchill was in the wilderness and then almost the only voice calling for the nation's rearmament in view of Hitler's policies. It was during this time that I first heard his voice. Answering the telephone one day a voice said, 'I am Winston Churchill. They tell me you know all about the German Navy.' To my reply that I wished I did, he went on, 'Do you know where the *Gneisenau* and *Scharnhorst* are?' On receiving the necessary information, he went on, 'Keep an eye on those ships. They are dangerous.'

ii *High level vertical photography*

The first indication to me that photographic reconnaissance could be an invaluable source of Intelligence was the fortuitous receipt of a high altitude photograph taken by a Fleet Air Arm aircraft during the Spanish Civil War of a pocket battleship – I think it was the *Admiral Scheer* off Majorca.

Many years previously I had become acquainted with Sidney Cotton, an Australian, who had served in the Air Force in World War I....I discovered that his Company had been employed by the Secret Service for certain clandestine photography. The aircraft they used were twin-engined Lockheeds with not particularly high performance. Two or three RAF pilots had been seconded to fly them. Just two days before the outbreak of war one of them who had been on a visit to Germany was returning to England when he noticed warships anchored in Schilling Roads outside Wilhelmshaven; intuitively he took an oblique photograph of them. When examined they turned out to be the *Scharnhorst*, a *Koln* class cruiser, the cruiser *Emden* and Hitler's yacht, the *Grille*....

The Royal Air Force did not take kindly to the use of unarmed aircraft on photographic missions, maintaining that such intelligence could only be obtained by combat aircraft. Sidney Cotton, pioneer and keen advocate of air photography, had already in mind the use of the Spitfire cleaned up and streamlined, stripped of its armament and fitted instead with cameras which would be able to operate above and outfly any known fighter. This, however, took time to materialise....

The value of the intelligence which could be obtained from high level overlapping vertical photography was established but the RAF were reluctant to take over Sidney Cotton's unit. Churchill, who had himself seen its value, swung the day by announcing that if the Air Ministry would not take it over the Navy would. Eventually the matter was put before Chiefs of Staff and they agreed that the Air Force should assume responsibility for it....

So was born a source of Intelligence which later, together with Special Intelligence, was to provide the greater part of our Intelligence.

iii *One hundred U-boats*

It was sometime during the early part of 1940 that the First Sea Lord came back from a War Cabinet meeting and informed us that the Chief of Air Staff was requesting permission to bomb the port of Emden as well over a hundred U-boats were in port there. This statement was, of course, nonsense, but I was informed that Bomber Command had photographs to prove it. I said we should like to see them and suggested that they be sent to the laboratory at Wembley. When I arrived there I was met by Michael Spender who laughingly said, 'Look at these U-boats'; just one glance at the photographs and one saw through the puffy wisps of cloud nothing more sinister than Rhine barges.

iv *A Foreign Secretary's long hair*

When I returned to my room about midnight, Winston was sitting there. I showed him the photographs and then he became interested in the work of the laboratory and the technique of interpreting air photographs from the stereoscopic effect of overlapping photography. At length he summed it up by saying this looked like an amalgam of two points of view which would undoubtedly give a more precise evaluation than just one. Then he went on to relate the following story which I only wish I could tell in his own phraseology. It might serve as a moral for many of us though not always borne in mind even by Churchill.

There was once in the Cabinet a Foreign Secretary. He was of middle age, shortish, and with silvery hair which he allowed to grow down over his collar. He was noted for the lack of tidiness in his dress; for instance, when he went out of doors he always wore a long coat which hung down almost to his ankles and a battered 'trilby' hat with a feather stuck in the band. He was a bachelor, so it was a surprise to his colleagues when one day he announced that he was getting married. After he returned from his honeymoon his colleagues noted that he never gave them an opportunity to meet his bride and eventually one of them mustered up courage to tell him that it would give them great pleasure to meet her. Whereupon he replied as follows: 'Well, it is like this. When I am out with my wife it is always very embarrassing to me. You see, she is very young and attractive and I am getting old and look it, particularly with my white hair. Only yesterday when we were walking in St. James's Park, a young lad approached us and pointing behind us said, 'Excuse me sir, but your daughter has dropped her gloves'. Glaring at him, I turned to retrieve them and suggested to my wife that for security it would be better if she wore them and so I relieved her of her handbag and umbrella whilst she put them on. During the course of it, I became aware that two women walking behind us, were discussing us. They had evidently taken me in wearing my long coat, battered 'trilby', white hair hanging down over my collar and carrying a lady's handbag and umbrella, and I heard one of them say, "Mother and daughter, I presume". You see, the same subject, two different points of view, two different judgments – both wrong'.

v *The failure of Dieppe in 1942*

Whereas photographic intelligence can often be very precise and accurate, nevertheless it may at times be inclined to mislead depending upon the skill and dedication of the interpreting officer. For instance, one of the several reasons for the failure of the raid on Dieppe was that the tanks could not get off the beaches and this was partially due to the fact that what had been interpreted from photographs as ramps leading from the beach to the promenade were in fact steps which the tanks could not negotiate.

vi *The nightcap*

It was not long before Winston Churchill left the Admiralty to become Prime Minister that he came down as usual to the Admiralty basement on his way to his underground bedroom. His practice was to visit the OIC for any up-to-date Intelligence and then the Duty Captain's room where there was a small bar from which Winston sometimes indulged in a nightcap – even I was sometimes invited to go along. News had just been received of a rather heavy bombing raid – it may have been the raid on Rotterdam – which had caused many civilian casualties. Sitting in a chair he pondered quietly for a few moments. Then said, as if to himself: 'Unrestricted submarine warfare, unrestricted air bombing – this is total war'. I still remember the scene vividly. He sat gazing at a large map which covered all one side of the room. Then said – I suppose he was quoting – 'Time and the Ocean and some guiding star and high cabal have made us what we are'. Then he paused a short time and continued, if I remember his words correctly: 'Our defence must now lie in the skies above but the Ocean is our only lifeline. They must be the highest priority in our strategy'.

4 The second breakthrough

i *The German cypher machine*

The Germans had an extremely efficient cypher machine called *Enigma*. They used it to communicate with their ships at sea and with their submarines. If only that could be obtained, it would be invaluable. Norman describes how it was done.

In the early months of 1941, OIC had located and plotted the positions of two weather reporting vessels which were operating in an area north of the Faroe Islands. This gave rise to a proposal to mount an operation to endeavour to capture one in order to obtain cyphering equipment. The operation was successfully carried out in that cyphering keys in connection with *Enigma* were obtained.

More importantly, in the middle of May, the U-boat U.110 was captured and before she sank the *Enigma* machine and keys were recovered intact.

Patrick Beesly tells the story in his book *Very Special Intelligence* (page 71):

On May 8, U.110, commanded by one of Dönitz's aces, Kapitän Leutnant Julius Lemp, had attacked an outward bound convoy south of Greenland, but had been heavily counter-attacked by the Senior Officer of the 3rd Escort Group. Captain Baker Cresswell saw the chance of securing not only a prize but also cypher material, of whose vital importance he was very conscious. He had no OIC expert with him, but a boarding party under Sub-Lieutenant David Balme, RN, reached U.110 and not only managed to prevent the U-boat from sinking but recovered, intact and undamaged, its cypher machine with all its accompanying material and many other secret documents. Baker Cresswell took great pains to prevent his prisoners from seeing what was happening, and the capture of U.110 was successfuly kept a secret not only throughout the war but right up to 1958. The fact that the U-boat eventually sank before she could be towed to Iceland, although a disappointment at the time, may well have contributed to the maintenance of the secret.

ii *The* Bismarck

Norman continues:

All the material thus captured was put to good use at Bletchley so that soon they were able to decypher the current *Hydra* cypher traffic. This cypher was used for communication to and from all surface vessels operating in German, Norwegian and French home waters. Initially it was also used for communication to and from U-boats.

Thus it came about that during *Bismarck*'s final action we were able to know the orders to U-boats to proceed towards her and to one in particular to endeavour to retrieve her war log. Also we read the signals made to her that the German Air Force had been ordered to give protection.

iii *The traffic in Intelligence*

The fact of being able to read the *Hydra* traffic altered the whole picture of Naval Intelligence.

The spate of traffic which subsequently flowed into the OIC from Bletchley almost continually day and night enabled us to build up the whole background of German naval operations around the coasts of German and German-occupied territories. Operations by surface vessels in the Atlantic were revealed by the traffic to and from U-boats.

It was extremely rare that the interception of a single message revealed the nature and intentions of a naval operation. This could only be determined through a laborious study of many inter-related messages and weighing them against what experience showed was the normal activity.

5 Special Intelligence

i *'The other side of the hill'*

Norman evidently had in mind Wellington's saying about 'the other side of the hill' (page 108), for he goes on in this way:

The onset of Special Intelligence – usually referred to in the OIC as 'Z' traffic because all teleprinter intercepts received from Bletchley were numbered with a 'Z' prefix – gave one, for the first time, the opportunity to begin reading the minds of those who worked on 'the other side of the hill'. This is an asset no other source of information can provide. To know how an opponent thinks is the key to anticipate his future actions. To aid my thoughts in this respect, I had a map of Europe specially prepared so that it was centred on Berlin instead of the normal one centred on London; I thought it might concentrate my thoughts looking outwards from Berlin rather than London.

When ships were in harbour and we were receiving no information about them, fortunately photographic reconnaissance kept a continuous watch and with the introduction of the *Mosquito* photographic aircraft even ports as far away as Tromsö and Gdynia were eventually covered.

ii *The Channel dash*

In 1941 the *Gneisenau* and the *Scharnhorst* had been on a raiding sortie in the Atlantic and returned to Brest. There they were joined by the *Prinz Eugen*. These three ships presented a continual threat to Atlantic shipping. Norman had information from which he suspected that they were contemplating a probable return to German home waters rather than a raiding sortie:

The question was – what route would they take, via the Atlantic or the Channel? The picture soon began to clear. We knew from Special Intelligence that intensive sweeping of the channels off the Frisian Islands and the Dutch coast had been taking place. German fighter aircraft had been re-disposed to airfields nearer the Channel. On 2 February 1942 I produced my appreciation that *Gneisenau*, *Scharnhorst* and *Prinz Eugen* would transfer from Brest to Germany via the Channel within a matter of days. The appreciation was received very dubiously by some but was accepted by the Vice-Chief of the Naval Staff and was re-issued as an Admiralty appreciation....

A series of misfortunes aborted all steps taken to detect the departure from Brest and passage up Channel and as they were keeping (W/T) wireless telegraphy silence no information was available from Special Intelligence. It was not until late in the forenoon of 12 February that my telephone rang; it was the Staff Officer to the Vice-Admiral, Dover, saying that some mysterious large blips had appeared on the radar screen between Boulogne and Calais and were moving up Channel, and what did I make of them. I dare not repeat my reaction but it led to almost instantaneous action to initiate the various measures that had been planned to attack them. Attacks made by aircraft and surface craft had no effect on their passage homewards. However, for several nights beforehand Bomber Command had, on our information, been laying mines in the swept channels off the Dutch coast and I implored them, as they still had time, to lay further mines in a new channel which we knew from Special Intelligence had been swept off Terschelling.

During the course of the night we learnt from Special Intelligence that *Scharnhorst* had been damaged by two mines and *Gneisenau* by one and it appeared that much difficulty was being experienced in getting *Scharnhorst* into port at Wilhelmshaven.

Several months were taken in repairing *Scharnhorst* for further operations but as regards *Gneisenau* in dock at Kiel, Bomber Command at last achieved the success which had eluded them at Brest because, as confirmed by photographic reconnaissance, her bows were hit and so badly damaged that she never put to sea again.

iii *The Arctic Ocean*

I would like to dwell for a few moments on the Arctic Ocean where the battle raged to transport war supplies of all kinds to North Russia. The sea route had to traverse a sea with the most appalling climatic conditions – almost continual gales, blizzards, fog and ice, nearly perpetual darkness in winter and nearly perpetual daylight in summer. In view of their occupation of

Norway, the Germans had complete air superiority over the area and easy and short access by U-boats operating from bases in Northern Norway. Moreover, the Germans had surface forces operating in the North, amongst which at varying times were *Tirpitz*, two pocket battleships, two heavy cruisers and about eight or more destroyers.

Despite the more treacherous weather conditions, passage during the nearly perpetual nights of winter was less hazardous than during summer's nearly perpetual daylight, as air reconnaissance was less effective and U-boat operations were more limited. Even so, many losses were sustained. Undoubtedly, passage during the summer months made operational non-sense but despite representations to that effect made by the Admiralty, political expediency ruled the day. Disaster was bound to occur and losses were very severe, particularly to Convoy PQ.17 (in July 1942). The question might well be asked: did the rewards merit the risks? The easier and less hazardous route to supply Russia was across Persia (now Iran) – why was this not chosen? What political reasons prevented it?

6 Convoy PQ.17

i *The judgment of the Court of Appeal*

The fate of Convoy PQ.17 came up before us in the Court of Appeal. I venture to set out part of my judgment which the Lord Chancellor, Lord Hailsham, referred to as a graphic description:[1]

Early in July 1942 a large convoy of 35 merchant ships – it had the code number PQ.17 – was sailing in the Arctic seas laden with materials of war for Russia. They were between North Cape and Spitzbergen, near the ice-fields. At that time of the year there was no nightfall. It was light all the time. The convoy was approaching the most dangerous part of the voyage. The German battle fleet had come up swiftly and secretly. It was lying in wait in Altenfjord just by North Cape. It consisted of the most powerful warship afloat – the *Tirpitz* – with the cruisers *Hipper* and *Scheer*, and six destroyers. Nearby, at Banak, was an airbase whence the German aircraft could make sorties of 400 miles to bomb the convoy. Under the sea there were German submarines watching through their periscopes for a chance to strike.

The convoy would seem an easy target. It could only make eight knots. It had to steam at the pace of the slowest. But it was in good hands; it was guarded by the Royal Navy. The close escort was under the command of Commander Broome, RN, in the destroyer *Keppel*. It consisted of six destroyers, which were very fast, and several converted merchantmen as naval escorts, which were much slower. In support was a cruiser covering force under Rear-Admiral Hamilton in the *London*. It consisted of four cruisers and three destroyers. Further behind, ready to do battle, was the Home Fleet under Admiral Tovey in the *Duke of York*.

4 July 1942 saw the climax. Enemy air attack was imminent....

Later that day the expected attack came. Suddenly at 8.22 p.m. 25 enemy

1 *Broome v Cassell* [1971] 2 QB 354.

aircraft appeared flying fast and low at the enemy. They were torpedo bombers and pressed home their attack with great determination. They sank two of the merchantmen. But the convoy and escort gave a good account of themselves. They shot down four of the attackers and went on in perfect formation. They were brave men. Commander Broome said to those nearby: 'Provided the ammunition lasts, Convoy PQ.17 can get anywhere'.

Soon after beating off this attack, there came a warning of fresh danger. This time it was the onset of enemy surface ships. The Admiralty sent out three signals which arrived one after the other on the bridge of the *Keppel*, and of the other ships. The signals were, of course, in cypher:

'9.11 p.m. Secret. Most Immediate. Cruiser force withdraw to westwards at high speed.

9.23 p.m. Secret. Immediate. Owing to threat from surface ships convoy is to disperse and proceed to Russian ports.

9.36 p.m. Secret. Most Immediate. My 9.23 p.m. Convoy is to scatter.'

The last message arrived so close on the heels of the one before that, when they had been deciphered, the signalman handed them both together to the commander. They spelt only one thing. The German battle fleet was about to attack. Everyone expected to see masts appearing on the horizon. The order to 'disperse' meant that the convoy was to split up into smaller formations, which were still under escort able to defend them. The next order to 'scatter' was more urgent still. It had never been given before, except once by the captain of the *Jervis Bay*, and he gave it only when the enemy cruisers were opening fire. It meant that the ships of the convoy were to scatter fanwise, each by himself, in every direction without escort. Leaving the escorting force to engage the enemy....

But the threatened attack never came. The enemy fleet never appeared over the horizon. The order from the Admiralty was a mistake. The First Sea Lord, Admiral of the Fleet Sir Dudley Pound, had convinced himself that the *Tirpitz* must have put to sea, whereas the Intelligence reports indicated that she had not. But the order was given. The convoy scattered to the four winds. Without protection, they were attacked by the enemy from the air and from beneath the sea. Many were sunk. Out of the 35, only 11 reached Russian ports: 153 merchant sailors were lost and vast quantities of war material went to the bottom. It was a tragedy. A severe blow to the allied cause.

ii *'Why was PQ.17 such a failure?'*

Now I would turn to Norman's explanation:

Why was PQ.17 such a failure? We knew from information received through Swedish sources that an attack on the convoy by surface ships was planned and that *Tirpitz* would be moved northwards from her base at Trondheim, probably to Narvik to be in readiness to operate against the convoy. After the convoy had been located by German air reconnaissance, photographic reconnaissance revealed that *Tirpitz* had left Trondheim.

At this time the German naval signals were being decrypted for a period of forty-eight hours at a time but the time lag between periods was from a few hours to a day or two. From the traffic we knew that the pocket *Admiral*

Scheer and some destroyers had arrived at Altenfjord and later we knew that *Tirpitz* had joined her there. Undoubtedly, the intention was to make a sortie to attack the convoy. When the First Sea Lord visited my room no positive intelligence had been received that the squadron had left Altenfjord but the timing was such that if *Tirpitz* had already sailed, an attack on the convoy could be expected within a matter of hours. From all my previous experience I was convinced that if *Tirpitz* had sailed we would have had certain indications. Admittedly this was all based on negative intelligence but when the First Sea Lord left my room I was satisfied that he had accepted my explanation of the situation. What made him change his mind if he had so accepted the situation, no one will ever know. Alas! – his decision firstly to disperse, amended a few minutes later to scatter the convoy, was his and his alone. As a consequence the convoy was decimated by U-boat and aircraft attack....

Since that time, I have never lost sight of the fact that the lack of my impact upon the First Sea Lord was such that he did not have sufficient confidence in my judgment. This seemed strange to me, as over the months I appeared to have built up the confidence of so many others even including that of the Commander-in-Chief, Home Fleet.

iii *The sinking of the* Ulm

A more successful occasion for the OIC in northern waters came a month or so later with the sinking of the minelayer *Ulm*....

My plotting of the probable course and position of the *Ulm* together with the estimate by Operations of the convoy's position were accurate enough to ensure the sighting and subsequent sinking of the *Ulm*.

7 Winston's handshake

I would conclude by stressing that the ability to read the signals of one's opponent – a marvellous achievement in itself and meriting the highest credit to all the skilled personnel involved – is nevertheless not entirely an end in itself. I would endorse what was said by those members of Room 40 OB who wrote so long ago:

> 'It is rare for Intelligence to be handed out on a plate. Information is not Intelligence until it has been refined in the crucibles of intellect, experience and common-sense'.

My own reward for whatever I may have contributed to the war effort came one evening two or three days after 'VE Day'. I was having a drink with a friend of mine, the personal assistant to the Chief of Staff to the Prime Minister, in the annex to the Prime Minister's war room, when the door opened and the Prime Minister entered. 'Still celebrating I see. May I join you?' He walked round the room talking to one or two people until he came to where I was standing. My friend asked him, 'Have you met Commander Denning, Sir?' He looked at me quizzically and said, 'Yes, when I was a former Naval Person we sometimes kept the middle watch together in the dungeons of the Admiralty'. Then his face hardened and he glared, 'Were you not the young officer who had the temerity to tell me that total war demanded total intelligence?' Taken aback, I was speechless, but his face cleared and softened. He held out his hand and said, 'We drank an occasional posset together in time of war; now we will drink a posset together in time of peace'.

That handshake was for me accolade enough for the never-ending stress, strain and toilsome labour of the previous eight years.

8 After the war

i *The higher ranks*

After the war, Norman reached higher ranks in the Navy. He became the Admiralty's Director of Administrative Planning and its Director-General of Manpower, 'both of them positions' (says Commander Peter Kemp, RN) 'demanding a rare combination of skill, tact, and understanding to keep the machinery of a big and complex structure working smoothly and efficiently'. In 1961 he became Director of Naval Intelligence and was promoted to be Vice-Admiral. In the words of Lord Mountbatten he was 'one of the finest DNIs the Navy has ever had'. When the armed forces were reorganised Lord Mountbatten chose him for the important new appointment as Deputy Chief of Defence Staff (Intelligence). In Lord Mountbatten's own words: 'Once again he did a superb job'.

ii *'D' Notices*

After he retired, he became responsible for the 'D' Notices. That was the informal arrangement made by the press with the Government – under which the press agreed not to publish information which might be prejudicial to national security. It was a post which called for a man of undoubted mastery of his subject but also one of diplomacy and understanding. Norman filled it, I believe, to the entire satisfaction of all. He won the complete confidence of the press. He was never pompous or dictatorial, but always helpful and fair.

iii *Home life*

Although he did all this work of such great import, you would never think it if you met him. He was modesty itself. He never spoke of what he had done. He was very happy in his home life. He and his dear wife Iris had two sons and a daughter. He was devoted to them – and they to him.

After his retirement he spent most of his time at his delightful cottage in Micheldever – not far from Whitchurch. It was a village which we knew well: as father used to take us there as children. Norman was a churchwarden and read the lessons each Sunday. He did much to preserve the attractiveness of the village – against intrusion by developers. From time to time he was invited to give lectures at home and overseas. He went to London occasionally on directorships. He came over each Saturday to see us.

iv *The loss of his elder son*

But his retirement was saddened by the loss of his elder son John. He was in the Royal Fleet Auxiliary and died in 1975 after a fall. Norman wrote this line to his daughter-in-law, Catherine. I give it here because it shows his outlook – very like that of Gordon:

Catherine.

  I have marked four passages:

Psalm 23 'The Lord is my shepherd....'

Joshua 1:9 – which has upheld me through many vicissitudes. 'Have not I commanded thee? Be strong and of a good courage; be not afraid, neither be thou dismayed: for the Lord thy God is with thee whithersoever thou goest'.

I *Corinthians* 13 – which is one of the loveliest passages in the whole English language. But remember when this translation was made – charity meant very different from the present meaning. It meant the love of one's neighbour as Jesus Christ preached. 'And now abideth faith, hope, charity, these three; but the greatest of these is charity' (verse 13).

Also *Revelation* 14:13 – 'And I heard a voice from heaven saying unto me, Write, Blessed are the dead which die in the Lord from henceforth: Yea, saith the Spirit, that they may rest from their labours; and their works do follow them.'   Love.

                                     Father and Mother.

v *Norman's death*

As Norman was the youngest of us, it was to be expected that he would survive the rest of us. But it was not to be. He had a dog of which he was very fond. It fought with another dog. Norman separated them but was bitten in the hand. He was given an injection against tetanus. But the reaction set off a sudden heart attack. So he died. In December 1979. He was buried in the churchyard at Micheldever – next to his elder son John.

vi *A moving tribute*

A memorial service was held in St. Martin's-in-the-Fields – the parish church of the Admiralty. Commander Peter Kemp, RN, gave the address. He was an old friend who had worked with Norman in Intelligence all through the war: and has since become an authority on Naval History. He paid a moving tribute to Norman from which I would take this extract:

Starting from the dismal failures of Operational Intelligence during the First World War, and working entirely on his own appreciation of what was needed, he created an organisation whose contribution to the final victory in 1945 was immeasurable. For security reasons its work was kept from public knowledge for many years after the war, and even today, when much more is known of its work, there are a few secrets of those wartime years which must remain untold. And because of that there are still many who will never be able to appreciate quite how much we owe, in our victory and our survival, to Norman Denning's work of creation and operation of this vital link in the Operational Intelligence chain.

...Looking back now, it might appear a little strange, though utterly understandable to those who worked with him, that a young lieutenant-commander should have so dominated the work of the Operational Intelligence Centre. But never strange to us, because behind the brilliance of operation and the sureness of touch we could see and appreciate the dedication to the simple and powerful principles which were ever the guiding stars of his naval life.

vii *So he passed over*

At the memorial service Reg and I each read a portion. I read the chapter – which Norman loved – from *Corinthians* on Charity. Reg read the passage from John Bunyan's *The Pilgrim's Progress*. Norman treasured that copy of Bunyan. It was the very copy we had at home when we were children – and Norman had retrieved it. Reg read the words about the passing of Mr. Valiant-for-Truth. They are so right for Norman:

Then said he, 'I am going to my Father's; and though with great difficulty I got hither, yet now I do not repent me of all the trouble I have been at to arrive where I am. My sword I give to thim that shall succeed me in my pilgrimage, and my courage and skill to him that can get it. My marks and scars I carry with me, to be a witness for me, that I have fought his battle, who now will be "my rewarder"'.

When the day that he must go hence was come, many accompanied him to the river side, into which as he went he said, 'Death, where is thy sting?' and as he went down deeper, he said, 'Grave, where is thy victory?' So he passed over, and all the trumpets sounded for him on the other side.

2 Reg continues in service

1 Awaiting the outcome

i *'Everything a British officer should be'*

At the end of the First World War Reg was on the staff – a staff captain – at headquarters. But a year or so later he got back to the regiment. (By this time it had been combined into the Bedfordshire and Hertfordshire Regiment.) He was glad of it. He gradually recovered from his severe wound and was able to take part in all the rigorous training of the troops. He was a regimental officer of the first quality. That was shown by his appointment as adjutant – the officer who is responsible (under the commanding officer) for discipline and leadership. He was adjutant – most exceptionally – of the two regular battalions. Each of a period of three years. Six years altogether. Then, as always happens to the best men – he was nominated to attend the staff college. He passed out with distinction. And then returned to the regiment. Serving with them in England and in India. I cannot forbear from setting out this tribute to him by the commanding officer of his regiment in 1936 in Dehra Dun:

I have known this officer for a number of years. He is in my opinion outstanding and well above the average of his rank and age, both tactically and administratively. He is a fine leader and an equally good instructor.

His loyalty and integrity of character are marked characteristics.

He is a good horseman, plays cricket and polo; in fact I consider him to be everything a British officer should be.

ii *England in danger*

After his time with the regiment, Reg was back on the staff. He was there when the Second World War broke out. During the 'phoney war', he helped to prepare the division to join the expeditionary force in France. He was constantly on the move, visiting the troops and seeing to their training and their welfare. But he never got to France before Dunkirk. Then there was a complete change. There was a great and impending danger of invasion. There was the bombing of London, our cities and our ports. There were the enemy aircraft and tanks on the other side of the Channel ready to pounce upon us.

iii *England defended*

At this critical time Reg was appointed to the staff of the 11th Corps. It was entrusted with the defence of the most vital area of England – the South East. Reg was in charge of administration. Everything came under his supervision. The troops themselves. The anti-aircraft guns. The Home Guard. The building of concrete emplacements. Constantly in danger. Constantly under bombardment. Those were the days in which we could say with Shakespeare:[1]

> This England never did, nor never shall,
> Lie at the proud foot of a conqueror, ...
> Come the three corners of the world in arms,
> And we shall shock them: nought shall make us rue,
> If England to itself do rest but true.

iv *Reg's part*

In all this he did his part. He does not speak of it himself, but I would quote the words in March 1941 of General Sir John Crocker who commanded the 11th Corps District:

Brigadier Denning has been in charge of Administration for the past year or more. Upon him has fallen the administrative organisation and management of this important and complex area. He has carried out these duties with conspicuous ability....

Great credit is due to him for his firm and efficient control, which has undoubtedly created great confidence amongst commanders and has contributed largely to the well-being and contentment of the troops during this difficult transition period.

2 Over to the offensive

i *The 'D' Day landing*

By 1943 the threat of invasion had gone. Plans had to be made for the allied forces to invade France. Reg was promoted Major-

1 *King John*, Act V, sc. 7.

General. There were three-quarters of a million troops in his area. They included the Canadian Army. He was keen to take part in the Normandy landing itself but there was no vacancy for a Major-General. He asked to be reduced to a Brigadier in order to go, but it was not allowed. So, to his disappointment, he did not take part in the 'D' Day landing. Nevertheless, he had much to do with it. 'D' Day had been decided and acted upon. Some of the troops had already sailed from Tilbury. The weather was so bad that the date was changed. Reg had to take urgent measures to bring the troops ashore – ready to sail again later.

ii Out to South-East Asia

Yet his disappointment was not for long. Within a few days after 'D' Day he was ordered to proceed at once to Lord Mount-batten's headquarters in South-East Asia. The allied forces came to one million men. At first he was Deputy Administrative Officer under General Wheeler of the US Army. When he went elsewhere, Reg became the Principal Administrative Officer for the whole of the allied forces in South-East Asia. Their head-quarters were at Kandy in Ceylon (now Sri Lanka). He flew long distances. He visited troops in the jungle. He went everywhere seeing to their welfare – and ensuring their supplies.

iii Planning the recapture Malaya

He worked closely with Lieutenant-General Browning who was Chief of Staff. Together under Lord Mountbatten they were responsible for the planning of the operations to recapture Malaya and Singapore by land, sea and air. All was set – ready to launch an invasion from ports and airfields in India and Burma. Then there came a signal from Lord Mountbatten. He was at the Potsdam Conference with Mr. Churchill and Mr. Truman:

Atom bomb dropped on Hiroshima and Nagasaki. Japanese Emperor has surrendered his country and armies.

iv Unconditional surrender

There followed many negotiations with the Japanese. It was feared that the Japanese Generals would commit hara-kiri rather than agree to the terms of surrender. At Rangoon the room in Government House was protected by troops at the ready in case of attempted hara-kiri. General Browning, speaking for the Allies, demanded unconditional surrender. At last they agreed.

125

A few days later the final ceremony was held at Singapore. Lord Mountbatten was flanked by General Browning and General Denning. The Japanese Generals delivered up their swords to the British Generals. Reg has his at home to this day.

3 Problems of peace

i *Allied prisoners of war*

But there remained much to be done. As Milton said in his sonnet *To the Lord General Cromwell, May 1652*:

> Yet much remains
> To conquer still; peace hath her victories
> No less renown'd than War.

First priority was given to the release of Allied prisoners of war in Japanese camps. They had suffered terribly – more even than the prisoners in German camps had suffered. There was the notorious railway in Burma where so many had died.

Next the gradual demobilisation and return of the armed forces. They came from all the world over. They had to be returned there.

ii *Near starvation*

At the same time there was near starvation in Malaysia – because they got their supplies of rice from Siam (now Thailand). After intense difficulty, General Browning and Reg got the rice supplied.

iii *Oil*

In the Netherlands East Indies (now Indonesia) the British Army required oil for its operations. They took it from the oil wells then operating. Years later the Indonesian Government demanded payment for it from the British Government. Mr. Diplock KC (for the Crown) submitted that it was taken as an act of war. Reg went over to Singapore to give evidence about it.

iv *Final assessment*

This is the commendation of Reg given by the Supreme Allied Commander Lord Mountbatten in conjunction with General Browning his Chief of Staff:

He has carried out his duties with outstanding success during an extremely arduous period. This period included the campaign and planning which culminated in the Japanese surrender in SEAC (South-East Asia Command) and the even more complex administrative problems in connection with the terms and the carrying out of the surrender. He has the widest knowledge of all matters connected with administration and has displayed fertile imagination, great drive and, above all, common-sense, in dealing with the difficult problems which have arisen. He inspires the utmost confidence in all with whom he comes into contact and always gets and demands the highest standard.

Lord Mountbatten endorsed everything and described him as 'an outstanding officer in every way'.

So you see that in the Army Reg excelled in Administration: because of his proven ability in that field. As Norman was outstanding in Intelligence – so Reg was in Administration. He would have been equally outstanding in the field – had the opportunity arisen.

4 Northern Ireland

In 1947 Reg was appointed Chief of Staff of the Eastern Command. Then in 1949 came his appointment as General Officer Commanding the British troops in Northern Ireland. He was promoted to be Lieutenant-General. At the time there was an under-current of unrest – owing to the conflict between Protestants and Roman Catholics. But there was no show of violence or resort to it, such as has disturbed the province over the last ten years. Reg tried more than on one occasion to bring the communities together in non-denominational gatherings, but did not always succeed. He says:

I could not then understand, nor do I now understand why Churches who devoutly worship God should be so bitterly opposed – on what is, it seems to me, only a difference of ritual. Surely it is not ritual which appeals to God, but a heartfelt worship of His Being.

5 Retirement

i *The reorganisation of the Army*

In 1952 Reg went on retired pay. He held the rank of Colonel of the Regiment. He was intensely proud of the British Army and kept up his close connection with it. He took part in the re-organisations in which county regiments were amalgamated into larger units. He himself formed the Royal Anglian Regiment and became its first Colonel. He did much to foster an esprit de corps within it. And succeeded.

ii *SAAFA*

Also he had already become the Chairman of the Soldiers', Sailors' and Airmen's Families Association: and for the next twenty years he – with his wife Eileen – rendered outstanding service to this important charity. They visited the Forces in all parts of the world – and also the many branches of the Association in the United Kingdom. He spoke at meetings. Eileen and he arranged functions to raise money. Reg went up to London most days to the headquarters of SSAFA. He put his administrative ability to good use – in peace – as he had done in war. He continued until the age of 80. The Queen Mother supported him at all times. It was a proud moment when the Queen conferred on him the honour in her own gift – Knight Commander of the Royal Victorian Order.

iii *Home*

Like others in the Services, Reg and Eileen had no settled home until he retired. They had two sons and a daughter – all now married. They found a charming house – Delmonden Grange, near Hawkhurst in Kent. Here they settled – with their children and grandchildren often to visit them. Here they had their golden wedding. Here they spend their days in peace – after a lifetime of service.

If I were to name his qualities, I would put above all his courage. His courage when severely wounded. His courage against all odds. Next his military prowess – equal to any. Sustained always by his faith in God. From his earliest days he has quoted – and still quotes – and follows – the precept of the great military commander Oliver Cromwell:

> Put your trust in God and keep your powder dry.

3 Tom – again in service

1 In defence of the Realm

i *To the North-East*

When the Second World War broke out on 3 September 1939, I had only been one year in silk. I was aged 40. I volunteered at once for service of any kind. Too old for a combatant role. I was invited to go and see Sir Alexander Maxwell, the Permanent Secretary to the Home Office. He told me that England was to be divided into regions. They envisaged that, owing to the war, one region might be cut off from others. Each region was to be self-governing. Each was to have its own Regional Commissioner in charge. Each was to have its own legal adviser. Would I be the legal adviser for the North-East Region? No pay, but travelling expenses would be allowed. I accepted without the slightest hesitation. I was only too glad to do it as my war service. Other young silks did likewise. Hartley Shawcross KC was legal adviser for the South-East Region. Charles Romer KC for the North Midlands. And so forth.

ii *Under bombardment*

Leeds was the headquarters of my region. I travelled up there many times when invasion threatened. In 1940 and 1941. Always by train: but the journeys were appalling. In peacetime it would take three hours. In wartime it took seven or eight hours or more – owing to bombs, alerts, and the like. Well do I remember the night when London was set on fire. I was returning in the train from Leeds. A few miles out of London a great red glare covered the sky. The train plodded on. Stopping every few yards. At last we reached Kings Cross. There were the fires. There were bombs and explosions all the time. People were still carrying on. Even a few taxi-drivers. I found a taxi and asked the driver to take me to Victoria. He managed to get me there – by going devious ways. But no trains moving at all. I went into a shelter for the rest of the night. Together with others. The bombs were exploding near us. Nobody said anything. We all hoped that no bombs would hit us. No sleep. Just waiting for morning. It was about midday that a train left for Haywards Heath. I got home to Mary and Robert. They were safe. I was so relieved that I broke down and cried. It was the strain of it all.

Many other nights I remember too. Some in trains. Some in London and in Leeds. We all carried on. We had Winston Churchill's words ringing in our ears:

We shall defend our island, whatever the cost may be, we shall fight on the beaches, we shall fight on the landing grounds, we shall fight in the fields and in the streets, we shall fight in the hills; we shall never surrender.

iii *Detaining 'fifth-columnists'*

Most of my work in Leeds was to detain people under Regulation 18B. We detained people, without trial, on suspicion that they were a danger. The military authorities used to receive – or collect – information about any person who was suspected: and lay it before me. If it was proper for investigation, I used to see the person – and ask him questions – so as to judge for myself if the suspicion was justified. He could not be represented by lawyers. As an instance I would tell of a parson who was called the 'Nazi Parson' in a village in Yorkshire. He had often spent his holidays in Germany. The military authorities arrested him, and detained him. They were fearful that German parachutists might come down to his lonely vicarage. They might sabotage our war effort by blowing up bridges, and the like. Although there was no case against him, no proof at all, I detained him under '18B'. The Bishop of Ripon protested, but we took no notice. This power was discretionary. It could not be questioned in the Courts. It was so held by the House of Lords in *Liversidge v Anderson*. But Lord Atkin gave a famous dissent – after my own heart – in which he said:[1]

In this country, amid the clash of arms, the laws are not silent. They may be changed, but they speak the same language in war as in peace. It has always been one of the pillars of freedom, one of the principles of liberty for which on recent authority we are now fighting, that the Judges are no respecters of persons, and stand between the subject and any attempted encroachments on

1 [1942] AC 206, 244.

his liberty by the executive, alert to see that any coercive action is justified in law.

2 The law carries on

i *The 'ghosts of the past'*

In between my work in the North-East Region, I carried on my practice in London – as best I could. It was essential that the Courts should continue to function: and that there should be barristers to conduct the cases. So it was also in a way part of my war work. A plan had been devised for the Courts to be moved to Oxford. But it was never put into effect. The Courts in the Strand kept open for business as usual: but sitting in the basement from time to time. The House of Lords sat for judicial work: but sitting in the King's Robing Room. If you care to look into the *Law Reports* you will see that during those critical days in May and June 1940 – when our troops were being driven back to the beaches at Dunkirk – I was arguing in the Lords the important case of *United Australia v Barclays Bank*. I appeared in robes. Geoffrey Streatfeild KC appeared in uniform, being in the Army. The Law Lords gave their reasoned judgments just as carefully and just as effectively as if there had been no war. Lord Atkin made his celebrated denunciation of the old forms of action:[1]

When these ghosts of the past stand in the path of justice clanking their mediaeval chains the proper course of the Judge is to pass through them undeterred.

You may be interested to know that I did that case for nothing. There was no legal aid in those days, but I thought the Court of Appeal were so wrong that I offered to conduct it for no fee. It was a subject on which I had done much research and knew much.

Likewise I did a case of medical negligence for nothing. In the Court of Appeal. It was *Gold v Essex County Council*.[2] It was in June 1942 and was the turning-point of the law on the subject.

ii *'False to your oaths'*

Not only in London but also on circuit I carried on my practice.

1 [1941] AC 1, 29.
2 [1942] 2 KB 293.

Many of the cases had a wartime setting. In particular one tried in the Great Hall of the Castle at Winchester. It was in July 1942 whilst the war was very much in the balance. I was instructed by the Attorney-General – he gave a few briefs around to the silks – to defend a young sailor who was charged with murder. He had strangled a girl on Southampton Common. I went to see him the night before in the cells in Winchester. There he was, dirty and unkempt. I asked him what his defence was. He said the girl had slapped his face. He had put his hands round her throat, and she died. Was there any defence? Not much of a defence of provocation so as to reduce it from murder to manslaughter. But I thought I would put it to the jury. I told the young man to clean himself up before the next day. There he was, when he was arraigned, as smart and nice a young sailor as ever you did see. The Judge was Mr. Justice Charles, also of the Western Circuit. He ran dead against my client. I put him into the box and asked him: 'Did you have your ship torpedoed under you three times?' The Judge boomed out: 'Many a sailor has had his ship torpedoed under him and he doesn't go and strangle a woman!' Next, when I was going to put my defence of provocation to the jury, the Judge said he was not going to put it. There was not sufficient provocation here to reduce it to manslaughter. Was I, as Counsel, to put it? I did. It is the duty of Counsel to put every legitimate defence. I put the defence of provocation to the jury. The Judge did as he said he would. He told the jury that there was no defence of provocation here. That was virtually a direction to find him guilty of murder, because, if there was no provocation, it was clearly murder. Well, it was a Hampshire jury, and I am a Hampshire man! The jury found him guilty of 'manslaughter only'. The Judge turned to the jury, and said: 'Get out of the box. You've been false to your oaths. You're not fit to be there'. As they left the box, they were heard to say, 'The Judge was biased'. (He is not the first Judge to find that, if he goes too far one way, the jury will go the other way. That is what the juries on the Western Circuit have done ever since Judge Jeffreys' day – though they gave in to him!) But, to finish the case – the Judge, addressing the sailor, said that he had to accept the verdict: but he went on and sentenced him to thirteen years' imprisonment. I thought that was too long, seeing it was manslaughter only, as the jury had found. So I told the sailor he could appeal if he liked, but I had to warn him that in those days the Court of Criminal Appeal could increase the sentence if they so wished. Afterwards (I think I have lost it now), I received a little note which he wrote to me from the prison in pencil. He thanked me. He said: 'In view of the possibility of an increase, I have decided not to appeal'. I am sure he has been restored to his friends and relations long since. The moral of that story is: Stick up to the Judge. It is one of the duties of Counsel to be courageous on behalf of his client, using all proper weapons, but no improper ones.

iii A Commissioner of Assize

It was in December 1943 – when the tide of war was beginning to turn – that I first sat as a Judge. Mr. Justice Wrottesley was taken ill on circuit at Manchester. The Lord Chancellor (Lord Simon) asked me to go as a Commissioner of Assize to take his place. I was young for it – only 44. In those days, being a Commissioner was regarded as a 'trial run'. If a man did it well, he could reasonably expect to be appointed a Judge. It is not so now. Nowadays being a Commissioner leads to nothing. And less pay than a practising barrister would earn. I sat as a Commissioner in Manchester for three weeks. The leader of the circuit was George Lynskey KC (afterwards Mr. Justice Lynskey). It is often the practice of a Lord Chancellor to ask the leader of the circuit how a man gets on. George Lynskey told me afterwards that I had won 'golden opinions'.

That period of my life – being a KC and also a Commissioner of Assize – put me on a par with Chaucer's 'Man of Lawe':[1]

> A Sergeant of the Lawe, war and wys, ...
> Justyce he was ful often in assyse,
> By patente, and by pleyn commissioun;
> For his science, and for his heigh renoun
> Of fees and robes hadde he many oon....
> No-wher so bisy a man as he ther nas,
> And yet he semed bisier than he was.
> In terms hadde he caas and domes alle,
> That from the tyme of king William were falle....
> And every statut coude he pleyn by rote.

3 The last 18 months

i Appointed a judge

After that 'trial run' as a Commissioner I was offered one of the

---

1 *The Canterbury Tales*, Prologue.

next vacancies for a judge. It was on 6 March 1944. Whilst I was actually arguing a case in the House of Lords – about war damage – *Reville v Prudential Assurance*.[1] Lord Simon appointed me a judge and attached me to the Probate, Divorce and Admiralty Division. Divorce cases were then much in arrear. Many marriages had broken down during the war. To cope with the problem, the Lord Chancellor appointed three new judges. I was one of them.

ii *The flying bombs*

So I was a judge for the last eighteen months of the war. It was in the days of the 'flying bombs'. The first of them came down near us – the other side of Cuckfield. It destroyed a house. You would hear a flying bomb approaching before it reached you. You would hold your breath – hoping it would not come down on you. You only breathed freely when it had gone past. Sometimes we would hear one coming – rush out and see it being chased by a Spitfire – watch it being shot down in smoke – and rendered harmless. So we carried on in wartime.

iii *Arnhem*

On one bright summer evening, in the clear sky we saw wave after wave of our aircraft – in regular formation – flying directly over us, going East. There must have been 20 or more aircraft in each wave. In all, hundreds of them sparkling like silver arrows. They took at least half-an-hour to fly over us. We watched and watched. We asked ourselves: Where are they going? And what for? Only afterwards did we learn that it was to Arnhem – where so many young lives were lost – and nothing achieved. I wonder whether the enemy Intelligence had got prior information of what was afoot.

Such was the last year of the war. It did not affect us directly – but it did indirectly: because of the rationing of food and petrol and so forth. We kept bees for honey. We kept chickens for eggs. We had no car. We went without. We won through.

1 [1944] AC 135.

Whitchurch – the draper's shop as it was in 1900 *(reproduced by Rosemary Eastman, Whitchurch)*

Capt. J.E.N.P. Denning (Jack), with Capt. Berkeley in France, 1916

Capt. R.F.S. Denning (Reg) as
adjutant of his regiment

Gordon, the midshipman, 1916

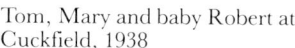

Tom, Mary and baby Robert at
Cuckfield, 1938

Tom, the young barrister,
1924

Wedding of Tom and Joan at Cuckfield
Church, December 1945

Mr. Justice Denning with Robert –
on being sworn in, March 1944

Master of the Rolls, 19 April 1962

Time off from the Commonwealth Magistrates' Conference in Nairobi *(photograph: Equatone)*

The Judge, the Admiral and the General – Tom, Norman and Reg, 1978

Marjorie, their sister

The family, 1970

Lord and Lady Denning at 'The Lawn'
(photograph: *The Sunday Times*)

Book Two

After the Wars

Tom at home

Introduction

The Second World War ended on 2 September 1945. The armies came back. England had to be rebuilt. Its cities, its houses and the factories. Most people thought that Winston Churchill would win the Election – and guide the country into peace. But he lost it. The Labour Party were returned to power: and by a series of statutes created the Welfare State. These statutes were based upon Sir William Beveridge's Report – in which he attacked the giants of idleness, disease, squalor, and want. There was created a vast system of Social Security. Together with the Planned State. All this meant vast new powers being entrusted to the executive. A challenging time for all. In this section I hope to tell how we lived through it – at home – and at work.

1 Cuckfield

1 Remarriage

i Sad and lonely

After Mary's death in November 1941, my life was darkened. I was sad and lonely without her. I felt it grievously. I sought refuge in my work. There was much to do because it was wartime. And there was our son Robert. He was only three years and four months when she died. In the evenings and at weekends I devoted myself to him. For he too – even at his age – felt the loss of his mother. Old Nanny looked after him well. So did the new Nanny who took her place. But nothing could replace my Mary. The war years passed. Peace came. In September 1945. There were all the celebrations. But I had no heart in them.

ii The clouds lift

All of a sudden the clouds lifted. A chance meeting. There was a small preparatory school near us called Parkfield. The headmaster and his wife arranged a party. To it they invited the parents – and prospective parents – of boys. There we met – my future wife and I. She was a widow. I a widower. She had known Mary. They were both members of the wives' fellowship at our parish church. She was Joan Stuart. Charming and captivating. No hesitation on either side. Instinctively we were attracted one to the other. Instinctively we fell in love. At first sight. Not in the headlong heedless way of youth. But in the deep sincere affection of maturity. We saw more and more of each other. We were like a couple of young lovers – meeting whenever there was the least opportunity. Naturally we talked of our children. Of my son Robert and of her daughters Pauline and Hazel and her son John. Some might have hesitated – at the problems these might bring – but not we two. Our love was so strong that it would solve all problems and overcome all difficulties. We were not of an age for there to be any great expectation of children. But that did not trouble us. Our love for one another was so great. Soon we became engaged. Soon we arranged our marriage. But not quite at once. Because I was to go out as the Judge of Assize on the Midland Circuit and be out from October to December 1945. We were married in the parish church at Cuckfield on 27 December 1945 – quietly – with all the children and the families on both sides there.

iii *Joan and I set out together*

So together we set out on a partnership which has lasted ever since – these last 35 years. Henceforward whenever I say in this book that I did this, that or the other, will you please remember that it is not me alone. I could have done none of those things except for the support and encouragement of Joan, my wife. It is she who sees to all those things which make for a happy home life: and it is on a happy home life that each one depends for his achievements. Not only in the home itself, but in the many things that go with it. Together to see to the well-being of the children: and to arrange for their schools and universities. Together to take them for holidays. Together to welcome friends and to visit them. Together to go on circuit. Together to travel. Together to do everything. That is how we have lived our lives together. It is no small achievement. The two families are united as one. And all because my Joan has the qualities sought by William Wordsworth:[1]

> And now I see with eye serene,
> The very pulse of the machine; ...
> The reason firm, the temperate will,
> Endurance, foresight, strength, and skill;
> A perfect woman, nobly planned,
> To warn, to comfort, and command;
> And yet a spirit still, and bright
> With something of angelic light.

2 What's in a name?

i *Pronounced 'cook'*

Joan gave up her home in Haywards Heath and came the one

[1] *She was a Phantom of Delight.*

mile up the hill to my home in Copyhold Lane at Cuckfield. I pause for a moment on the pronunciation. It is not spoken as the 'u' in 'Tuck' or 'Uckfield'. It is spoken as the 'u' in 'cuckoo'. A similar difference occurs in respect of the great Lord Coke. At the present time many people pronounce the 'o' as in 'coal' or 'coke'. But in his time in the 1600s it was invariably pronounced 'cook' like the cook in the kitchen: because that was its origin. He it was who professed to divide up each day into

> Six hours in sleep,
> In law's grave studies six,
> Four spend in prayer,
> The rest on Nature fix.[1]

But his output on law was so great that no one believes he spent any time on the muses: and very little on prayer. Some may say the same about me!

ii *Copyhold*

Our home, as you know, was in a lane called Copyhold Lane. That very name goes back to mediaeval times: when there was a Lord of the Manor who had his own court called the Court Baron. Copyhold was then a usual form of tenure. In order to get a good title to land, the buyer had to go to the Lord's Court. His purchase would be recorded: and he would get a 'copy' of the Court Rolls in so far as they affected his 'holding'. He 'held' his estate by 'copy' of court roll. So it was 'copy held'.

iii *'Fair Close'*

My holding in Copyhold Lane was by modern conveyance. A simple conveyance by the Archdeacon of Lewes (The Venerable Smythe) to me. He had called the house by a word of his own invention – 'Monandale'. That was a pun because it was built on a 'mount' – a rise in the land – and sloped down to a 'dale' – a valley. I disliked it. So I changed it to 'Fair Close'. That too has a mediaeval origin. I took it from land at my home town of Whitchurch where the 'fair' used to be held. I described such a 'fair' in a judgment in the Court of Appeal. The case was *Wyld v Silver*:[2]

The inhabitants of the village had a right by ancient usage to hold a fair or wake on the waste lands of the parish. This fair or wake was held on the

1 *Pandects*, lib.II, tit.iv, *De in Jus vocando*.
2 [1963] 1 Ch 243, 254.

Friday in Whitsun week in every year. It had its origin, no doubt, in the vigil which used to be held on the eve of a festival in the church. The fair was a gathering of buyers and sellers. The wake was the merry-making which went with it. There can be no doubt that this right of the inhabitants was a customary right to which the courts would give effect.

After the Enclosure Act of 1800 the waste lands of a parish were 'enclosed' by fences. At Whitchurch the ground on which the fair was held became the 'Fair Close'. I took that mediaeval name and used it in a modern dress: 'fair' meaning beautiful; and 'close' an enclosure.

3 The house

i *East and west*

It was indeed beautiful. It was an ideal home in which to bring up our family. It faced east and west – the best of ways. In the morning the sun streamed through to wake us. In the evening it set over a lovely peaceful view – looking across the wooded valley to the village of Cuckfield and the graceful spire of its church. (In May 1980 the spire was burnt down completely.) On summer evenings we delighted to sit there as the sun went down. Often, often have I murmured to myself the words of Arthur Hugh Clough:[1]

> And not by eastern windows only,
> When daylight comes, comes in the light,
> In front the sun climbs slow, how slowly,
> But westward, look, the land is bright.

ii *The library*

The house was built in 1933. Good to look at and to live in. The Archdeacon of Lewes had designed it himself. He had bought an old Sussex barn – and used the oak timbers and tiles to build it. It was just the right size. Three large bedrooms and two smaller ones. We turned a room downstairs into my library. We put in shelves and bookcases and housed all the *Law Reports* – and the *English Reports*. The house was set in two acres. We bought the adjoining two acres – so as to save it being built upon. We bought another 12 acres of the field – towards the village. The farmer put his cows there. Afterwards we planted trees. We still have it.

1 *Say not the struggle naught availeth.*

iii 'Sussex by the sea'

The setting was perfect. In the Sussex Weald 'with its checker-work of woods' (Wilfrid Blunt) – looking to the south where there was

> Along the sky the line of the Downs
> So noble and so bare (*Hilaire Belloc*)

We came to love our Sussex. Indeed, we could say with Rudyard Kipling:

> Each to his choice, and I rejoice
> The lot has fallen to me
> In a fair ground – in a fair ground –
> Yea, Sussex by the sea!

4 The things we did

i *Commuting to London*

It was 'commuter country'. We were 1½ miles from the station of Haywards Heath – with the best train service to London. 45 minutes. (Talking of names – that town was built on the heath land frequented by Hayward the highwayman.) Most of the men went to and fro each day. I walked in the morning. It was down-hill almost all the way. Joan met me in the car in the evening. I usually had a heavy bag with papers.

> Does the road wind up-hill all the way?
> Yes, to the very end.[1]

I caught the morning train – at 7.55 or 8.25. I got back in the evening by the earliest possible train. I rose in Court at 4.15. I caught the 4.45 from Victoria. Most of my fellow-travellers read their newspapers in the train. I never did. I glanced at the pleadings in our next case – and thought about the next judgment. In those days I rarely stayed late in London. I wanted to get home – to Joan and the family. Apart from my work, they were my great interest in life – where I found my happiness.

ii *Country life*

There we did all the things that count so much – as one looks back. Often we walked across the fields to the village. Halfway there was a wooden stile with a wide seat. We used to sit on it

1 Christina Rossetti, *Up-Hill*.

144

and contemplate. The family named it the 'contemplatious stile'. In the summer evenings we would play tennis. It was my job to cut the grass. Or we would go down Copyhold Lane – always lovely. On Fridays (when I was in the Lords and had the day off) we would play golf – on the hilly downland course at Pyecombe. On Sunday mornings we went to Church at 8 o'clock. In the mornings (when we had Rose to cook the lunch – she had come back after the war) we would go for long walks. We knew every footpath and lane for miles around. In the holidays the boys and I would do all the outdoor things that are so good for them – cut down trees – make a terrace of stone – bridge the rivulet – extend the tennis court – explore our stream to the source – search out the 'hammer ponds'. (You should know what they are. In former times Cuckfield had iron-ore and charcoal furnaces. The streams were dammed up so as to create a head of water – to work the hammers.) On hot days in summer we would drive over the downs to Hove – to swim in the sea. On spring and autumn days, up to the downs – 'Our blunt, bow-headed, whale-backed Downs' as Kipling calls them – to Ditchling Beacon – or to the windmills Jack and Jill – and walk along the ridge.

iii *Holidays*

We always took the children away for the summer holidays – on the first day after the term ended. They sang in the car the current song: 'We're off to see the Wizard – the wonderful Wizard of Oz'. To Cornwall mostly. Sometimes to Ireland. Only once to Scotland. Surfing which all enjoyed. Sailing at which I was no good. The boat nearly capsized in the Helford river. Fishing when we caught nothing. Walking along the cliffs or the shore. All the usual things that families do. Often I have quoted Sir Isaac Newton's description:

I do not know what I may appear to the world, but to myself I seem to have been only like a boy playing on the sea-shore, and diverting myself in now and then finding a smoother pebble or a prettier shell than ordinary, whilst the great ocean of truth lay all undiscovered before me.

5 Travelling

i *Joan with me on circuit*

During the first three years after our marriage, I was a trial

145

judge, that is, trying cases at first instance. Often out on circuit. Joan came with me whenever she could. How we enjoyed it! I will tell you later of my own circuit, the Western. But I would mention now a few of the incidents that come to mind. Oxford – where the Vice-Chancellor came with the proctors to the lodgings, a lovely house in St. Giles, to present to the Judge a handsome pair of white kid gloves edged with gold tassels. I have mine still. Warwick – with the oldest and most charming Court I know; the Judge had a key to the Castle grounds – where there were peacocks. Brecon – where we were lodged in the Cathedral precincts – and the beds were so damp that we had to dry them out ourselves in front of the fire. Carmarthen – where the snow was so deep that I walked to the Court in gum-boots; the clerks rode with the books – and were greeted by the trumpeters.

And so on and so on. Many the tales I could tell.

ii *To Lewes for Quarter Sessions*

But when I became a Lord Justice of Appeal, I never went on circuit. My work was in London. Our home in Cuckfield. We had many friends in the village and in the county. So much so that in 1957 when I went to the Lords, I was asked to become Chairman of the Quarter Sessions for East Sussex. I was pleased to do it. It could be fitted in. Joan drove me to Lewes in the morning – and fetched me in the evening – 12 miles of our countryside. We sat only about five days in the long vacation and two or three in other vacations. It enabled me to keep in touch with the criminal law – to sum up to juries – and to sentence prisoners. But best of all – to sit with the magistrates of the county – to have the benefit of their advice – to lunch with them at the lodgings – to get to know them. None of it possible now that there are no longer any Quarter Sessions or any Chairmen of them.

iii *An after-dinner story*

I used my experience as a basis for an after-dinner story. With some exaggeration! The first case I had was a man charged with driving a car while under the influence of drink. I summed up in my most impartial and impeccable manner. The jury came – I won't say to the just result – they came to the usual result. They found him 'Not Guilty'. So in the next case I thought I would try different tactics. This was a man who was charged with being in possession of house-breaking implements by night. There I put on my most sarcastic and ironic manner. I said to them: 'Members of the jury. If you think the accused was at the door at midnight intending to present these implements to the house-holder – as a gift! – as a tribute of the esteem in which he held him – then of course you will find him "Not Guilty" '. At this point I paused for effect. Then – 'They did'. It always went down well.

2 Lincoln's Inn

1 How we live

i *The flat in Old Square*

So we lived until I became Master of the Rolls in 1962. Then everything changed. No longer could I be a commuter. So many engagements after Court – meetings of committees – dinners with speeches – night after night. We had to have a flat in London. We found it in my own Inn of Court, Lincoln's Inn. No. 11 Old Square. No lift. 62 stairs to climb. Three rooms of good size (excluding the tiny kitchen). Here we have since stayed all the weekdays in term-time. Only weekends at home in the country.

ii *'Gentlemen, you may sit'*

Every morning I make the tea at 6.45. We hear the news at 7 a.m. We get up. I walk down Chancery Lane at 7.45 a.m. Always through the great gateway of Lincoln's Inn in Chancery Lane. The huge oak doors – and the wicket gate – are just as they were when built 400 years ago. Through that gateway came the King – Charles II – to celebrate his restoration to the Monarchy. The revels lasted two days. The Inn has a book called the 'Golden Book' in which he wrote his name. The others with him wrote theirs too. Prince Rupert, the gallant cavalry leader in the Civil War. James, the brother of Charles, who afterwards became James II. Monmouth, the supposed son of Charles, who afterwards led the rebellion. All signed the 'Golden Book'. All drank far too much. So much so that none could stand. When the toast was made to the King, he exclaimed, 'Gentlemen, you may sit'. From that day to this – over 300 years – the Benchers of Lincoln's Inn do not rise for the Loyal Toast. They sit.

2 The buildings

i *The Old Hall*

As I walk from the flat to the Courts, I daily pass the Old Hall. It is here that the Lord Chancellor sat for three centuries administering Equity. He sat in this old Hall in vacation. He sat in term-time in Westminster Hall. It is just the same as it has always been – from the year 1506 when it was built – until today. I have beside me a picture of it in the time of Lord Eldon. It is in a treasured book in my library called *The Microcosm of London* published by Rudolph Ackermann in the year 1808. It describes the Hall then, as it is now, 'a noble, well-proportioned room: at the upper end is a painting by Hogarth, which represents St. Paul preaching before Felix'. The picture by Rowlandson and Pugin shows Lord Eldon with twenty barristers in wigs before him. I feel sure it is the same scene as Charles Dickens describes in *Bleak House* at the hearing of *Jarndyce v Jarndyce*:

On such an afternoon, some score of members of the High Court of Chancery bar ought to be – as here they are – mistily engaged in one of the ten thousand stages of an endless cause, tripping one another up on slippery precedents, groping knee-deep in technicalities, running their goat-hair and horse-hair warded heads against walls of words, and making a pretence of equity with serious faces, as players might.

I know some members of the Chancery bar of whom the same might be said today!

ii *The Chapel*

Hard by the Old Hall is the Chapel. It is a 'peculiar', that is, exempt from the jurisdiction of the bishop. It was consecrated in 1623 and the preacher on that occasion was John Donne. There are still the old pews, each with its door, where the benchers sit, and separate pews for the ladies. This custom is still carried on. The Inn has its own preacher who conducts services in term-time. Always there is a memorial service for a bencher who dies. Very often it includes this prayer of John Donne which many like but, while the words are poetic and well chosen, does not express my vision of eternity:

Bring us, O Lord, at our last awakening into the house and gate of heaven, to enter into that gate and dwell in that house, where there shall be no darkness nor dazzling but one equal light, no noise nor silence but one equal music, no fears nor hopes but one equal possession, no ends nor beginnings but one equal eternity; in the habitations of thy glory and dominion, world without end. Amen.

iii *Stone Buildings*

From our windows in the flat, we look across to Stone Build-ings. This fine structure has a magnificent façade looking across the North Garden of the Inn. It was completed in 1794 when the Treasurer was William Pitt, then aged 35. High up on the west front there is a lovely sundial with the classic inscription of unknown origin: *'Horas non numero nisi serenas'* (I count only the shining hours). William Pitt was the greatest of the sons of Lincoln's Inn. It was a 'shining hour' in 1805 when after Trafalgar he said, in his last public speech (it was at Guildhall):

England has saved herself by her exertions, and will, as I trust, save Europe by her example.

Only the next year dark clouds obscured everything when he said after Austerlitz:

Roll up that map; it will not be wanted these ten years.

He died soon afterwards.

iv *The library*

When I was studying for the Bar, I spent hours and hours in the library – just as students do now. After I was called, I still spent much time there, looking up cases. It is the power-house of our case-law. It is part of the complex with the New Hall. Alcove upon alcove. Books upon books. Reports kept up to date by diligent noting-up by the librarian. In the centre a statue of Thomas Erskine – perhaps the greatest advocate of all time – whose words I have often repeated to the students:

I will forever, at all hazards, assert the dignity, independence and integrity of the English Bar, without which impartial justice, the most valuable part of the English Constitution, can have no existence.

v *The New Hall*

When I was young, the general opinion was critical of the New Hall and library. It was built in 1843 and was regarded as an ugly building. How times change! and fashions change! Now it is regarded as a superb piece of Victorian architecture. It is indeed so. The Great Hall is spacious and impressive. The council-room and drawing-room are of a good size, pleasing and comfortable. All around are the portraits of the great men of the Inn, painted by the greatest artists of their day. Of Sir Thomas More there is a charming miniature by Holbein. (More's father and grandfather were both butlers of the Inn.) Of William Pitt there is the painting by Gainsborough. Covering the whole side of one wall of the Hall, there is a mural by George Watts of the Lawgivers of the World. Alfred Tennyson sat as a model for one of them! There are pictures of worthies right down to the present day. It even includes one of me. But I will make no further comment! You should see for yourselves and make your own comment. I would say as Oliver Cromwell said to Peter Lely:

I desire you would use all your skill to paint my picture truly like me, and not flatter me at all; but remark all these roughnesses, pimples, warts, and everything as you see me, otherwise I will never pay a farthing for it.

vi *The garden alongside*

One of the great privileges of a flat in the Inn is the pleasure of the garden. In the very heart of London are the well-kept lawns, studded with trees and bordered with flowers. A lovely row of pink cherries topping the bank of the old wall. Magnolias and white cherries in the garden of New Square. Camellias in hundreds behind the War Memorial. Crocuses in profusion opposite the New Hall. Flowers changing with spring, summer and autumn. Joan and I walk here in the evenings. Often we meet our friends. For the Inn is full of our friends. As Hilaire Belloc says:

> From quiet homes and first beginning.
> Out to the undiscovered ends,
> There's nothing worth the wear of winning,
> But laughter and the love of friends.[1]

1 *Dedicatory Ode.*

3 Back to Whitchurch

1 The return

i *A difficult problem*

Late in 1960 we heard from my sister (who still lived at 'The Hermitage') that 'The Lawn' might be sold. It had been used by the Army as an officers' mess but they were giving it up. Were we interested in returning to Whitchurch?

This posed a difficult problem. We loved Sussex but we could not get help in the house. It was a residential area and we were far from the village. The family were all grown up and off our hands. Whereas 'The Lawn' at Whitchurch was close to the church, the grocer, the post office and the doctor. Everyone knew our family. We could get help there. And, after all, I was Lord Denning of Whitchurch. So after much deliberation we bought 'The Lawn' and sold 'Fair Close'. As I have said, we kept the land and woodland plantation at Cuckfield. So we still have a stake in Sussex. We go back once or twice a year.

ii *A conservation area*

I have told you of Whitchurch when I was young. Now I will tell you of it as it is now. It has doubled its size. New housing estates have been built about it. But we have sought to keep the old town – and our part of it – much as it was. It is a conservation area. Unless I had returned, it would, I expect, have been 'developed' by builders – and its character lost.

iii *The Town Hall*

The town has, as its centre piece, the Town Hall. We are proud of it. It was built in the time of Queen Anne – the successor to a previous Town Hall which is shown in the Town Crest. Our old home was the very next door to it. So I knew it well. When I was a boy, the Town Hall housed the fire engine. It was a hand-pump – with hoses – and drawn by horses. Above the roof was the fire bell. (We used to shoot at it with pellets from an airgun.) When there was a fire, one man pulled the rope to ring the bell. The firemen – all volunteers, unpaid – rushed up with their brass helmets and leather buckets. They harnessed up the horses: and galloped away – to the rick or the cottage, whatever it was. Very exciting for us boys to watch.

iv *The freeholders of Whitchurch*

In 1963, when we returned, the Town Hall was in danger of falling down. The roof was leaking like a sieve: and there was no money to repair it. To whom did it belong? 'The freeholders of Whitchurch', said the ancient records. But who were they now? No one could tell. So a parish meeting was held. Trustees were appointed. Later I became Chairman. We set about raising money. We got it. The repairs were done. Recently it was taken over by the Town Council. Saved. Back to its original purpose – the place where the Mayor and Council decide the affairs of the town.

2 'The Lawn'

i *When we took over*

Next – the house which became our home. It was taken over during the war – at first by the Bank of England who evacuated their staff here – and afterwards by the Army Pay Corps. It was very dilapidated. No repairs had been done for years. The garden was utterly neglected. It was a wilderness.

ii *In Regency times*

It was very different from what it was when it was built – in Regency times. We restored it and modernised it and made it – although I say it – a very desirable residence. Just as desirable as it was in the year 1868. For I can give you a good description of it then – from Particulars of Sale when it was sold by auction at Garraway's Sale Rooms, Change Alley, Cornhill, in the City of London. It was sold for £7,000 – a fortune in those days. The description is so apt – and so much of it still appropriate for today – that I will set out the wording of it. I would invite you to read it with care. To notice that there was accommodation for the butler, the housekeeper, the housemaids, the horses and carriages, the cows and the pigs. Remember also that the buildings were still the same, unaltered, when I was a boy. The house was occupied by an old lady and her daughter. They used to drive out every afternoon in their carriage and pair – with the coachman in his top hat and a feather in it.

iii *The particulars of 1868*

This is what the Particulars of 1868 said:

A very desirable FREEHOLD RESIDENCE occupying a most
attractive position on the outskirts of the Town

It presents a very handsome and imposing elevation and stands in VERY TASTEFULLY ARRANGED PLEASURE GROUNDS, which with its Plantations, Paddock, Shrubbery and Kitchen Gardens, extend to upwards of FIVE ACRES, studded with fine old timber of great beauty.

The charm and character of the Property is greatly enhanced by THE RIVER TEST, a Stream abounding with Trout, fringing the Property, affording endless sport to the Angler within the precincts of his own Residence.

This very delightful Property stands close to the Church, and to the Entrance of Lord Portsmouth's Park.

THE RESIDENCE contains a handsome and spacious HALL, on entering which a very beautiful vista of the Pleasure Grounds presents itself.

ON THE GROUND OR PRINCIPAL FLOOR, DRAWING ROOM AND DINING ROOM – these Rooms are both beautifully decorated and well fitted, from which the Grounds are entered through French Casements. LIBRARY, Bath Room, BILLIARD ROOM. Small Sitting Room, Butler's Pantry, Housekeeper's Room, Two Kitchens and other conveniences. The principal Staircase leads to eight Bed Rooms of good dimensions, Water Closet, Housemaid's Closet, and large Attic Bed Room.

THE OUTBUILDINGS enclosed by a large Court Yard, comprise 3-stall Stable, Loose Box, Harness Room, Coach-house for three or four Carriages, Brewhouse, &c. Another Yard embraces 2-stall Stable, Cow-house, Tool and Wood Houses, Cart Shed, Piggeries, &c.

iv *How judges used to live*

That is the sort of establishment which judges of olden days used to have. They used to live in style befitting their standing. In the 17th century Lord Coke had his great house at Stoke Poges and 1,000 acres. Near the house a stream was dammed to make a lake, after the fashion when a man improved his country-place. His domestic accounts showed his attraction to pleasant country living – sheep to crop the turf, cows grazing near the house, the stables within sight and sound, and so forth. He loved it. Just as I love 'The Lawn'. In the 18th century Lord Mansfield had 'Kenwood' (or Caen Wood) high up on the hill at Hampstead, with a splendid view over London. He made extensive altera-tions to it – with the help of Robert and James Adam. He added a beautiful library – as I have mine at 'The Lawn'. But he was not a countryman at heart. I am.

3 We convert it

i *The house*

Yes. The house as described in 1868 was too large for us. We converted it to suit ourselves. We pulled down more than half the house but added a new wing instead. We turned the drawing-room into a beautiful library for me. We turned the stables into dwellings. We altered the outbuildings. We designed the house so as to be used in two self-contained halves – one for ourselves – the other an annexe for our younger genera-tion – when they came to stay – with the grandchildren. So that they could make as much noise as they liked.

ii *The pleasure of a garden*

Our greatest pleasure was in restoring the garden and remaking it. As Bacon said long ago in his Essay *Of Gardens*:

God Almighty first planted a garden. And indeed it is the purest of human pleasures. It is the greatest refreshment to the spirits of man; without which, buildings and palaces are but gross handyworks.

We followed the advice of John Parkinson in his splendid book in 1629, *Paradisi in Sole*:

Although many men must be content with any plat of ground, of what forme or quantity soever it bee, more or lesse, for their Garden, because a more large or convenient cannot bee had to their habitation: Yet I perswade my selfe, that Gentlemen of the better sort and quality, will provide such a parcel of ground to bee laid out for their Garden, and in such convenient manner, as may be fit and answerable to the degree they hold.

Our garden is, I hope, fit and answerable to the degree of Master of the Rolls.

iii *Our garden*

Let me try to describe our garden and what we did. From the French casements of my library, you walk out to a wide open

lawn which slopes down to the water. It is why the place is called
'The Lawn'. You then come to an island in the river. It is crossed
by two charming old bridges – one of wood in an arch – the
other of wrought ironwork. The island has many fine trees.
Beyond the island is the main stream – and the far bank is full of
willows, poplars and hazels. When we took the place over, the
island, the paddock and the paths were all thick with dense
undergrowth. You could not get along at all. The banks of the
river were falling in.

> Nothing teems
> But hateful docks, rough thistles, kecksies, burs,
> Losing both beauty and utility.[1]

iv *What we did*

We set to work – Joan and I and the family. We cut away the
undergrowth – hacking our way through it. We cleared the
paths. Joan and I ourselves wheeled down rubble to fill in the
banks of the river. The strong youngsters of the family got old
railway sleepers and lined the banks – driving in stakes to do so.
At first the far bank was in other hands: but we acquired 20 acres
and planted poplars there. The youngsters made a bridge across.
We used big stones which had been discarded on the repair of the
old gateway of Lincoln's Inn. We all worked, remembering
Kipling's *The Glory of the Garden*:

> Our England is a garden, and such gardens are not made
> By singing:– 'Oh, how beautiful!' and sitting in the shade…
> And when your back stops aching and your hands begin to harden,
> You will find yourself a partner in the Glory of the Garden.

Then there is the kitchen garden, walled, and running down
to the river: fine soil and very fertile. The border of box hedges
well clipped. A large Victorian greenhouse – very expensive to
maintain. Few people can find gardeners nowadays. We have a
good man. More than enough fruit and vegetables for our own
use.

v *Well worth it*

It has been well worth it. The garden gives all the greatest
pleasure. The children have a swing – high from a tree – across
the stream. They have a canoe to paddle along it. In the summer
we have a fete for the Church and one for the Cricket Club –

1 Shakespeare, *Henry V*, Act V, sc. 2.

when 800 or more people come and revel in the delights of the place.

4 Beyond the house

i *The 'tithe' barn*

So much for our house and garden. But near us – just beyond the Church – there is the Parsonage Meadow. In it there is the old 'tithe' barn. 'Tithe' means the tenth part – of the produce of the land. The landowner had to take to the parson one-tenth of the corn that he produced. Our old barn has still its thatched roof. It has still the wooden partitions – dividing it into six large bins – to receive the corn. It still stands on the staddle stones – shaped like mushrooms – to stop the rats getting up into it. It goes back to Tudor times. But when we returned to Whitchurch, it had fallen into decay. The thatch had gone. The rafters were exposed. It was about to be pulled down. We took a lease from the Lords of the Manor – the Hospice of St. Cross at Winchester. We restored it. We thatched it. It stands beautiful in its setting.

ii *The little barn*

There was another old barn too – just beyond our land. It was derelict and about to be pulled down. On staddle stones too. We had it moved to our own meadow. Brick by brick. Stone by stone. It makes a pretty picture.

iii *Woodlands and fields*

These are only instances of the things that we have done since our return. We have opposite us a fine old house, 'The Mount', set in finely-timbered grounds. We have converted it into flats for elderly retired people. We have planted woodlands – poplars in the water-meadows – which I pruned myself. On the hill at Upper Wyke (three miles away) we have planted larch, Norway spruce and beech. We have let the farmer put his cows in our fields. We have, like Lord Coke, the pleasures of country living.

iv *A period piece*

So you see I am back in the place where I was born. It is good for a man to have his roots deep down. It is good for him to return to the place of his childhood. It is good for him to meet and to talk with those whom he knew when he was a boy. And to feel that he has done something to keep its character as a period piece.

Tom in the Courts

1 A judge of first instance

1 Early days

i *Shakespeare's justice*

> And then the justice,
> In fair round belly with good capon lin'd,
> With eyes severe, and beard of formal cut,
> Full of wise saws and modern instances;
> And so he plays his part.

Very little of that fits me. I became a justice, yes – a justice in the High Court of Justice; but not the sort of justice Shakespeare had in mind. He was thinking of a country justice like Robert Shallow:[1]

Shallow He shall not abuse Robert Shallow, esquire.

Slender In the county of Gloster, justice of peace, and *coram*.

Shallow Ay, cousin Slender, and *Cust-alorum*.

Slender Ay, and *ratolorum* too.

(Shakespeare of course was making a play on the words *custos rotulorum*, the custodian of the rolls, as I am now of the rolls of England: and the Lords Lieutenants are of the rolls of the counties. *Coram* is the Latin word which barristers still use when endorsing their briefs, such as '*coram* Denning J' meaning 'in the presence of'.)

I had no 'fair round belly.' I was tall – 6 feet 1½ inches – and slim. My inside was not fed with a 'capon' – which means a castrated cock. My eyes have never been severe – but kindly. I have never had a beard of any sort. But I would like to think, or, rather, for others to think – that I was full of wise sayings and everyday examples.

1 *Merry Wives of Windsor*, Act I, sc. 1.

At any rate I played my part. I have already described my work as a judge in Divorce. It is in *The Due Process of Law* (pages 187–193). Now I would describe my work as a judge of the King's Bench.

ii *Trial by jury*

When a judge sits to try a case with a jury, he is himself on trial – before his fellow-countrymen. It is on his behaviour that they will form their opinion of our system of justice. He must be robed in the scarlet of the Red Judge – so as to show that he represents the majesty of the law. He must be dignified – so as to earn the respect of all who appear before him. He must be alert – to follow all that goes on. He must be understanding – to show that he is aware of the temptations that beset everyone. He must be merciful – so as to show that he too has that quality which 'droppeth as the gentle rain from heaven upon the place beneath'. Nowadays juries have almost disappeared in civil cases. But they are retained in all criminal cases of serious import. I have always strongly supported this retention. Sir William Blackstone put it well over 200 years ago:[1]

But the founders of the English laws have with excellent forecast contrived, that no man should be called to answer to the king for any capital crime, unless upon the preparatory accusation of twelve or more of his fellow subjects, the grand jury: and that the truth of every accusation, whether preferred in the shape of indictment, information, or appeal, should afterwards be confirmed by the unanimous suffrage of twelve of his equals and neighbours, indifferently chosen, and superior to all suspicion.

In the United States they still retain the Grand Jury. We have abolished it. They still retain the requirement of unanimity. We have now majority verdicts. By 10 to 2. But still trial by jury remains as the grand bulwark of our liberties. Sir Patrick Devlin in his book *Trial by Jury* put it eloquently when he said (page 164):

The first object of any tyrant in Whitehall would be to make Parliament utterly subservient to his will; and the next to overthrow or diminish trial by jury, for no tyrant could afford to leave a subject's freedom in the hands of twelve of his countrymen. So that trial by jury is more than an instrument of justice and more than one wheel of the constitution: it is the lamp that shows that freedom lives.

1 *Commentaries on the Laws of England*, Book IV, page 349.

iii *Summing-up*

At the Bar I had watched judges at work. I had heard them sum up to juries. That is how I learned to do it – or rather how not to do it. Only too often you will hear a judge go through the whole of the evidence given by the witnesses. He will read out his notes from beginning to end. It takes a long time. It is quite unnecessary: because the jury have heard all that evidence. All that a judge should do – or at any rate all that I did – was to give a short outline of it: and hope that the Court of Appeal would not find fault with it.

iv *Quashed*

In the long vacation of 1947 I tried a case at the Old Bailey. Six men were charged with 'black market' offences during the war. The case took six weeks. Many witnesses: and masses of documents. I summed up in three hours. Five were convicted and one acquitted. The five appealed. Their convictions were quashed. But not on the ground of any fault in my summing-up. Only on the ground that the indictment was erroneous. It is a reported case, *Rex v West*,[1] decided in March 1948. I was sorry about this result. After all our hard work. The jury were a good intelligent group of businessmen. They and I knew all about the case. The Court of Appeal said (page 720):

The most serious aspect of the present case was the creation of false documents brought into being and used for the purpose of deceiving the Board of Trade.

Yet they reversed our decision. I feared at the time that their ruling might imperil my chances of going to the Court of Appeal. It did not. Within the next six months – as soon as the next vacancy occurred – in October 1948 I was promoted to be a Lord Justice. At the age of 49. Moral for trial judges: Don't be disturbed when you are reversed by the Court of Appeal.

2 On circuit

i *Shorn of his trappings*

As a trial judge, I often went on circuit. In those days the Judge of Assize was treated with the respect of centuries. He went with

1 [1948] 1 KB 709.

his own butler and cook: his clerk and his marshal. (The marshal is always a young barrister or student whom the Judge chooses to accompany him on the circuit. He or she gets two guineas a day.) The Judge was greeted by the High Sheriff and his trumpeters, and guarded by the javelin-men. He was accommodated in lodgings which befitted his lordly state. Nowadays, since the reforms embodied in the Courts Act 1971 all has changed. No longer does a High Court Judge go on assize. He has been shorn of much of his trappings – and with it, I regret to say, some of the esteem in which the Judges of the past were held. More's the pity of it.

ii *The good sense of the case*

It was one of my most instructive experiences to be a Judge of Assize on an English circuit. In those days, different from now, capital punishment was the order of the day. Flogging was the order of the day. Was it wrong? I remember a youngster of 18 coming behind an old woman of 80 and hitting her over the head and injuring her badly, and stealing her savings of £20 in money. I ordered him twenty-five strokes of the birch. Was I wrong? I remember also trying a case at Gloucester when an Army officer, a captain, was charged with murdering his wife. He was a small-arms instructor. His wife led him an awful life, nagging and going for him continually. One day, coming back from his course, she went at him so much that he picked up his revolver and shot her dead – pregnant as she was! Was he guilty of murder or manslaughter? Obviously of murder. Words are not sufficient provocation to reduce it to manslaughter. I so directed the jury. I don't know whether it was the tone of my voice or not, but I did tell them that it was to be their verdict and not for me. It was for them to come to their own decision. The jury found the officer guilty of manslaughter. I sentenced him to two years' imprisonment. All those in the gallery cheered. They had watched the case. They had heard the evidence, as I had done. They knew perfectly well that this man did not deserve capital punishment. That is why the jury found manslaughter only. They do not go by the strict law at all. They go by the good sense of the case.

iii *Is capital punishment right or wrong?*

I suppose that I am one of the few judges left now who have passed sentence of death. I have on many occasions, using the formula: 'You shall be hanged by the neck until you are dead: and may the Lord have mercy on your soul.' The Chaplain says, 'Amen.' It is never done now.

Is capital punishment right or wrong? In giving evidence before the Royal Commission on Capital Punishment I was in favour of it – for murder most foul. That was many years ago now. Some years afterwards I changed my mind. It is not a legal question. It is a question of policy. It is an ethical question. Is it right that we, as a society, should do a thing – hang a man – which none of us individually would be prepared to do, or even to witness? On such grounds I changed my mind. Parliament was right to abolish capital punishment. It was right to abolish flogging. Those days are past.

3 Civil cases

i *Fit for service. Fit for pension*

As a trial judge, I had also to try civil cases. I have already described the most famous of these – the *High Trees case*[1] – in *The Discipline of Law* (pages 203–205. Here I would turn to what was perhaps the most rewarding series of cases in my career. It was the Pensions cases. I was the nominated Judge for Pensions Appeals – the sole judge – and what is more a judge from whose decision there was no appeal to the Court of Appeal or anyone else. Never before or since have I been entrusted with such absolute power. I made good use of it. I found that the Minister of Pensions himself, and the tribunals also, had been applying the wrong principles. They had put upon the man the burden of proving that his injury or illness was *due* to his war service: whereas I held that, if the man was fit when he joined the armed forces — and unfit when he came out – the burden was on the Minister to prove that it was not due to his war service, and that this burden on the Minister was a heavy burden which he would hardly ever be able to discharge, see *Miller v Minister of Pensions*.[2] The current slogan was 'Fit for service. Fit for pension'. So I overruled the tribunals. In case after case I awarded a man a pension when it had been rejected by the Minister and by the tribunal. The leading case was *Starr v Minister of Pensions*.[3]

1 [1947] 1 KB 130.
2 [1947] 63 TLR 474.
3 [1946] 1 KB 345.

ii *Overruling the Attorney-General*

But then what was to be done about the past cases – where pensions had been refused and the men were out of time to appeal? In those cases I extended the time for appeal. The Attorney-General, Sir Hartley Shawcross, came to my Court and argued that I had no power to extend the time. I held that I could extend the time; and I did so. (I was glad that there could be no appeal from my decision.) The effect was magical. Many men obtained pensions which had previously been refused. This is what I said in *James v Minister of Pensions*:[1]

The statute entrusts this court with a reserve power to grant leave to appeal in proper cases, and this power is not to be cut down by the rules or actions of the Pension Appeal Tribunals. This reserve power has often proved a decisive force in obtaining for servicemen their rights. When I first sat to hear cases under this Act on 11 January 1946, the very first application was by a man named Phillips for leave to appeal after the tribunal had refused to extend the time for applying to them. I heard arguments and held that I had jurisdiction to give leave, and gave it. The effect was decisive. When the appeal came on for hearing on 1 April 1946, the Minister conceded the claim. Later in that year there was a series of cases in this court and the Court of Session which showed that tribunals had been acting on the wrong principles. This led to many applications to me for leave to appeal after the tribunals had refused to extend the time. They were in my list for hearing on 29 July 1946. The effect was again decisive. The Minister stated that all men whose claims had been rejected by tribunals up to 31 July 1946 should have the right to have their cases reviewed by the Minister with an appeal to a Special Tribunal. I am told by counsel for the British Legion that this system has worked exceedingly well, and that many men, whose claims had been previously rejected, have now been allowed their rights under the Royal Warrant. Cases have often occurred where I have given leave to appeal after the tribunal have refused it and then the Minister concedes the claim before the appeal comes on for hearing. A striking case occurred the other day. The widow of a warrant officer named Finnerty who died of cancer of the lung, was refused a pension by the Minister and by the tribunal, who refused leave to appeal. I granted leave and when the appeal came on for hearing on 1 July 1947, the Minister conceded the claim because a careful study of the history showed that the man in the course of his service had been subjected to radium which might have had an influence on the onset or progress of the cancer.

iii *A judge's lot*

I was only a trial judge in the King's Bench Division for three years from October 1945 to October 1948. But I would have liked to stay longer. I found much human interest in hearing and seeing the witnesses – in summing-up to juries – and in deciding

1 [1947] 1 KB 867, 871.

cases. I enjoyed especially going on circuit. Joan nearly always with me. That was unusual in those days. A junior judge could not take his wife unless she was invited by the senior judge: and he rarely invited her. It was simply not done for a judge to take his wife. Mr. Justice Byrne broke through that rule. He always took his wife on circuit – or, shall I say, she took him. She made her presence felt – a little too much. Not so with my Joan. She did not overdo it. She was most discreet. She did not come and sit on the bench. She saw us off and welcomed us back. She won all hearts. If the list collapsed – and we had a free afternoon – or at a weekend, we would enjoy the countryside of our lovely England. The lot of a Judge of Assize was indeed a happy one.

4 The Western Circuit

i *Its glories*

On becoming a Lord Justice of Appeal, I missed most the chance of going my own circuit – the Western Circuit. Other circuits have their glories and their traditions. But none can excel the Western. On which I started – on which I learned my trade – on which I practised for over 20 years – and which I have come to love. I know all the places so well. They are Salisbury – with its spire – the incredible pinnacle pointing to heaven: Devizes – with its Market Cross commemorating Ruth Pierce who declared 'May God strike me dead if I have told a lie'. He did! Dorchester – where I sat in the Court where Judge Jeffreys sat (but I did not have it draped with red curtains): Wells – with the beautiful West front – and the moat with the swans to pull the bell: Taunton – with its lovely vale: Bodmin – with its bleak moor: Exeter – with its ancient Guildhall – and the Recorder's blue gown: Bristol – with its coach and four for the Judges: and Winchester in the county of my birth – with its Round Table of the Knights.

ii Pie-Powder

Whenever there is a Circuit Dinner the Bar invite me to join them. I recall for them that best of circuit books, *Pie-Powder*, meaning 'the wayfarer', by that dishevelled circuiteer, J. A Foote. (You may be interested to know that Foote takes that title from the old Court of *Piepoudre* which was probably a court held at fairs for deciding disputes arising there in which the suitors were the wayfarers with their dusty feet. Blackstone describes it:[1]

> The lowest, and at the same time the most expeditious, court of justice known to the law of England is the court of *piepoudre, curia pedis pulverizati*: so called from the dusty feet of the suitors; or according to Sir Edward Coke, because justice is there done as speedily as dust can fall from the foot.

I also recall for them the circuit toast *Cras animarum* – To the morrow of All Souls. The reason for it is that after the long vacation the judges went out on circuit on 3 November – the day after All Souls' Day. So the toast is 'To when we meet again'.

iii *The touching farewell*

I finish by reciting – I can do it by heart – the touching farewell of that old circuiteer. It gives a picture of life at the Bar – on the circuit 100 years ago:

> The dust of seventy circuits past,
> On ways well worn by frail humanity –
> And shall the traveller at last
> Say naught, except that all was vanity?
>
> From London town, a jovial crew
> We travelled all the Western Counties;
> Nor recked we much when fees were few,
> And clients chary of their bounties.
>
> How many miles of iron rail!
> How many briefs, in many places!
> What sturdy struggles to prevail!
> And O! how many vanished faces!
>
> Voices of once familiar tone,
> That often cheered my poor endeavour,
> Footsteps that sounded by my own,
> Are silent now, and hushed for ever.
>
> Through Taunton's meads, by Avon's tide,
> On Cornish moors, we strolled and jested;
> And if with Fate dissatisfied,
> It was but seldom we confessed it.
>
> The Table Round in Winton's hall,
> Fair Dorchester and bleak Devizes,
> The front of Wells – I see them all,
> When still in dreams I go assizes.
>
> So here to all who shared the strife
> By towers of Exe or spire of Sarum,
> I pledge, in hope of larger life,
> The Circuit toast – *Cras Animarum!*

---

1 *Commentaries on the Laws of England*, Book III, page 32.

2 In the Court of Appeal

1 Hard labour

i. *The entrée*

When I was appointed a Lord Justice of Appeal, I had only been a trial judge for 4½ years. That was a very short time in those days. Lord Simon (who had appointed me in 1944 to be a trial judge) wrote to me on 14 October 1948:

My dear Denning,
  I am delighted that my choice is so soon a winner. How absurdly ill-informed the newspapers are – a 'divorce expert' no doubt, but what about the Common Law?

Yours v. sincerely,
Simon

It did not mean any increase in pay. It only meant that I was made a Privy Councillor – to be addressed as 'Right Honourable' instead of 'Honourable' – and to have the privilege of the entrée – of entering Buckingham Palace by the side-door instead of the front. But it meant a very different kind of work – to sit on appeals from others – not trying cases myself.

ii *Beware of logic*

Mark you, I do not regret my time as a trial judge. In order to be a good Appeal Judge, you should have served for a time at first instance as a trial judge. There are a few notable exceptions. Some outstanding leaders at the Bar have felt it beneath their dignity to become a trial judge. Ex-law officers such as Sir Henry Slesser and Sir Donald Somervell have sometimes been thought to have a built-in claim to be appointed straight to the Court of Appeal. As to all these I would say simply this. They would have been much better Appeal Judges if they had served a term previously as a trial judge. It is only by experience that a man can get to know the problems which beset a trial judge. He has to keep his eyes on the witness and also on counsel – ready to intervene at any moment. He has to take down notes of any relevant evidence or point – so as to be sure he does not overlook it. At the conclusion he has to sum up to the jury or give judgment straightaway after counsel have finished their speeches – without any transcript to go by. Very rarely does the case permit of a reserved judgment. Such experience is good for a man who becomes an Appeal Judge. Sir Wilfred Greene, my predecessor as Master of the Rolls, lacked it. He was pre-eminent as an advocate in points of law. He was appointed straight from the Bar to the Court of Appeal. He had been brought up in Chancery where every word of a witness is believed unless the judge says otherwise. In the Court of Appeal Wilfrid Greene would try cases on the transcript. He would take the shorthand notes, read out an answer of a witness and say to us at the Bar: 'How can you say that in view of that evidence?' We would answer: 'The judge may not have accepted it'. He would reply: 'Then he ought to have said so'. Not having said so, his decision was reversed. Irrefutable logic. Unanswerable from the Bar. But leading to a wrong determination of the appeal. Moral for an Appeal Judge: Beware of logic. It has misled better men than you.

iii *'Their own many shortcomings'*

During all my time at the Bar – and even until 1947 – there were only six Judges in the Court of Appeal on the civil side. One division of three took the common law cases. The other division of three took the Chancery cases. In 1947 it was increased to nine. Now it is 18. And even so, we cannot keep up with the work.

There is no doubt that the Court of Appeal (on the civil side) is the hardest-worked court in the land. Three Judges sit in each division. (Much better than five.) Five days a week. All day. Judgment given at the end of the argument – in most cases. Only about one in ten are reserved. They have to be prepared at weekends. Equally there is no doubt that it is as good an Appeal Court as you could find anywhere. The Judges are picked from the best talent available – at an age when they are able to give good and valuable service.

In 1882 when the Royal Courts of Justice were opened by Queen Victoria, the address of the Judges contained this phrase (which is set out in a Memorandum of the *Law Reports* 10 QBD at page 3):

Your Majesty's Judges are deeply sensible of their own many shortcomings.

Lord Justice Bowen suggested an amendment. Instead of 'their own' it should read 'one another's'. Each Judge was aware of the shortcomings of his colleagues: but not of his own.

That little piece of irony has no place today. Each Judge of the Court of Appeal is sensible of his own shortcomings. Each works with the other as part of a team. Differences of opinion – yes – as there are bound to be. But never such as to affect in the least the friendship of each for the other. To prove this, I will tell you of the comradeship which has always prevailed.

iv *Delicate wit*

I call to mind the delicate wit and insight of Cyril Asquith – the gifted son of the Prime Minister. It was he who made play of the House of Lords:

The ideal Judge of first instance is one who is short, simple and wrong: but that is not to say that the Court of Appeal should be long, tedious and right: because that would be to usurp the prerogative of the House of Lords.

It was he also who came to me one morning and made a sly allusion to the maxim of equity that 'he who comes to equity must come with clean hands'. We had all noticed that Sir Donald Somervell (a good common lawyer) had been sitting term after term in the Chancery side of the Court of Appeal (where they are supposed to do equity). Cyril Asquith said to me: 'I can't think what has come over our brother Somervell lately. Always before he goes into Court, he will keep washing his hands!'

That quip was such fun that Donald Somervell (who himself had a pretty wit) made use of it. He had been delayed by a puncture and had to change the wheel. His hands were all dirty. We asked him: 'Aren't you going to wash your hands before going into Court?' 'No', he said, 'it doesn't matter. We're in the Divorce Court today'.

And whilst I am telling stories about my colleagues, Norman Birkett was a great advocate – and the best after-dinner speaker of his time. As we were going along the corridor towards the Court, he would often regale us with his latest story. On his return from America he told us of the English visitor addressing the students at Harvard. He took each letter H A R V A R D. 'H' for Honesty – 10 minutes on Honesty. 'A' for Ambition – 10

171

minutes on Ambition. 'R' for Reliability – 10 minutes on Reliability. 'V' for Virtue. Then came a voice from the back of the hall: 'Thank goodness we are not at the Massachusetts Institute of Technology'.

v *A philosophy of my own*

It is in the Court of Appeal that a Judge has the chief opportunity of influencing the law – always supposing that he can get his two colleagues (or at any rate one of them) to agree with him. Many of the cases raise a point of law of some kind or other. The decision of the Court settles it. Very few cases go to the Lords.

Not many of the Judges – even of the Court of Appeal – have any conscious philosophy of the law: but subconsciously each develops his own philosophy. During my term as a Lord Justice of Appeal – from 1948 to 1957 – I found myself evolving a philosophy of my own. I applied it in the cases that came before us. You will find them in the *Law Reports*. I also gave expression to it in lectures and addresses. These are not readily available for you. So please bear with me if I tell you of them. My philosophy can be summarised under three headings: (i) Let justice be done; (ii) Freedom under the law; (iii) Put your trust in God. I will take them in order.

2 Let justice be done

i *As done in Rome*

In my coat of arms, I took as my motto, *Fiat justitia* – Let justice be done – believing it to have a respectable origin. I have since discovered that it was first used to excuse the most outrageous injustice. It comes from a story told by Seneca.[1] Piso sentenced a soldier to death for the murder of Gaius. He ordered a centurion to execute the sentence. When the soldier was about to be executed, Gaius came forward himself alive and well. The centurion reported it to Piso. He sentenced all three to death. The soldier because he had already been sentenced. The centurion for disobeying orders. And Gaius for being the cause of the death of two innocent men. Piso excused it by the plea, *Fiat justitia, ruat coelum* – Let justice be done, though the heavens should fall.

1 *Dialogues*, III, 18.

ii *Lord Mansfield's fine words*

Afterwards Lord Mansfield used the same phrase in the celebrated case of John Wilkes: but he did it also with his tongue in his cheek. John Wilkes had published, so it was said, a seditious libel in a paper called *The North Briton*. He had fled abroad and been outlawed. He returned and himself asked for the outlawry to be reversed, but he was cast into prison meanwhile. He was a popular hero and many supported him and urged his release. Numerous crowds thronged in and about Westminster Hall. Pamphlets were issued in the name of the people, dictating to the Judges the way they should decide. Reasons of policy were urged emphasising the danger to the kingdom by commotions and general confusion. This is how Lord Mansfield answered them when he came to give judgment:

> Give me leave to take the opportunity of this great and respectable audience, to let the whole world know, all such attempts are vain. Unless we have been able to find an error which will bear us out, to reverse the outlawry, it must be affirmed. The Constitution does not allow reasons of State to influence our judgments: God forbid it should! We must not regard political consequences, howsoever formidable they might be: if rebellion were the certain consequence, we are bound to say *'Fiat justitia, ruat coelum'*. The Constitution trusts the King with reasons of State and policy: he may stop prosecutions: he may pardon offences: it is his, to judge whether the law or the criminal should yield. We have no election....We are to say, what we take the law to be: if we do not speak our real opinions, we prevaricate with God and our own consciences....Once for all, let it be understood, that no endeavours of this kind will influence any man who at present sits here.

iii *He finds a flaw*

These are fine words but I ought, perhaps, to add that Lord Mansfield went on to find a flaw on which he could and did reverse the outlawry. It was a most technical point. The sheriff had in the formal document referred to 'my county court' without adding the words 'of Middlesex' as he ought to have done – and for want of those two words the outlawry was held bad and John Wilkes was released. It would be *lèse-majesté* to suggest that Lord Mansfield was influenced by the public clamour. But his audience knew not which to admire the more – the eloquence by which he silenced the people – or the subtlety by which he set their hero free. For myself I prefer to take the first part – *'Fiat justitia'* – and discard the *'ruat coelum'*. If justice is done, the heavens should not fall. They should rejoice.

173

iv *The proper role of a judge*

My root belief is that the proper role of a judge is to do justice between the parties before him. If there is any rule of law which impairs the doing of justice, then it is the province of the judge to do all he legitimately can to avoid that rule – or even to change it – so as to do justice in the instant case before him. He need not wait for the legislature to intervene: because that can never be of any help in the instant case. I would emphasise, however, the word 'legitimately': the judge is himself subject to the law and must abide by it.

3 Consumer protection

i *The Buick motor-car*

You can see that philosophy at work throughout my time as a Lord Justice. Such as in *Candler v Crane Christmas*[1] and other cases which are considered in *The Discipline of Law*. But I would add one even more appropriate example. It is in the field of consumer protection. You will remember that in *L'Estrange v Graucob*,[2] when I was at the Bar, I succeeded in persuading the Court of Appeal that printed forms were binding. So that a supplier of goods could exempt himself from all liability by putting in an exempting condition in a printed form. But when I got to the Court of Appeal – presiding there – I was able, with my colleagues, to avoid that rule by introducing the doctrine of 'fundamental breach'. It was in *Karsales (Harrow) v Wallis*.[3] A hire-purchase company let to a customer a Buick motor-car which he had seen a week before. They inserted in the printed form an exempting clause:

No condition or warranty that the vehicle is roadworthy, or as to its age, condition or fitness for any purpose is given by the owner or implied herein.

When the car was delivered, it would not go. They had to tow it away. I said (page 940):

The law about exempting clauses has been much developed in recent years, at any rate about printed exempting clauses, which so often pass unread. Notwithstanding earlier cases which might suggest the contrary, it is now settled that exempting clauses of this kind, no matter how

1 [1951] 2 KB 164.
2 [1934] 2 KB 394.
3 [1956] 1 WLR 936.

174

widely they are expressed, only avail the party when he is carrying out his contract in its essential respects. He is not allowed to use them as a cover for misconduct or indifference or to enable him to turn a blind eye to his obligations. They do not avail him when he is guilty of a breach which goes to the root of the contract. The thing to do is to look at the contract apart from the exempting clauses and see what are the terms, express or implied, which impose an obligation on the party. If he has been guilty of a breach of those obligations in a respect which goes to the very root of the contract, he cannot rely on the exempting clauses….In the present case the lender was in breach of the implied obligation that I have mentioned. When the defendant inspected the car before signing the application form, the car was in excellent condition and would go: whereas the car which was subsequently delivered to him was no doubt the same car, but it was in a deplorable state and would not go. That breach went, I think, to the root of the contract and disentitles the lender from relying on the exempting clause.

ii *The legislature intervenes*

That doctrine was accepted in the Court of Appeal for many years but in *Suisse Atlantique*[1] the House of Lords said it was erroneous. We revived it in *Harbutt's 'Plasticine' v Wayne Tank and Pump*[2] but that too, in turn, was reversed by the House of Lords in *Photo Productions v Securicor Transport*.[3] The reason is because they have a different philosophy of the law from me. They give priority to the strict letter of the law: whereas I give priority to the doing of justice. Incidentally, I no longer mind their decision in this case; because the legislature has now intervened so as to give the consumer adequate protection against these exempting conditions. They are only to be enforced if they are just and reasonable. That was done by the Unfair Contract Terms Act 1977. Thus making our doctrine of 'fundamental breach' unnecessary.

4 The need for a new equity

i *My lecture*

This philosophy of mine is very akin to the philosophy upon which the doctrine of equity is founded. During my time as a Lord Justice, I gave a lecture which I like to think had some impact. It was in 1952 in University College, London, under the title *The need for a new equity*.

1 [1967] 1 AC 361.
2 [1970] 1 QB 447.
3 [1980] 2 WLR 283.

ii *What is equity?*

Every student knows what equity is. It arises out of the tendency of all law to become rigid. The rules of law, when enunciated by legislators or judges, are usually founded on reasons which appear satisfactory at the time. Once these rules are given the force of law, however, they must be obeyed for their own sake, and not for the goodness of the reasons which prompted them. No society can permit its members to disobey its laws simply because they disapprove of the reasons for them. The rule therefore becomes the important thing, not the reasons for it. In the course of time the reasons may cease to be valid: but the rules remain binding. New days may bring the people into new ways of life and give them new outlooks: and with these changes there may come a need for new rules of law, to control the new order and to reflect the new outlook. The old rules must then be modified or else the society itself will stagnate. This truth was observed and well stated by Sir Henry Maine nearly a hundred years ago:

> 'Social necessities and social opinion are always more or less in advance of law. We may come indefinitely near to the closing of the gap between them, but it has a perpetual tendency to reopen. Law is stable; these societies we are speaking of are progressive. The greater or less happiness of a people depends on the degree of promptitude with which the gulf is narrowed'.

iii *Past the age of child-bearing*

In those days in 1952 the gap might be closed (a) by equity or (b) by legislation. But these had been unavailing. As to equity I said:

We are much too modern and sophisticated to believe in a law of nature; and that is all that equity was. Whether you take Roman equity as administered by the praetors, or English equity as administered by the Lord Chancellor, in each case equity invoked the principles of natural justice. Equity claimed that these principles had priority over all the laws then existing: and therefore that these principles could be prayed in aid to mitigate their harshness or to soften their rigidity. Thus although a man might be entitled at law to use his land as he pleased, nevertheless equity would not let him do so if it would be contrary to good faith. So it invented the trust. Although a man might be entitled at law to insist on the binding force of a contract, nevertheless equity would not allow him to do so if it had been induced by a misrepresentation, even though it was an innocent misrepresentation. In the days of Lord Nottingham and Lord Hardwicke equity was very fluid and adaptable but in the hands of Lord Eldon it became rigid and technical: and it has remained so ever since.

When counsel sought to rely on the equity in a case, Lord Justice Bowen in 1890 said with judicial gravity:

When I hear of an 'equity' in a case like this, I am reminded of a blind man – in a dark room – looking for a black hat – which isn't there!

Harman J said in 1950 that 'Equity is presumed not to be past the age of child-bearing'. But in 1952 it had no child living which was not at least 100 years old.

As to legislation I said:

Parliament is much too busy to do all it should for law reform. Crisis follows upon crisis; and one major debate on another major debate. Foreign policy, economic affairs, defence and social services claim the attention of the legislature to such an extent that there is no time for them to consider the injustices caused by decisions of the courts of law. Even if they do find time, they can never remedy the injustice in the case itself. They cannot, or at any rate should not, legislate retrospectively. The aggrieved party must suffer under the injustice, and content himself with the reflection that his case has brought it to light. Then Parliament can remedy it for others in the future, if it can find time to do so, but it cannot remedy it for the original sufferer.

iv *Where is the new equity to be found?*

In 1952 I concluded the address with these words:

I repeat again: Where is the new equity to be found? Not in the Judges, for they are forbidden to legislate. Not in the House of Lords, for they are bound by their own mistakes or, to put it more accurately, bound by their past decisions even though they have become out of date. It is, I think, to be found in the new spirit which is alive in our universities. There must rise up another Bentham to expose the fallacies and failings of the past and to point the way to a new age and a new equity. We stand at the threshold of a new Elizabethan era. Let us play a worthy part in it.

v *Much has been done*

Since I gave the address in 1952 a good deal has been done. The universities have played the worthy part I besought of them. The teachers and the students – especially the students – have supported the cause of reform. Work of the first importance has been done by the Law Reform Commission established in 1965 by Lord Gardiner. We have also the Resolution of the Lords in 1966 that they would no longer be absolutely bound by their own decisions. But there remains a great deal that can yet be done by the judges. That is why I put my first priority – Let justice be done. The judges should so handle precedent – and should so interpret statutes – as to do justice – in a way fitted for the needs of the times in which we live.

6 Freedom under the law

i *A telling phrase*

Freedom under the law – it is a telling phrase. I make so bold as to claim to be 'the first and true inventor' of it. It was in 1949 shortly after I had become a Lord Justice. I was invited to give the first series of lectures under the Hamlyn Trust. Miss Hamlyn of Torquay had left the residue of her estate on trust to a charity to promote jurisprudence. I prepared the lectures in the long vacation. I worried about what to call them. Often I go to bed with a problem – and when I wake up I have it solved. I did so when I was studying Mathematics. I do so still. One morning I awoke and told my wife I had it. I felt like Archimedes when in his bath he cried 'Eureka.' It was 'Freedom under the law.' The lectures were well received. So well that ever since I have often been asked to give – and have given – addresses all the world over.

ii *The heritage of freedom*

I can best explain this philosophy by the opening paragraphs of my lectures:

I hope you have not come expecting a scholarly discourse replete with copious references. If you have, I fear you will be disappointed: for, I have come as the Hamlyn Trust bids me, to speak, as it were, to the common people of England and to further amongst them the knowledge of their laws, so that they may realise their privileges and likewise their responsibilities. So if I refer to matters which you know full well, I hope you will forgive me. Not that it is any discredit to any of us to be one of the common people of England. It is indeed the greatest privilege that any man can have: for the common people of England have succeeded to the greatest heritage of all – the heritage of freedom: and it is that which I have come to talk about – freedom under the law.

iii *Built up from procedure*

Let me start with an instance of how the courts approach the subject. Whenever one of the King's Judges takes his seat, there is one application which by long tradition has priority over all others. Counsel has but to say, 'My Lord, I have an application which concerns the liberty of the subject' and forthwith the Judge will put all other matters aside and hear it. It may be an application for a writ of habeas corpus, or an application for bail, but, whatever form it takes, it is heard first. This is of course only a matter of procedure, but the English law respecting the freedom of the individual has been built up from the procedure of the courts: and this simple instance of priority in point of time contains within it the fundamental principle that, where there is any conflict between the freedom of the individual and any other rights or interests, then no matter how great or powerful those others may be, the freedom of the humblest citizen shall prevail over it.

iv *To be balanced with duties*

These are fine sentiments which you will find expressed in the laws of other countries too; but rights are no good unless you can enforce them; and it is in their enforcement that English law has shown its peculiar genius. The task is one of getting the right balance. The freedom of the individual, which is so dear to us, has to be balanced with his duty; for, to be sure everyone owes a duty to the society of which he forms part....What matters in England is that each man should be free to develop his own personality to the full: and the only duties which should restrict this freedom are those which are necessary to enable everyone else to do the same. Whenever these interests are nicely balanced, the scale goes down on the side of freedom....

v *To be matched with social security*

Let me define my terms. By personal freedom I mean the freedom of every law-abiding citizen to think what he will, to say what he will, and to go where he will on his lawful occasions without let or hindrance from any other persons. Despite all the great changes that have come about in the other freedoms, this freedom has in our country remained intact. It must be matched, of course, with social security, by which I mean the peace and good order of the community in which we live. The freedom of the just man is worth little to him if he can be preyed upon by the murderer or thief. Every society must have the means to protect itself from marauders. It must have powers to arrest, to search, and to imprison those who break the laws. So long as those powers are properly exercised, they are themselves the safeguards of freedom. But powers may be abused, and, if those powers are abused, there is no tyranny like them. It leads to a state of affairs when the police may arrest any man and throw him into prison without cause assigned. It leads to the search of his home and belongings on the slightest pretext – or on none. It leads to the hated gestapo and the police state. It leads to extorted confessions and to trials which are a mockery of justice. The moral of it all is that a true balance must be kept between personal freedom on the one hand and social security on the other. It has been done here, and is being done. But how?

vi *Powers must not be abused or misused*

That is the question I asked in 1949. Now I give the answer. It is this: The law itself should provide adequate and efficient remedies for the abuse or misuse of power from whatever quarter it may come. No matter who it is – who is guilty of the abuse or misuse. Be it government, national or local. Be it trade unions. Be it the press. Be it management. Be it labour. Whoever it be, no matter how powerful, the law should provide a remedy for the abuse or misuse of power. Else the oppressed will get to the point when they will stand it no longer. They will find their own remedy. There will be anarchy. To my mind it is fundamental in our society that a judge should do his utmost to see that powers are not abused or misused. If they come into conflict with the freedom of the individual – or with any other of our fundamental freedoms – then it is the province of the judge to hold the balance between the competing interests. In holding that balance the judge must put freedom first. He must give priority to the freedom of the individual.

You can see that philosophy at work in many cases in my time. Such as in *Barnard v National Dock Labour Board*[1] and *Lee v Showmen's Guild of Great Britain*.[2]

vii *The powers of the executive*

In the Hamlyn lectures, I examined the powers of the executive and showed how they were being misused at that time. This is how I concluded:

Reviewing the position generally, the chief point which emerges is that we have not yet settled the principles upon which to control the new powers of the executive. No one can suppose that the executive will never be guilty of the sins that are common to all of us. You may be sure that they will sometimes do things which they ought not to do: and will not do things that they ought to do. But if and when wrongs are thereby suffered by any of us, what is the remedy? Our procedure for securing our personal freedom is efficient, but our procedure for preventing the abuse of power is not. Just as the pick and shovel is no longer suitable for the winning of coal, so also the procedure of mandamus, certiorari, and actions on the case are not suitable for the winning of freedom in the new age. They must be replaced by new and up-to-date machinery, by declarations, injunctions, and actions for negligence: and, in judicial matters, by compulsory powers to order a case stated. This is not a task for Parliament. Our representatives there cannot control the day-to-day activities of the many who administer the manifold activities of the State: nor can they award damages to those who are injured by any abuses. The courts must do this. Of all the great tasks that lie ahead, this is the greatest. Properly exercised the new powers of the executive lead to the Welfare State: but abused they lead to the totalitarian State. None such must ever be allowed in this country. We have in our time to deal with changes which are of equal constitutional significance to those which took place 300 years ago. Let us prove ourselves equal to the challenge.

That lecture was given in 1949. Now, 30 years or so later, I think we can say that we have achieved what I then hoped for. We have now new and up-to-date machinery for the winning of freedom. We have declarations, injunctions, actions for negligence, and judicial review. All that is needed now is for the judges – and the Bar – to get to know how to use it.

7 Put your trust in God

i *'Keep your powder dry'*

'Put your trust in God and keep your powder dry'. That was the advice which Oliver Cromwell gave to his men as they were

1 [1953] 2 QB 18.
2 [1952] 2 QB 329.

about to cross a stream to attack the enemy. It was the watch-word which, as I have said, my Army brother Reg took for himself, and set down in letters to me.

So I would say: In coming upon legal obstacles, it is not enough to keep your law books dry. It is as well to have a Bible ready to hand too. It is the most tattered book in my library. I have drawn upon it constantly. So did Lord Atkin in the great case of *Donoghue v Stevenson*[1] which transformed the law of negligence. He drew (page 580) upon the Parable of the Good Samaritan in *St. Luke* 10:

The rule that you are to love your neighbour becomes in law you must not injure your neighbour: and the lawyer's question 'Who is my neighbour?' receives a restricted reply. You must take reasonable care to avoid acts or omissions which you can reasonably foresee would be likely to injure your neighbour. Who, then, in law is my neighbour? The answer seems to be – persons who are so closely and directly affected by my act that I ought reasonably to have them in contemplation.

ii *Agnostics are terrible*

I have for many years been President of the Lawyers' Christian Fellowship. Every year early in October we have a service in the Temple Church. It is full to overflowing with young barristers, solicitors and students. I have spoken to them from the pulpit. It is high up. The *acoustics* are deporable. Often after dinner I tell a story (told me by Arthur Goodhart) of the Lord Bishop coming to preach there. The verger gave him this advice: 'Pray, my Lord, speak very clearly and distinctly because the *agnostics* here are terrible'.

I gave an address to them in November 1954 at the Law Society in which I talked about 'Putting principles into practice' – by which I mean putting Christian principles into practice. This is what I said:

iii *Law and morals*

When William Temple on one occasion went to address a gathering of lawyers at the Inns of Court he opened his remarks by saying, 'I can't say that I know much about the law, having been far more interested in justice'. That was a piece of delicate irony directed at the lawyers then present. His hearers had been brought up in the philosophy of John Austin. That drew a clear and absolute line between law and morals. Law was simply a series of commands issued by a sovereign telling the people what to do or what not to do. Judges and advocates were not concerned with the morality of the law, but only with the interpretation of it and with its enforcement. This supposed division

1 [1932] AC 562.

between law on the one hand and morals on the other has been a great mistake.

iv *Law and religion*

So is the supposed division between law and religion. I know that a great number of people today think that law and religion have nothing in common. The law, they say, governs our dealings with our fellows. It lays down rigid rules which must be obeyed without questioning whether they are right or wrong. But religion, they say, concerns our dealings with God: it is concerned with the things of the next world, not with the things of this world in which we are living.

That was the philosophy of law in which I was brought up. It is a philosophy which still governs many of the lawyers of my generation. But it is a false philosophy. The truth is that although religion, law and morals can be separated, they are nevertheless very dependent on one another. Without religion there can be no morality: and without morality there can be no law.

v *State your case strongly*

William Temple himself proclaimed on many occasions the Christian precept of love – 'Thou shalt love thy neighbour as thyself' – and sought to apply it to the complexities of the modern life and he found that 'love finds its primary expression through justice.' 'Christian Charity', he wrote, 'manifests itself in the temporal order as a supra-natural discernment of, and adhesion to, *justice* in relation to the equilibrium of power.' He took the instance of a dispute between employers and workers on the verge of a strike. The Committee are to be actuated by love. Oh, yes, by all means. But towards whom? Are they to love workers or employers? Of course, both. But that will not help them much to determine what terms ought to be proposed or accepted. 'Love' means in practice that each side should state its case as strongly as it can before the most impartial tribunal available, with determination to accept the award of the tribunal. At least that puts the two parties on a level and is to that extent in accordance with the command 'Thou shalt love thy neighbour as thyself.'

Now just see how that illustration bears on the work of the lawyer. 'Each side should state its case as strongly as it can' – that is the task of the Advocate. 'Before the most impartial tribunal available' – that is the task of the Judge. 'With determination to accept the award of the tribunal' – that is the part of the ordinary man.

vi *Why do people obey the law?*

And speaking of the part of ordinary men, may I just say how wrong it is to apply the Austinian philosophy to them. The people of England do not obey the law because they are commanded to do so; nor because they are afraid of sanctions or of being punished. They obey the law because they know it is a thing they *ought* to do. There are of course some wicked persons who do not recognise it to be their duty to obey the law: and for them sanctions and punishment must be inflicted. But this does not alter the fact that the great majority of the people obey the law simply because they recognise it to be obligatory on them. They recognise that they are under a moral obligation to obey it.For this reason, it is most important that the law should be just. People will respect rules of law which are intrinsically right and just, and will expect their neighbours to obey them, as well of course as obeying the rules themselves: but they will not feel the same about rules which are unrighteous or unjust. If people are to feel a sense of obligation to the law, then the law must correspond, as near as may be, with justice.

vii *Return to religion*

So I ask you to accept with me that law is concerned with justice and that religion is concerned with justice. And thence I ask the question – What is justice? That question has been asked by many men far wiser than you or I and no one has yet found a satisfactory answer. All I would suggest is that justice is not something you can see. It is not temporal but eternal. How does man know what is justice? It is not the product of his intellect but of his spirit. Religion concerns the spirit in man whereby he is able to recognise what is justice: whereas law is only the application, however imperfectly, of justice in our everyday affairs. If religion perishes in the land, truth and justice will also. We have already strayed too far from the faith of our fathers. Let us return to it, for it is the only thing that can save us.

viii *Two to one against*

I was a Lord Justice of Appeal for nine years. It was a most rewarding time. Usually we were agreed, but sometimes I found myself in a minority. I was reluctant to dissent. But in the last resort I did so. It was for my own peace of mind. So long as I did what I thought was just, I was content. I could sleep at night. But if I did what was unjust, I stayed awake worrying. Afterwards, when I spoke to students I made fun about it. I used to tell them: 'When I was a Judge of first instance, sitting alone, I could and did do justice. But when I went to the Court of Appeal of three, I found that the chances of doing justice were two to one against!' That was quite untrue. In the great majority of cases, we were all agreed. It was only in very few that I dissented – and then I did so only for conscience sake – because I could not bring myself to agree.

3 In the House of Lords

1 Becoming a Lord

i *Not in any way ordinary*

It was in April 1957 that I went to the Lords. I was hesitant about it. We all know the quip: 'The House of Lords is like Heaven. Everyone wants to get there sometime but not just yet'. I was ambitious. I wanted to become either the Lord Chief Justice or the Master of the Rolls. And I feared that, if I accepted the Lords, it would lessen my chances. I went along the corridor and talked it over with Hubert Parker – then a Lord Justice like me. I decided to accept.

I became a Lord of Appeal in Ordinary. That odd description was introduced in 1876. It does not mean that the man is in any way ordinary. He is really extra-ordinary. The word 'Ordinary' is a technical term used in law to describe a judge who has jurisdiction to hear cases by virtue of his office. In contrast to other persons who have jurisdiction only by being peers.

ii *Not going into retirement*

To go from the Court of Appeal to the House of Lords is like going into retirement. It is rather like the senior partner retiring and becoming a consultant. In the Court of Appeal you are under continuous pressure. In the House of Lords you are relaxed and at ease. You sit four days a week. Sometimes less. Sometimes short days. You reserve every judgment, with ample time to think it over and to write it.

I rather think that when Shakespeare portrayed the sixth age, he was describing the age when a man retires:

> The sixth age shifts
> Into the lean and slipper'd pantaloon,
> With spectacles on nose and pouch on side,

> His youthful hose well sav'd a world too wide
> For his shrunk shank; and his big manly voice,
> Turning again towards childish treble, pipes
> And whistles in his sound.

But that does not describe me in the least on my 'retirement' to the House of Lords. I was aged 58. As active as ever. No shrunk shank. No childish treble. I took on a new role. Not only as a judge but as a legislator. Strictly speaking, a Law Lord is not a judge. He is a member of the House of Lords seconded for judicial duties. But in point of fact he is a judge – sitting in the Supreme Tribunal of the land – just as the Justices of the Supreme Court of the United States of America. But he differs from them in this: A Law Lord can and does sit in the Legislative Chamber when Bills are considered and passed. He can and does speak on them. He can and does vote on them. There is a convention that he should not speak or vote on matters which involve party politics. But otherwise he is free to vote on social questions and on legal questions.

iii *Opening with prayers*

On every day that the House sits, the proceedings are opened with prayers. Usually they are read by one of the Bishops. It takes five minutes. No strangers are admitted. A sprinkling of peers attend. I wish there were more. They turn round and kneel with their knees on the red-cushioned seats. The Bishop says the expressive prayer – with its lovely words – which has come down the centuries:

Almighty God, by whom alone Kings reign, and Princes decree justice; and from whom alone cometh all counsel, wisdom, and understanding; We thine unworthy servants, here gathered together in thy Name, do most humbly beseech thee to send down thy Heavenly Wisdom from above, to direct and guide us in all our consultations: and grant that, we having thy fear always before our eyes, and laying aside all private interests, prejudices, and partial affections, the result of all our counsels may be to the glory of thy blessed Name, the maintenance of true Religion and Justice, the safety, honour, and happiness of the Queen, the publick wealth, peace and tranquillity of the Realm, and the uniting and knitting together of the hearts of all persons and estates within the same, in true Christian Love and Charity one towards another, through Jesus Christ our Lord and Saviour. Amen.

In the Commons, the Chaplain says the same. I sometimes after dinner make a little fun, saying that: 'The Chaplain looks at the assembled members – with their varied intelligence – and then prays for the country!'

2 Speaking in debate

i *Always nervous*

When I look up Hansard again, I am surprised at the number of subjects on which I spoke and voted – during the five years in which I was a Lord of Appeal in Ordinary. I was always nervous. The other peers were among the most accomplished and able men of the time. You are not supposed to read your speech: but you can use notes. You must prepare beforehand what you are to say – otherwise you will muff it. I always prepared carefully. I did research. I made notes. I tried always to introduce some little story or incident – so as to give colour to my argument. But when I got up to speak, I put my notes aside. I did not look at them. I trusted to my memory. Your speech loses much of its effectiveness if you read it or if you keep looking down at notes. You should aim at a simple, easy presentation – addressing your audience directly – as if in conversation in a room. Above all, speak clearly and distinctly. To illustrate it, I will take from Hansard a couple of speeches which show my style – on matters of interest today as then.

ii *On suicide*

The first was on 2 March 1961 when the Government introduced a Bill to provide that suicide – and attempted suicide – should no longer be a crime. I said:

My Lords, if your Lordships approve this Bill, it will end a most interesting chapter of our English law, because for nearly a thousand years suicide has been regarded as the most heinous of felonies – the felony of self-murder. In consequence attempted suicide was a crime, a suicide pact was murder, and helping another to commit suicide was also murder. I say 'for nearly a thousand years', because it was King Edgar, nearly one thousand years ago, who decreed that it was a crime for a man to take his own life, denied him burial rights and laid down that all his goods were to be forfeited.

The reason for that law was stated by Blackstone to be founded, as it was, on our religion. The law of England, he said, wisely and religiously decreed that no man had power to destroy life except by commission of God, the author of it. He said that it was twofold; that one was spiritual. He said that to commit suicide was invading the prerogative of the Almighty, by rushing into His presence uncalled for. The other was temporal, against the King, because the King had an interest in the preservation of all his subjects. Those being the reasons for the law, the punishment which we inflicted for hundreds of years was twofold. First, on the corpse we inflicted ignominious burial. The suicide was buried at a cross-roads with a stake through his body and a stone on his face. Indeed, that continued until 1824, and the last suicide who was buried at the cross-roads was at Grosvenor Place. Even after that, until 1882, a suicide had to be buried by night; and ever since 1882 up to this day, according to the law of the Church of England, a suicide is not entitled to Christian burial. You will remember the gravediggers' scene in *Hamlet* and how Shakespeare puts into the mouth of the gravedigger these words:

'Is she to be buried in Christian burial that wilfully seeks her own salvation?'

It never has been so. I expect that now that suicide is to be no longer a crime – and I am glad to say it – a suicide will be permitted by Ecclesiastical Law a Christian burial, maybe with an alternative form of service recommended. That would be a final end to the law of dishonour in the courts. That was one angle of the punishment.

The other angle was to forfeit the goods, lands or leases of a suicide to the King. The great case, on which Shakespeare founded the scene of Ophelia, was the case in which Sir James Hale threw himself into the river at Canterbury, and the question was whether his widow would be entitled to his lease of the Graveney Marshes on his death. The Judges held that the widow was not entitled, and it went to the Crown. That forfeiture existed until 1870, when we abolished it. But there is one form of forfeiture which exists to this day and which I hope this Bill, when passed, will do away with – monies on insurance policies.

…One of the benefits of this Bill when it passes is that suicide will no longer be a crime and insurance companies will have to honour their liabilities on their policies; all forfeitures will be gone; all dishonouring of the corpse will be gone.

What about attempted suicide? Suicide was a crime, and attempting to commit suicide was also a crime. If suicide ceases to be a crime now, attempted suicide will cease to be a crime; and one is very glad of that. I have had cases of attempted suicide before me, and what one always did was to bind them over and arrange for medical treatment. But now, since the Mental Health Act 1959 to which the right reverend Prelate referred, it is unnecessary for any action to be taken in the courts. There is procedure laid down in that Act for application to be made through the relatives or the doctors and medical attention can be given. So there is no need for attempted suicide to be a crime any more. It will not be a crime, but will be treated medically and mentally.

That Bill was passed, and became law in the Suicide Act 1961. But the Statute contained express provision that it was an offence to aid or abet another to commit suicide – punishable with 14 years' imprisonment. That is a wise provision. Quite recently, however, there are people who have formed a Society called 'Exit', advocating the 'Right to Die with Dignity'. They have issued, or propose to issue, a booklet called *A Guide to Self-Deliverance* which will list five methods of painless suicide. Is this contrary to law? I would not say: for it may come before the Courts for decision.

iii *On right of privacy*

The other speech I would mention was on 13 March 1961 when Lord Mancroft introduced a Private Member's Bill to provide for a right of privacy. I said:

My Lords, if the law of England gives no remedy for an infringement of privacy then it becomes a duty at once to implement some Bill to put it right. Furthermore, if this Bill itself is not workable for the purpose then let us, in Committee, make it workable; because this problem has been with the courts for well over 100 years and our lawyers, 100 years ago and more, indicated a remedy, particularly in regard to the intrusion on the privacy of Royalty.

When King George III was ill it was said by Lord Eldon that if his physician had made notes in a diary of the King's illness, and what he had seen and heard, and had kept those notes and threatened afterwards to publish them, then the courts would have stopped him. Then later, there was the case when Prince Albert and Queen Victoria made a number of etchings, 63 in number, of their private lives, concerning their friends, their family, and children and dogs. A publisher managed to get hold of them and made a catalogue describing all these etchings, and threatened to publish them and to put a facsimile of Prince Albert's and Queen Victoria's signatures upon them. Thereupon Prince Albert brought an action to restrain the publisher. In that action it was held by the judges that the publisher ought to be restrained, and the Vice-Chancellor laid down a principle to protect privacy in these words. He said it was:

> 'an unbecoming and unseemly intrusion, offensive to that inbred sense of propriety natural to every man; a sordid spying into the privacy of domestic life, into the home of a family entitled to the most marked respect in this country'.

The decision was confirmed by the Lord Chancellor, who said that privacy was the right invaded. So, in 1848, the courts of this country were ready to give a remedy for the infringement of privacy.

In 1890, two lawyers in America (the noble Lord, Lord Mancroft, has mentioned them), wrote an article in the Harvard *Law Review* built on this very case of Prince Albert's, in which they said that this was just a single instance of the general right of privacy; and on that basis the courts of the United States, applying also Common Law, have founded a complete doctrine of the right of privacy. Just a little while ago a photographer surreptitiously took a photograph of a husband and wife in a loving embrace as the husband was leaving, and a periodical published it without consent. The courts of the United States gave a remedy in damages, and enunciated the principles of the right of privacy in a way which would surely do justice to anybody at Common Law. They said:

> '...the unwarranted ... publicising of one's private affairs with which the public has no legitimate concern, or the wrongful intrusion into one's private activities, in such a manner as to outrage or cause mental suffering, shame or humiliation to a person of ordinary sensibilities'.

That is the law as evolved in the United States from our Common Law. Why cannot we have something similar? I am not in despair. The Judges may well do it. There is nothing in any decision of this House, judicially, which prevents it, in that whenever any grievous cases come up we find that the lawyers produce a remedy....

This right of privacy, my Lords, is only one aspect of fundamental human rights which we have enunciated and put our name to, not only in the European Convention of Human Rights but in our very Constitution which we have framed, and also in that which we have helped frame for Nigeria and that which we are now helping to frame for Sierra Leone. We have the words:

> 'Every person has a right to respect for his private and family life, his home and his correspondence'.

Have we not any such right in England when it is being enunciated for us in countries overseas? Let us consider the question (it does not come into this Bill) of telephone-tapping, opening correspondence and so forth. Have we not a right to prevent infringement of privacy in that connection? All I would say is that if the law does not give the right of privacy, the sooner this Bill gives it the better.

That Bill was not passed into law. Since then, the subject of privacy was considered in 1972 by a Committee presided over by Mr. Kenneth Younger. It was against the establishment by statute of a general right of privacy. But in the Courts we have had a series of cases – especially on breach of confidence – which go some way towards protecting individuals against intrusion on their privacy.

3 The working of the Constitution

i *How I got to know it*

It was only when I was in the Lords that I got to know the working of our Constitution. The introduction of Bills – in the Commons or in the Lords; what happens on first reading, second reading and third reading; in committee and on report stages; the final assent of the Crown (by a Commission of Peers) which turns a Bill into a Statute and makes it the law of the land – by the simple phrase (still in our Norman-French) – 'Le Roy le Veult' or 'La Reyne le Veult'. Assent is never refused but, if it were, the formula would be 'Le Roy s'avisere' or 'La Reyne s'avisera', that is, 'It will be considered'.

But not only the procedure. The Palace of Westminster is itself the physical embodiment of our Constitution. I used always to enter and leave by Westminster Hall – and go to my small room – with no clerk or any assistance – except one clerk for all of us Law Lords. (It is better now. The Law Lords have good rooms with their own libraries close at hand and good assistance.) We used to sit judicially in a committee room, dressed in our ordinary lounge suits, with no ostentation whatever. But when the House sits in its legislative capacity, it sits in the Great Chamber of the Lords – carpeted and upholstered in red (the Commons is in green). It is here that one gets the 'feel' of the Constitution. So I would tell you of it.

ii *The great hall of William Rufus*

We have had many changes, but nevertheless the spirit of the Constitution remains the same. What is this spirit? Like other things of the spirit, it is more easy to recognise than to define. İt is to be felt rather than to be seen: and to be experienced rather than to be learnt. It is an atmosphere which springs out of our long experience and tradition. If you would catch something of it, you should go to Westminster Hall and remember the great scenes that have been enacted there.

The great hall of William Rufus, the hall which has resounded with the acclamations at the inauguration of thirty Kings ... the hall which witnessed the just sentence of Bacon and the just absolution of Somers ... the hall where Charles confronted the High Court of Justice with the placid courage which has half redeemed his fame ... the hall where the great proconsul Warren Hastings presented himself to his Judges.[1]

Such memories will bring back to you some of the great constitutional issues which have been decided by the English people. But you should also remember that, in this hall for nigh on seven hundred years, the judges of England laid down the common law which precisely defined the rights of the individual and made the life and liberty of every law-abiding citizen secure from injury on the part of others or of the State. Here sat the judges of England right from the days of King Henry II in 1189 till the year 1882 when the Courts were moved to their present situation in the Strand. The principles laid down by them have sunk deep into the mind of the nation and have been more powerful than anything else in creating the spirit of the British Constitution. If you reflect on all this in that hall, so strong and so well balanced, so built as if for all time, you will get a sense of wonderful history, and with it a knowledge that the English people are heirs of a spiritual worth which is a greater power in the world than armies or navies or atomic bombs.

1 Macaulay, *Essay on Warren Hastings*.

iii *The spirit of the Constitution*

Again, however, I ask the question – What is this spirit? It lies, I believe, first, in the instinct for justice which leads us to believe that right, and not might, is the true basis of society; and secondly, in the instinct for liberty, which leads us to believe that free-will, and not force, is the true basis of government. These instincts for justice and liberty are abstract ideas which are common to all freedom-loving countries: but the peculiar genius of the British Constitution lies in a third instinct, which is a practical instinct leading us to balance rights with duties, and powers with safeguards, so that neither rights nor powers shall be exceeded or abused. But who are the guardians of this spirit? Who are they who interpret it on our behalf?

They are twofold. On the one hand – Parliament. On the other hand – the Judges. Our Constitution is unwritten. But it is founded on two strong pillars. One is the sovereignty of Parliament. The other is the independence of the Judges.

iv *The sovereignty of Parliament*

In our constitutional theory, Parliament is supreme. Every law enacted by Parliament must be obeyed. Parliament can take us into the Common Market. It can also take us out of it. By a simple majority. Parliament can pass a Bill of Rights. But it can also repeal it or any clause in it. By a simple majority. We have no entrenched clauses. We have no fundamental Constitution by which other laws can be tested. No matter that a law may be unreasonable or unjust, nevertheless if it is clear on the point, the judges have no option. They must apply the statute as it stands. The people of this country, however, trust Parliament – and the members of it – always to be guided by those instincts for justice and liberty of which I have written.

v *The independence of the judges*

The keystone of the rule of law in England has been the independence of the judges. It is the only respect in which we make any real separation of powers. There is here no rigid separation between the legislative and the executive powers, because the ministers, who exercise the executive power, also direct a great deal of the legislative power of Parliament. But the judicial power is truly separate. The judges for nearly 300 years have been absolutely independent. And when I speak of judges, I include not only the High Court Judges, but also all the magistrates and others who exercise judicial functions. No member of the government, no member of Parliament, and no official of any government department, has any right whatever to direct or to influence or to interfere with the decisions of any of the judges. It is the sure knowledge of this that gives the people their confidence in the judges, and I would add also the chairmen of tribunals when they are independent of the executive, for then they too are judges. It does not depend on the name judge or chairman but on the substance. The critical test which they must pass if they are to receive the confidence of the people is that they must be independent of the executive.

Why do the English people feel so strongly about this? It is because it is born in them. We know in our bones that it will not do for us to allow the executive to have any control over the judges: and we know it because our forefathers learnt it in their struggles with the kings of England – the kings who in the old days exercised the supreme executive power in the land. Ever since the Act of Settlement in 1701 it has been part of our constitution that a judge of the High Court cannot be removed except for misconduct, and, even then, there must be a petition from both houses of Parliament for his removal. This means that a judge is virtually irremovable. No judge has ever been dismissed from that time to this. Secure from any fear of removal, the judges of England do their duty fearlessly, holding the scales even, not only between man and man, but also between man and the State. Every judge on his appointment takes an oath that he 'will do justice to all manner of people according to the laws and customs of England, without fear or favour, affection or ill-will'. Never since 1701 has any judge failed to keep that oath.

4 Conflict between Parliament and the Courts

In the ordinary way there is no conflict between our two great institutions – Parliament and the Courts. But in exceptional cases there has been. One such arose whilst I was a Law Lord. The Houses of Parliament enjoy certain privileges. One of them is freedom of speech. *Erskine May* says: 'What is said or done within the walls of Parliament cannot be enquired into in a court of law'. The Bill of Rights 1688, art. 9, s. 1, says:

That the freedom of speech, and debates or proceedings in Parliament, ought not to be impeached or questioned in any court or place out of Parliament.

This is how the conflict arose in my time.

i *Writ against Mr. Strauss MP*

On 8 February 1957 Mr. Strauss MP wrote a letter – on House of Commons paper – to Mr. Maudling, the Paymaster-General. He complained of the behaviour of the London Electricity Board. He said that they were disposing of scrap cables at too low a price. He said their conduct was a scandal. Mr. Maudling replied saying that it was a matter of day-to-day administration and, as such, the responsibility of the Board and not of the Minister. He passed the complaints on to the London Electricity Board. They said that the complaints against them were unfounded. They asked Mr. Strauss to withdraw them. He withdrew any imputation of dishonesty but retained the imputation of obstinacy and folly. The Board's solicitor on 4 March 1957 wrote saying:

Your letter is wholly unsatisfactory and we are instituting proceedings which we expect to serve upon you during the course of next week.

That simple solicitor's letter raised the great constitutional issue. Who was supreme? Parliament or the Courts of Law? Mr. Strauss said the letter (threatening a writ) was a breach of the privileges of Parliament, and that the Board and its solicitor were punishable by the House itself. The London Electricity Board said that they were entitled to have recourse to the Courts of Law and that the House of Commons could not stop them.

ii *I lose – by six to one*

The issue was referred to the Privy Council. Seven Law Lords sat to hear it. I was one of them. I found myself in a minority of one. Six of them, headed by Lord Simonds, avoided any direct ruling. They held that the House of Commons could treat the issue of a writ against a Member of Parliament – in respect of a speech or proceeding in Parliament – as a breach of its privileges. I thought otherwise. I prepared a memorandum of dissent. I held that every Englishman had a right to seek redress in the Courts of Law without interference by the House of Commons. On that ground I would have held that the London Electricity Board were entitled to issue a writ for libel against Mr. Strauss. When the case came before the Courts, it was for the judge to inquire into the matter: to see if Mr. Strauss had any defence by way of qualified privilege or by way of Parliamentary privilege –

as being a 'proceeding in Parliament' within the Bill of Rights, and that Parliament could not prevent the Courts from inquiring into it.

iii No dissent allowed

I took great pains over my memorandum of dissent. I attached to it learned appendices on 'The privilege of Members of Parliament from arrest or process' and 'The privilege of freedom of speech'. The six would have none of it. I asked that it should be published as a dissenting opinion. They would not have this either. I asked that the Report of the Privy Council should state that it was 'by a majority' or 'with one dissentient'. But they would not have this either. So if you read the Report in the *Law Reports*[1] – *re the Parliamentary Privilege Act 1770* – you would think that it was a unanimous opinion of all seven.

Nowadays it would be very different. Dissenting opinions are allowed. This being so I propose to lodge my papers in the case with the library of Lincoln's Inn: so that, if the point should arise again, my views upon it can be known.

iv The Commons are furious

In support of my view I would recall the great case of *Ashby v White*[2] in 1703. There was a conflict between the House of Commons and the Law. A 'poor indigent' man named Mathias Ashby went to the polling booth and claimed a right to vote for two members of Parliament: but the voting officers refused to allow him to vote on the ground that he was no settled inhabitant of the borough. Ashby brought an action for damages. The House of Lords then resolved that Ashby was entitled to bring his action and to recover his damages of £5. The House there not only vindicated the fundamental right of a citizen to vote, but it also established the great principle that wherever a man has a right, he shall have a remedy at law to enforce it. The decision, so clearly a broadening of freedom, was, however, furiously opposed by the House of Commons. They ordered the arrest of the solicitor who acted for Ashby; and they committed to prison five other men simply because they, like Ashby, brought actions against the returning officers. These men applied for a writ of habeas corpus. They had counsel to argue

1 [1958] AC 331.
2 1 *Smith's Leading Cases* 253.

for them. But the House of Commons thereupon took action against the counsel. The Sergeant-at-Arms actually arrested two of the counsel and would also have liked to have taken a third, Mr. Nicholas Lechmere, 'but that he got out of his chamber in the Temple, two pair of stairs high, at the back window, by the help of his sheets and a rope'. The controversy between the two Houses was only resolved because Queen Anne prorogued Parliament and the prisoners were released. No one, however, has doubted from that time to this that the principles established by the House of Lords were correct, and they are some of the most fundamental in our Constitution.

5 The Lords judicially

i *Was the policeman murdered?*

So much for constitutional matters. My primary role, however, in the Lords, was to sit judicially. I would recall now one of the most controversial decisions in the criminal law. It has excited students ever since. It is *The Director of Public Prosecutions v Smith*.[1] Smith had a load of stolen goods in the back of his car. A policeman stopped him to investigate. Smith drove off. The policeman jumped on to the bonnet of the car, calling on Smith to stop. Smith drove the car – with the policeman on it – straight into some oncoming cars. The policeman was knocked off. He was run over by an oncoming car, and killed. Smith was charged with murder, convicted and sentenced to death. The appeal to the Lords was heard by the strongest team that could be gathered together to decide a criminal appeal. Lord Kilmuir, the Lord Chancellor; Lord Goddard, who had been the Lord Chief Justice; Lord Tucker, one of the best criminal lawyers of the day; Lord Parker of Waddington, then the Lord Chief Justice; and me. We held unanimously that the conviction of murder was right. Yet it was attacked by the academic lawyers – none of whom had ever tried a criminal case in their lives. As an answer I took the case as my theme in a lecture I gave to the Hebrew University of Jerusalem. I called it *Responsibility before the law*. This is what I said:

Before I tell you the facts I would like to tell you a few dates, for they show how quickly justice is done in England or – as the critics would say, injustice

1 [1961] AC 290.

is done. On 2 March 1960, a police constable was killed. On the same day Jim Smith was arrested and charged with the murder of him. Just over one month later, on 7 April 1960, Smith was tried and found guilty by a jury of capital murder and was sentenced to death. Little more than another month passed when, on 10 May 1960, the Court of Criminal Appeal reversed the finding of murder, substituted a verdict of manslaughter, and sentenced Smith to ten years' imprisonment. Two and a half months later, on 28 July 1960, the House of Lords restored the conviction of capital murder. The House may have been wrong – though I dispute it – but no one can suggest that they were guilty of delay.

ii Or was he only shaken off?

Now let me tell you the facts: and I am going to take them … from the words of a head-note:

> 'The constable clung on to the side of the car, which pursued an erratic course, but he was finally shaken off and fell in front of another car, receiving fatal injuries.'

Now if the facts had been as there stated, I should have thought the jury would have found Smith not guilty of murder but guilty of manslaughter only: and I myself would have thought that manslaughter would have been the proper verdict: because the death of the policeman was, on this view, an accident. No one could reasonably be expected to have foreseen that the policeman would suffer really serious harm merely from falling off the car. The approach of the oncoming cars was an unforeseen event which unfortunately caused his death.

Now I must point out the insufficiency of those facts…. .

The head-note simply said 'he was finally shaken off'. But it was far more serious than shaking him off.

…The policeman had too firm a grip for that. He was stretched across the bonnet and banging on the window to tell Smith to stop. So what did Smith do? He drove his car right up close to the approaching traffic so that the policeman's body was struck up against the oncoming cars. Each of the drivers of those cars gave evidence. No one of them spoke of any zig-zagging at the time he was hitting them. They spoke of the car coming at them and swerving towards them. The policeman's body was struck against one car after another. A slight bump on the first. A heavier bump on the second. And a violent blow on the third, so violent that the offside front mudguard was knocked right in by the policeman's body – no marks being left on Smith's car. After that violent blow, the policeman was hurled off and came underneath the fourth car. That evidence had a great effect, I doubt not, on the jury's mind….No one suggested that Smith intended to kill the police officer. But the prosecution contended throughout that he intended to do the officer grievous bodily harm. And what stronger evidence could you have of grievous bodily harm than this driving of the policeman's body on to the sides of these approaching cars? One after the other, with such a violent impact on the third as to knock in the mudguard: and it was a very big dent.

iii *'The reasonable man' again*

...No doubt Smith had no *desire* to kill him: and it was not his *purpose* to kill him. But must he not have been aware that there was a very high probability that the policeman would suffer grievous bodily harm? And if so, was he not guilty of murder? The Judge so directed the jury: and the jury so found. And the House of Lords have said the direction was right. The Lord Chancellor summarised the direction in this way: 'If in doing what he did, *he must* as a reasonable man have contemplated that serious harm was likely to occur, then he was guilty of murder'. Note the words '*he must*' – that is – *this particular man* must have contemplated. Thus it must be brought home to *him* subjectively.

It was those words 'as a reasonable man' which offended the critics. Those words, they said, made the direction wrong: and also the conviction wrong. I would suggest that the jury would have come to the same conclusion anyway. How A. P. Herbert would have chortled – about 'the reasonable man' again – to overthrow the House of Lords!

iv *Don't despise the academics*

Smith was reprieved. But the academics persisted in their criticism. They succeeded. An Act was passed to take account of their criticism. It is section 8 of the Criminal Justice Act 1967. Moral for Judges: Don't despise the academics.

v *I move down*

In 1962 Lord Evershed, the Master of the Rolls, resigned and became himself a Lord of Appeal in Ordinary. Who was to succeed him? We all wondered. Then at lunch one day in the Lords, the Lord Chancellor, Lord Kilmuir (when the others had left the table) said to me: 'I hear that you would like to be Master of the Rolls yourself. Is that so?' Now I had mentioned it to no one – unless it were to Lord Parker – in 1957 – five years before. I said at once that I would. It was the opportunity I wanted. Lord Goddard often told me that he enjoyed his time in the Court of Appeal best of all. So had I. It was with a glad heart that I returned to it. Some would say that I moved down.

Tom — Master of the Rolls

1 The office in history

i *'I came, I saw, I conquered'*

I became Master of the Rolls in April 1962. I am still Master of the Rolls in 1981. Even so, and I trust you can see from this book – I have not reached Shakespeare's seventh age:

> Last scene of all
> That ends this strange eventful history,
> Is second childishness, and mere oblivion,
> Sans teeth, sans eyes, sans taste, sans everything.

I have been Master of the Rolls for nearly nineteen years. Not quite a record. Three have been for twenty-one years.

First, Julius Caesar was Master of the Rolls from 1614 to 1636 (not the Julius Caesar who wrote *'Veni, vidi, vici'* – 'I came, I saw, I conquered' – when, according to Plutarch, he announced his victory at Zela in 47 BC); our Julius Caesar MR never conquered anything.

Next, Joseph Jekyll from 1717 to 1738. (Pope described him as

> An odd old whig
> Who never changed his principles or his wig.)

Third, John Romilly from 1851 to 1873. (He was the son of Samuel Romilly who led the cause of Law Reform with zeal); our John MR never led anything.

ii *Beheaded for heresy*

Often I am asked: What is the office of the Master of the Rolls? What is its origin? What does it mean? I will try to explain.

There have been Masters of the Rolls ever since the year 1290 – there are records to prove it – and probably before that. He has always been one of the great officers of State. He was the Keeper of the Rolls or Records of the Chancery of England. The Rolls were the old rolls of parchment which contained the records of the proceedings of the Court of Chancery. Shakespeare speaks of the Master of the Rolls in *Henry VIII*. He tells how Thomas Cromwell was made Master of the Rolls. That was on 8 October 1534. Thomas Cromwell was, I believe, the only Master of the Rolls to have been beheaded. In June 1540. For heresy. He did not follow the advice given to him by Cardinal Wolsey:[1]

> Mark but my fall, and that that ruin'd me.
> Cromwell, I charge thee, fling away ambition;
> By that sin fell the angels; ...
>   be just, and fear not.
> Let all the ends though aim'st at be thy country's,
> Thy God's, and truth's.

I, too, was ambitious. I, too, was accused of heresy – and verbally beheaded – by Lord Simonds. You can read it in *Midland Silicones Ltd v Scruttons Ltd*,[2] quoted in *The Discipline of Law* (pages 288–289). But for the rest of the quotation from *Henry VIII* – 'Be just and fear not' and so forth – the advice of Wolsey accords with my philosophy – with the ends at which I have aimed.

iii *Only an old-time archivist*

You might think that – being merely keeper of the rolls of parchment – the Master of the Rolls was not a judge, but only an old-time archivist. Others have thought so too. In 1726 a book was published which called in question the judicial power of the Master of the Rolls. But it was answered two years later by a very learned book under the authority of Sir Philip Yorke, the Attorney-General (afterwards Lord Hardwicke, the great Lord Chancellor). It was called *A Discourse of the Judicial Authority belonging to the Office of Master of the Rolls in the High Court of Chancery*. It proved conclusively that for time out of mind 'the Master of the Rolls hath his place amongst the Judges between the two chief of them' — next to the Chief Justice of the King's Bench – and above the Chief Justice of Common Pleas. He has remained so to this day. Next after the Lord Chief Justice and above all the others.

1 Act III, sc. 2.
2 [1962] AC 446.

iv *A good example to follow*

There have been many distinguished holders of the office. But none more than Sir George Jessel, the Master of the Rolls from 1873 to 1883. He was the first Jew – after their emancipation in 1841 – to become an English judge. A judge, too, after my own style. As a student, he had received a gold medal for Mathematics. He used short, staccato sentences. *The Times'* obituary described him as 'one of the most erudite of case lawyers and also the most courageous of Judges in handling authorities....Unlike the ordinary authority-monger, he was the master, not the slave of precedents'. A good example to follow!

v *He received a fortune*

Over the centuries the office of Master of the Rolls was most rewarding financially. He had his own Court – called the Rolls Court – off Chancery Lane. He had his own mansion house – Rolls House. His own chapel – the Rolls Chapel – with two chaplains. He owned sixty houses in the streets round about – all let at good rents. It was called the Rolls Estate. Many of the houses were destroyed in the Great Fire of London in 1666. He got compensation and rebuilt them. But in 1837, in the time of Lord Langdale, an Act of Parliament was passed transferring them all to the Crown. In return for £7,000 a year free of tax. (That was a fortune in those days.) His mansion house was pulled down. On the site was erected the Public Record Office.

vi *A play on his title*

In time his salary was diminished. It was reduced so as to be on a level with the other judges. He became subject to tax – he became an ordinary mortal – or rather, shall I say, with nothing to distinguish him from the rest of mankind except his title – The Master of the Rolls. That is unique. There is now no other Master of the Rolls the whole world over. Even his title is not understood. It is mixed up with the motor-car called the Rolls. This is a letter which I received from International Students' House:

Dear Lord Denning,

I am an Indian citizen. I graduated in Mechanical Engineering in the University of London and was awarded a Master of Science degree. I feel I have the necessary qualifications, motivation, energy, drive and personality to begin a successful career in an automobile industry. I will ever remain grateful to you if you would kindly help me to begin my professional career with your Company, the Rolls Royce Motor Company... .

vii A Jack-of-all-trades

Yet the Master of the Rolls is still one of the most coveted posts in the land. He presides in the Court of Appeal on the civil side: where he has much influence on the development of the law – or its retardation. He still retains the remnants of his historical origin. He is, by Statute, Chairman of the Advisory Council on Public Records. He is Chairman of the Royal Commission on Historical Manuscripts. He has, by Statute, a fatherly eye on the Roll of Solicitors. He is a Jack-of-all-trades and Master of *One* – the 'Master' as he is affectionately known in the profession. The Bar still write to me – 'Dear Master'.

2 Presiding in the Court

i Time's up

Every Court of Appeal in England hears arguments by word of mouth. It has been done for centuries. The Court sits *in banco* (Latin) or *en banc* (Norman-French). A Court of three (or more) judges sitting together to hear an appeal: and deciding by a majority. The mediaeval pictures show them sitting on a bench – a long seat without a back. But the later ones show them sitting in chairs behind a long bench on which they have their papers and books. It is so today. But sometimes each judge has his own desk.

Go over to the United States of America. You will find there is little argument by word of mouth. In the Courts of Appeal the lawyers prepare printed 'briefs'. These contain their full arguments and submissions. The judges are supposed to read them beforehand. Then on the day appointed for hearing the argument is limited to a very short time. Half-an-hour is the most for each side. Then the Presiding Judge switches on a red light to show that 'Time's up'.

ii The way of Socrates

Ever since I have been Master of the Rolls there has been great pressure on me to adopt the United States system. I have steadfastly resisted it. To my mind the best way of getting at a correct decision is that which was pursued by Socrates some 2,400 years ago. He did it by word of mouth – by asking questions – and getting the answers he wanted. I would give you an instance from *The Republic of Plato*:[1]

Socrates: Do you admit that it is just for subjects to obey their rulers?
Thrasymachus: I do.
Socrates: But are the rulers of states absolutely infallible, or are they liable to err?
Thrasymachus: To be sure, they are liable to err.
Socrates: Then in making their laws they may sometimes make them rightly, and sometimes not.
Thrasymachus: True.

Now put that into modern dress. For Socrates read the Master of the Rolls. For the rulers read the House of Lords. For Thrasymachus read Queen's Counsel. And I get the answer I want.

But in the Court of Appeal a judge should not ask questions too soon: nor too many. He should let the advocate open the case in his own way. Not interrupting him until a convenient moment arrives. And for myself I do not read the papers beforehand. Only a glance at them to see what the case is about. Lord Atkin used to read them in detail. With the result that he made up his mind before counsel opened his mouth, and asked devastating questions from the outset. The litigants thought that the case was prejudged before their counsel was heard. Better by far to follow Lord Bacon's advice in his *Essay on Judicature*:

Patience and gravity of hearing is an essential part of justice; and an over-speaking judge is no well tuned cymbal. It is no grace to a judge first to find that which he might have heard in due time from the bar; or to show quickness of conceit in cutting off evidence or counsel too short; or to prevent information by questions, even though pertinent.

iii *How to stop him*

There is one thing that Bacon does not tell us, and that is – How to stop an advocate who goes on too long? The best method is to sit quiet and say nothing. Let him run down. Show no interest in what he is saying. Once you show any interest, he will start off again. Other methods have their uses. Take a few hints from Touchstone.[2] There is the *Retort courteous*: 'I think we have that point, Mr. Smith'. There is the *Quip modest*: When counsel

1 I.339 (Jowett's translation).
2 Shakespeare, *As You Like It*, Act V, sc. 4.

complained that he had been stopped by the Judge below, the Master of the Rolls said, 'How did he do that, Mr. Smith?' 'By falsely pretending to be "with me"', was the answer. There is the *Reply churlish*: 'You must give us credit for a little intelligence, Mr. Smith'. To which you may get the answer, 'That was the mistake I made in the Court below'. Next there is the *Reproof valiant*: When the advocate said, 'I am sorry to be taking up so much of Your Lordship's time' – 'Time, Mr. Smith', said the Master of the Rolls, 'You've exhausted time and trespassed upon eternity'. Next there is the *Countercheck quarrelsome*: 'You've said that three times already'. Finally the *Lie circumstantial* and the *Lie direct*: 'We cannot listen to you any longer. We will give judgment now'. Against him.

iv *The Master starts off*

One thing a judge must never do. He must never lose his temper. However sorely tried. Nor must he be sarcastic to counsel or to witness. Never discourteous. He may – indeed must – reprove counsel or witness when the occasion calls for it. Firmly and calmly.

All these, I know, are counsels of perfection. We must try even if we never attain.

> Ah, but a man's reach should exceed his grasp,
> Or what's a heaven for?[1]

After the conclusion of the argument, the members of the Court confer together. Often in whispers on the bench itself. Sometimes a talk for five minutes outside. Then straightway they give judgment. Usually the Master of the Rolls starts off. The others follow. Occasionally, if the case is difficult, it is reserved for two or three weeks and put into writing.

3 The giving of judgment

The giving of judgment is an art which is only learned by experience. To describe it, I will take first the usual kind of judgment. Second, my kind of judgment.

i *The usual kind*

I will not use names but I can tell of a judge who is regarded by his contemporaries as a good judge and is much respected. In giving judgment he is cold and impassive. Not swayed by emotion or prejudice. Impersonal and inhuman. He does not call the litigants by their known names – John Doe or Richard Roe. But by their *noms de litis* – plaintiff or defendant – appellant or

1 Robert Browning, *Andrea del Sarto*.

respondent. Quite often he gets them transposed – saying plaintiff when he means defendant – but the shorthand writer puts it right. He is indifferent to the merits. Going by the strictness of the law. Heedless of hardship to one side or the other. No raising or lowering of his voice. No ornament or colour in his words. Precise and accurate. Even when it leads to obscurity. Even when it means long sentences – punctuated by parentheses and qualifications – rather than short ones. He drily sets out the pleadings: and the orders already made. In order of date. He gives a detailed recital of facts, omitting nothing, relevant or irrelevant. He makes endless references to authorities – with long quotations of what other judges before him have said. Coming ultimately – and with professed reluctance – to a decision contrary to the justice of the case. Wiping the crocodile tears from his eyes.

ii *My kind*

It is against that kind of judgment that I set my face. The parties come in with a living problem. I try to make my judgment live – so that it can readily be understood – by the parties in particular: and by others who hear it. Let me tell you how I do it – for better or for worse – so that you can say whether you approve or not.

I start my judgment, as it were, with a prologue – as the chorus does in one of Shakespeare's plays – to introduce the story. Then I go on from act to act as Shakespeare does – each with its scenes – drawn from real life. But I do it by dividing my judgment up into main headings (corresponding to the acts) and sub-paragraphs (corresponding to the scenes) – each with a caption – so as to catch the eye. I draw the characters as they truly are – using their real names – so that I never get them mixed up. Never plaintiff or defendant, or appellant or respondent. In telling the story, I set out the merits – I rely on them – I do not scorn them. Because the merits go to show where justice lies. I use every argument that appears to me to be valid. I am not afraid of the rebuke, 'That is mere prejudice': for I know that only too often it is used only as a way of escape – from the merits. I avoid long sentences like the plague: because they lead to obscurity. It is no good if the hearer cannot follow them. I strive at all costs to be clear. Not ambiguous or prevaricating. I refer sometimes to previous authorities – I have to do so – because I know that people are prone not to accept my views unless they have support from the books. But never at much length. Only a sentence or two. I avoid all reference to pleadings and orders – unless something turns on them. They are mere lawyer's stuff. They are unintelligible to anyone else. I finish with a conclusion – an epilogue – again as the chorus does in Shakespeare. In it I gather the threads together and give the result. I never say, 'I regret having to come to this conclusion but I have no option'. There is always a way round. There is always an option – in my philosophy – by which justice can be done.

4 Judgments as short stories

i *Each is a landmark*

I hope you will not think me boastful but I will try to illustrate my method by giving a few instances. I state the facts, I give the merits, and then show the way to a just result. If you are a lawyer you may know them already. If so, you can skip them. But if you are not a lawyer, they will, I hope, interest you. Each has a useful lesson. Each is a landmark in our law. Each is a short story. Not fiction. But true. Based on evidence.

ii *The widow's annuity*

It had been held for over 100 years that no man could sue on a contract to which he was not a party. Even though it was expressly made for his benefit, he could not recover on it. That doctrine would have deprived a widow of her annuity – unless we had intervened. It was in *Beswick v Beswick*:[1]

Old Peter Beswick was a coal merchant in Eccles, Lancashire. He had no business premises. All he had was a lorry, scales and weights. He used to take the lorry to the yard of the National Coal Board, where he bagged coal and took it round to his customers in the neighbourhood. His nephew, John Joseph Beswick, helped him in the business.

In March 1962, old Peter Beswick and his wife were both over 70. He had had his leg amputated and was not in good health. The nephew was anxious to get hold of the business before the old man died. So they went to a solicitor, Mr. Ashcroft, who drew up an agreement for them. The business was to be transferred to the nephew: old Peter Beswick was to be employed in it as a consultant for the rest of his life at £6.10s. a week. After his death the nephew was to pay to his widow an annuity of £5 per week, which was to come out of the business....

After the agreement was signed, the nephew took over the business and ran it. The old man seems to have found it difficult at first to adjust to the new situation, but he settled down. The nephew paid him £6.10s. a week. But, as expected, he did not live long. He died on 3 November 1963, leaving his widow, who was 74 years of age and in failing health. The nephew paid her

1 [1966] 1 Ch 538, 549.

the first £5. But he then stopped paying her and has refused to pay her any more.

...The action came for hearing before the Vice-Chancellor of the County Palatine of Lancaster, who held that she had no right to enforce the agreement. He dismissed the action.

If the decision of the Vice-Chancellor truly represents the law of England, it would be deplorable. It would mean that the nephew could keep the business to himself, and at the same time repudiate his promise to pay the widow. Nothing could be more unjust....

The general rule undoubtedly is that 'no third person can sue, or be sued, on a contract to which he is not a party': but at bottom that is only a rule of procedure. It goes to the form of remedy, not to the underlying right. Where a contract is made for the benefit of a third person who has a legitimate interest to enforce it, it can be enforced by the third person in the name of the contracting party or jointly with him or, if he refuses to join, by adding him as a defendant. In that sense, and it is a very real sense, the third person has a right arising by way of contract....The widow is entitled to an order for specific performance of the agreement, by ordering the defendant to pay the arrears of £175, and the instalments of £5 a week as they fall due.

iii *The picnic at bluebell-time*

At one time it was held that damages could not be allowed for nervous shock. That doctrine would have deprived another widow of her compensation – unless we had intervened. It was in *Hinz v Berry*:[1]

It happened on 19 April 1964. It was bluebell-time in Kent. Mr. and Mrs. Hinz had been married some ten years, and they had four children, all aged nine and under. The youngest was one. Mrs. Hinz was a remarkable woman. In addition to her own four, she was foster-mother to four other children. To add to it, she was two months pregnant with her fifth child.

On this day they drove out in a Bedford Dormobile van from Tonbridge to Canvey Island. They took all eight children with them. As they were coming back they turned into a lay-by at Thurnham to have a picnic tea. The husband, Mr. Hinz, was at the back of the Dormobile making the tea. Mrs. Hinz had taken Stephanie, her third child, aged three, across the road to pick bluebells on the opposite side. There came along a Jaguar car driven by Mr. Berry, out of control. A tyre had burst. The Jaguar rushed into this lay-by and crashed into Mr. Hinz and the children. Mr. Hinz was frightfully injured and died a little later. Nearly all the children were hurt. Blood was streaming from their heads. Mrs. Hinz, hearing the crash, turned round and saw this disaster. She ran across the road and did all she could. Her husband was beyond recall. But the children recovered.

An action has been brought on her behalf and on behalf of the children for damages against Mr. Berry, the defendant. The injuries to the children have been settled by various sums being paid. The pecuniary loss to Mrs. Hinz by reason of the loss of her husband has been found by the judge to be some £15,000; but there remains the question of the damages payable to her for her nervous shock – the shock which she suffered by seeing her husband lying in the road dying, and the children strewn about.

1 [1970] 2 QB 40, 42.

The law at one time said that there could not be damages for nervous shock: but for these last 25 years, it has been settled that damages can be given for nervous shock caused by the sight of an accident, at any rate to a close relative....Somehow or other the court has to draw a line between sorrow and grief for which damages are not recoverable, and nervous shock and psychiatric illness for which damages are recoverable. The way to do this is to estimate how much Mrs. Hinz would have suffered if, for instance, her husband had been killed in an accident when she was 50 miles away: and compare it with what she is now, having suffered all the shock due to being present at the accident. The evidence shows that she suffered much more by being present....

At the trial, five years after the accident, she frequently broke down when giving her evidence. She brought the children to court. They were very well turned out. The judge awarded £4,000 on the head of nervous shock. I do not think it is erroneous. I would dismiss the appeal.

iv *Yew Tree Farm*

It was long held that if a customer signed a bank guarantee, he could not get out of it. No matter that it operated most harshly on him. The law took no notice of inequality of bargaining power. But we managed to help the customer in *Lloyds Bank v Bundy:*[1]

Broadchalke is one of the most pleasing villages in England. Old Herbert Bundy, the defendant, was a farmer there. His home was at Yew Tree Farm. It went back for 300 years. His family had been there for generations. It was his only asset. But he did a very foolish thing. He mortgaged it to the bank. Up to the very hilt. Not to borrow money for himself, but for the sake of his son. Now the bank have come down on him. They have foreclosed. They want to get him out of Yew Tree Farm and to sell it. They have brought this action against him for possession. Going out means ruin for him. He was granted legal aid. His lawyers put in a defence. They said that, when he executed the charge to the bank, he did not know what he was doing: or at any rate that the circumstances were such that he ought not to be bound by it. At the trial his plight was plain. The judge was sorry for him. He said he was a 'poor old gentleman.' He was so obviously incapacitated that the judge admitted his proof in evidence. He had a heart attack in the witness-box. Yet the judge felt that he could do nothing for him. 'There is nothing', he said, 'which takes this out of the vast range of commercial transactions'. He ordered Herbert Bundy to give up possession of Yew Tree Farm to the bank. Now there is an appeal to this court. The ground is that the circumstances were so exceptional that Herbert Bundy should not be held bound.

...

Gathering all together, I would suggest that through all these instances there runs a single thread. They rest on 'inequality of bargaining power'. By virtue of it, the English law gives relief to one who, without independent advice, enters into a contract upon terms which are very unfair or transfers property for a consideration which is grossly inadequate, when his bargaining power is grievously impaired by reason of his own needs or desires, or by

1 [1975] 1 QB 326, 334.

his own ignorance or infirmity, coupled with undue influence or pressures brought to bear on him by or for the benefit of the other....

...I have no doubt that the assistant bank manager acted in the utmost good faith and was straightforward and genuine. Indeed the father said so. But beyond doubt he was acting in the interests of the bank – to get further security for a bad debt. There was such a relationship of trust and confidence between them that the bank ought not to have swept up his sole remaining asset into its hands – for nothing – without his having independent advice.

We rejected the claim of the bank. We allowed Herbert Bundy to stay.

v *The street trader's indiscretion*

At one time the Courts never interfered with the disciplinary powers of administrative authorities. They allowed those authorities to punish misbehaviour in whatever way they thought fit. But we managed to save Harry Hook the street trader. It was in *R v Barnsley Council, ex parte Hook*:[1]

To some this may appear to be a small matter, but to Mr. Harry Hook it is very important. He is a street trader in the Barnsley market. He has been trading there for some six years without any complaint being made against him; but, nevertheless, he has now been banned from trading in the market for life. All because of a trifling incident. On Wednesday, 16 October 1974, the market closed at 5.30. So were all the lavatories, or 'toilets' as they are now called. They were locked up. Three-quarters of an hour later, at 6.20, Harry Hook had an urgent call of nature. He wanted to relieve himself. He went into a side street near the market and there made water, or 'urinated', as it is now said. No one was about except one or two employees of the council, who were cleaning up. They rebuked him. He said: 'I can do it here if I like'. They reported him to a security officer who came up. The security officer reprimanded Harry Hook. We are not told the words used by the security officer. I expect they were in language which street traders understand. Harry Hook made an appropriate reply. Again we are not told the actual words, but it is not difficult to guess. I expect it was an emphatic version of 'You be off'. At any rate, the security officer described them as words of abuse. Touchstone would say the security officer gave the 'Reproof valiant' and Harry Hook gave the 'Countercheck quarrelsome' (*As You Like It*, Act V, sc. 4).

On the Thursday morning the security officer reported the incident. The market manager thought it was a serious matter. So he saw Mr. Hook the next day, Friday, 18 October. Mr. Hook admitted it and said he was sorry for what had happened. The market manager was not satisfied to leave it there. He reported the incident to the chairman of the amenity services committee of the council. He says that the chairman agreed 'that staff should be protected from such abuse'. That very day the market manager wrote a letter to Mr. Hook, banning him from trading in the market....So there he was on Friday, 18 October, dismissed as from the next Wednesday, banned for life....

1 [1976] 1 WLR 1052, 1055.

Now the law is that the stallholder has to have the permission of the marketholder to start with. But once he has it and has set up his stall there, then so long as he pays the stallage, he has a right to keep it there. It is not to be taken away except for just cause and then only in accordance with the provisions of natural justice. I do not mind whether the marketholder is exercising a judicial or an administrative function. A stallholder counts on this right in order to enable him to earn his living. It is not to be taken away except for just cause and in accord with natural justice.

So it was quite right for the committee to hold the hearings....But, nevertheless, each of the hearings was, to my mind, vitiated by the fact that the market manager was there all the time. He was the one who gave evidence – the only one who did – and hearsay evidence, too. His evidence was given privately to the committee, not in the presence of Mr. Hook or his representatives. Mr. Hook was not himself in the room. And when the committee discussed the case and came to their decision, the market manager was there all the time. His presence at all their deliberations is enough to vitiate the proceedings. It is contrary to natural justice that one who is in the position of a prosecutor should be present at the deliberations of the adjudicating committee....

...So in this case if Mr. Hook did misbehave, I should have thought the right thing would have been to take him before the magistrates under the byelaws, when some small fine might have been inflicted. It is quite wrong that the Barnsley Corporation should inflict upon him the grave penalty of depriving him of his livelihood. That is a far more serious penalty than anything the magistrates could inflict. He is a man of good character, and ought not to be penalised thus. On that ground alone, apart from the others, the decision of the Barnsley Corporation cannot stand. It is said to be an administrative decision: but even so, the court has jurisdiction to quash it. Certiorari would lie to quash not only judicial decisions, but also administrative decisions.

vi *21 are killed and 161 injured*

Six Irishmen were convicted – on their own confessions – of murder. Yet they afterwards sued the police for damages on the ground that they were assaulted and beaten up whilst in custody – so much so that their confessions were involuntary. Could these actions be stopped? The case was *McIlkenny v Chief Constable of the West Midlands:*[1]

The Birmingham Bombers
Thursday, 21 November 1974.

Eight minutes past eight in the evening. The telephone rang in a newspaper office in Birmingham. A young man picked it up. It was from a call-box. 'Is that "The Birmingham Post"?' asked a voice with an Irish accent. 'Yes'. The voice went on: 'There is a bomb planted at the Rotunda. There is another in New Street near the tax office'. That was all. At once the young man dialled the police. He repeated the message to them. The police were quick as lightning. Their cars rushed to those addresses – screeching their way. But

1 [1980] 2 WLR 689, 696, 706, 707.

they were too late. The bombs went off before the police could get there. Each in a crowded public house. One in 'The Mulberry Bush'. The other in 'The Tavern in the Town'. Both were devastated. Dead and dying lay everywhere. Twenty-one people were killed and 161 injured.

Outside the police were going into action swiftly. To catch the terrorists. They sent out squads to every exit from Birmingham, by road, rail or air. They went to the railway station at New Street. It was quite close to the bombed premises. They found that a train had left New Street for Belfast. It had left at 7.55 p.m., about 20 minutes before the bombs went off. It had many Irish passengers on it. It was due at Heysham – 200 miles away – a little before 11 o'clock at night. The passengers would then take the boat to Belfast. The police then did a fine piece of detective work. As a result they had reason to suspect five of the passengers on that train. They telephoned to the Lancashire police. They met the train. Four of the men came through the barrier at Heysham. They were arrested by the Lancashire police. The fifth was arrested on the boat. They were taken the four miles to the police station at Morecambe. The men told the Lancashire police that they were on their way to attend the funeral in Belfast of James McDade. He was a prominent member of the IRA. He had made a mistake while setting a bomb in Coventry. It had exploded too soon and killed him. He was to be buried in Belfast.

Friday 22 November 1974

During the night the Birmingham police went post haste to Morecambe, arriving early on the next day. It was a Friday. They interviewed the five men that day. In the evening, with an escort, they drove the men back by car the 200 miles to Birmingham. The men were then detained at the Queen's Road Police Station. Later the same night the police arrested a sixth man, called Callaghan, at his home in Birmingham. They took him also to the Queen's Road Police Station.

Saturday, 23 November 1974

The six men were further interviewed. They all made statements. Some in writing. Some by word of mouth. In them they admitted their parts in placing the bombs. Now here is the crucial point in the whole case: Apart from the confessions, the police had no sufficient evidence on which to charge the men, let alone convict them. There was nothing but suspicion of the vaguest kind quite unsupported by any concrete evidence. So the statements were vital. Were they obtained voluntarily or not? That was to be the decisive point at the trial.

....

In this case at the 'trial within a trial' there was an issue whether the police had been guilty of violence or threats towards the six men so that their confessions were not made voluntarily. The judge on the issue made a clear finding that they were voluntary. He found *against* the six men after a trial of eight days in which the six men had full and fair opportunity of being heard – and were in fact heard – and were represented by leading counsel. At the trial the same evidence about violence and threats was given all over again before the jury....Again the jury found against the men.

This case shows what a civilised country we are. Here are six men who have been proved guilty of the most wicked murder of 21 innocent people. They have no money. Yet the state lavished large sums on their defence.

They were convicted of murder and sentenced to imprisonment for life. In their evidence they were guilty of gross perjury. Yet the state continued to lavish large sums on them – in their actions against the police. It is high time that it stopped. It is really an attempt to set aside the convictions by a side-wind. It is a scandal that it should be allowed to continue. The issue was fully tried out and decided by Bridge J at the 'trial within a trial'. His finding on that issue is decisive unless there are circumstances which make it fair or just to reopen it. I see no such circumstances. I would allow the appeal and strike out these actions on the ground of issue estoppel.

vii *Who was the 'mole'?*

Granada Television obtained some very confidential papers belonging to the British Steel Corporation and made great play with them on television. The British Steel Corporation wanted to know the name of the 'mole' who disclosed the papers to Granada. It raised the important point: How far is a newspaper or a television company bound to disclose its source of information? This is how I put it in *British Steel Corporation v Granada Television Ltd*:[1]

After studying the cases it seems to me that the courts are reaching towards this principle: The public has a right of access to information which is of public concern and of which the public ought to know. The newspapers are the agents, so to speak, of the public to collect that information and to tell the public of it. In support of this right of access, the newspapers should not in general be compelled to disclose their sources of information. Neither by means of discovery before trial. Nor by questions or cross-examination at the trial. Nor by subpoena. The reason is because, if they were compelled to disclose their sources, they would soon be bereft of information which they ought to have. Their sources would dry up. Wrongdoing would not be disclosed. Charlatans would not be exposed. Unfairness would go unremedied. Misdeeds in the corridors of power – in companies or in government departments – would never be known. Investigative journalism has proved itself as a valuable adjunct of the freedom of the press. Notably in the Watergate exposure in the United States: and the Poulson exposure in this country. It should not be unduly hampered or restricted by the law....

Nevertheless, this principle is not absolute. The journalist has no privilege by which he can claim – as of right – to refuse to disclose the name. There may be exceptional cases in which, on balancing the various interests, the court decides that the name should be disclosed. Such as in *Garland v Torre* in the United States and *Attorney-General v Mulholland* here. Have we any scales by which to hold the balance? Have we any yardstick by which to determine which cases are exceptional? It seems to me that the rule – by which a newspaper should not be compelled to disclose its source of information – is granted to a newspaper on condition that it acts with a due sense of responsibility. In order to be deserving of freedom, the press must show itself

1 [1980] 3 WLR 774.

worthy of it. A free press must be a responsible press. The power of the press is great. It must not abuse its power. If a newspaper should act irresponsibly, then it forfeits its claim to protect its sources of information.

To show what I mean by irresponsibly, let me give some examples. If a newspaper gets hold of an untrustworthy informant – and uses his information unfairly to the detriment of innocent people – then it should not be at liberty to conceal his identity. If it pays money to an informant so as to buy scandal – and publishes it – then again it abuses its freedom. It should not be at liberty to conceal the source. But, if it gets hold of a trustworthy informant – who gives information of which the public ought to know – then, even though it originated in confidence, the newspaper may well be held to act with a due sense of responsibility in publishing it. It should not be compelled to divulge its source. All that I have said applies equally to television. The like principles apply to them.

I have been much troubled whether Granada acted with a due sense of responsibility. Many things they did are disturbing. Not so much in the decision to use the information in the public interest, but in the way they went about it. True it is that they did not pay any money to the un-named informer. If they had – if they had bought his disloyalty with a bribe – it would have put them out of court at once. At any rate out of this court. But they did something equally irresponsible. They made an unfair use of this confidential information. Mr. Alexander Irvine QC admitted that if it was 'blatantly unfair' they might have to disclose the name. I think it was.

Granada appealed to the House of Lords. The House dismissed the appeal. We all wondered what would happen. It was said that Granada would disobey the order of the Court. They would not disclose the name of the 'mole'. What then? Would someone be sent to prison? Or would their funds be sequestrated? As luck would have it, however, British Steel discovered the name. So the issue was settled without recourse to the Court. What a pity! It would have been exciting to watch a battle between the Courts and the media!

Since then *The Sunday Times* has discovered the name of the 'mole' and of the researcher for Granada. It has become public knowledge. But nevertheless the episode has been well worthwhile. It has made clear that in the last resort the media can be compelled to give the source of their information if it is necessary in order that justice should be done.

5 Gems in ermine

i *Judges and judgments*

Now I would tell you more of judges and of judgments. The judges wear the fur of the ermine as the mark of their calling.

They give their judgments by word of mouth. These judgments have been taken down and recorded in our law books for nearly 700 years. There are to be found there 'full many a gem of purest ray serene'. When great issues have been at stake, the judgments are marked by eloquence, wisdom, and authority. They have laid the foundations of freedom in our land. It is due to the judges, more than to anyone else, that this England is a land where:

> A man may speak the thing he will,
> A land of settled government,
> A land of just and old renown,
> Where Freedom slowly broadens down
> From precedent to precedent.[1]

Judges do not speak, as do actors, to please. They do not speak, as do advocates, to persuade. They do not speak, as do historians, to recount the past. They speak to give judgment. And in their judgments you will find passages which are worthy to rank with the greatest literature which England holds. John Buchan at one time desired to make an anthology of them. 'It would', he said, 'put most professional stylists to shame'.

ii *'Style is the dress of thought'*

I will pick out some of my efforts for you to judge. I hold firmly to the view that – in speeches – or in judgments – if you are to persuade your hearers – or your readers– you must cultivate a style which commands attention. No matter how sound your reasoning, if it is presented in a dull and turgid setting, your hearers – or your readers – will turn aside. They will not stop to listen. They will flick over the pages. But if it is presented in a lively and attractive setting, they will sit up and take notice. They will listen as if spellbound. They will read you with engrossment. That is how Winston Churchill helped us so much to win the war. It was by his speeches and his writings – rather than by his strategy or mental capacity. They were good enough but they would not have carried the day by themselves.

Samuel Wesley put it well:[2]

> Style is the dress of thought; a modest dress,
> Neat, but not gaudy, will true critics please.

Sir Walter Scott gives good advice to lawyers. On style. He was himself called to the Scottish Bar. So he knew. He describes

---

1 Tennyson, *You ask me, why*.
2 *An Epistle to a Friend concerning Poetry*.

how the lay client Colonel Mannering goes to the chambers of the lawyer Counsellor Pleydell. The walls were lined – not with law books – but with books of history and literature – and on the walls a painting or two by Jamieson, the Caledonian Vandyck. The lawyer points to the books of history and literature:

These are my tools of trade. A lawyer without history or literature is a mechanic, a mere working mason; if he possesses some knowledge of these, he may venture to call himself an architect.[1]

iii 'A poor thing: but mine own'

My style is 'a poor thing: but it is mine own'. My judgments throughout carry my style. Many illustrations you will find in *The Discipline of Law* and in *The Due Process of Law*. But I would add here just one more. I will take my word portraits of some of the characters in the *Profumo Inquiry*. That was over 17 years ago now. So many of you may not have read it; and may find it interesting. I have described my method of working in *The Due Process of Law* (pages 67–73). But not my style. And here I am concerned with style:[2]

iv Stephen Ward

The story must start with Stephen Ward, aged 50. The son of a clergyman, by profession he was an osteopath with consulting rooms at 38 Devonshire Street, W.1. His skill was very considerable and he included among his patients many well-known people. He was also an accomplished portrait artist. His sitters included people of much eminence. He had a quick and easy manner of conversation which attracted some but repelled others. It pleased him much to meet people in high places, and he was prone to exaggerate the nature of his acquaintanceships with them. He would speak of many of them as if they were great friends when, more often than not, he had only treated them as patients or drawn their portraits.

Yet he was at the same time utterly immoral. He had a small house or flat in London at 17 Wimpole Mews, W.1., and a country cottage on the Cliveden Estate next to the River Thames. He used to pick up pretty girls of the age of 16 or 17, often from night clubs, and induce them to come and stay with him at his house in London. He used to take these girls down at weekends to his cottage. He seduced many of these himself. He also procured them to be mistresses for his influential friends. He did not confine his attention to promiscuity. He catered also for those of his friends who had perverted tastes. There is evidence that he was ready to arrange for whipping and other sadistic performances. He kept collections of pornographic photographs. He attended parties where there were sexual orgies of a revolting nature. In money matters he was improvident. He did not keep a banking account. He

1 Sir Walter Scott, *Guy Mannering*.
2 Cmnd. 2152, paras. 10–12, 16, 228–229.

got a firm of solicitors to keep a sort of banking account for him, paying in cheques occasionally to them and getting them to pay his rent. More often he cashed his incoming cheques through other people; or paid his bills with the incoming cheques. He had many cash transactions which left no trace.

Finally, he admired the Soviet régime and sympathised with the Communists. He used to advocate their cause in conversation with his patients, so much so that several became suspicious of him. With others he was more discreet. He became very friendly with a Russian, Captain Eugene Ivanov.

v *Christine Keeler*

Christine Keeler is a girl, now aged 21, whose home is at Wraysbury. She left home at the age of 16 and went to London. She was soon employed at the Murray Cabaret Club as a show-girl, which involved, as she put it, just walking around with no clothes on. She had only been at the Cabaret Club a short time when Stephen Ward came there and they danced together. Thereafter he often telephoned her and took her out. After a very few days he asked her to go and live with him. She went. She ran away from him many times but she always went back. He seemed to control her. She lived with him at 17 Wimpole Mews from about June 1961 to March 1962. He took her to his country cottage at Cliveden and he introduced her to many men, sometimes men of rank and position, with whom she had sexual intercourse. (A jury has since found him guilty on a charge of living on the earnings of her prostitution.) She had undoubted physical attractions. Later on he introduced her also to the drug Indian hemp and she became addicted to it. She met coloured men who trafficked in it and she went to live with them.

vi *The story ends, as it began, with him*

On 1 April 1963, the police started their investigation into Ward's activities. Many statements were taken and a report was made in May to the Director of Public Prosecutions. A conference was held with counsel on 7 June. On that very evening information reached Scotland Yard that Ward was about to leave the country. In consequence Ward was arrested on Saturday 8 June. He applied for bail but was refused it. He remained in custody throughout the hearings before the magistrate. These were not concluded until 3 July 1963. He was then committed for trial, but allowed bail, in spite of objections by the police.

The trial of Ward started on 22 July and continued for eight days. He was allowed bail throughout. On 30 July 1963, the Judge started his summing-up, but had not finished it when the court adjourned. On the morning of 31 July Ward was found unconscious, having taken an overdose of drugs. The Judge concluded his summing-up in Ward's absence. He was found guilty of living on the earnings of prostitution between 1 June 1961 and 31 August 1962 (Christine Keeler being the woman concerned) and between 1 September 1962 and 31 December 1962 (Marilyn Rice-Davies being the woman concerned). The Judge postponed sentence till Ward was fit to appear. But Ward never regained consciousness and died on 3 August 1963. The story ends, as it began, with him.

218

6 Not Yet The Times

The frog gets an injunction

My style of writing and of giving judgment has become so well known that a delightful skit was made about it. It was whilst *The Times* was not appearing owing to a strike. Someone produced a paper in the same get-up and headed it *Not Yet The Times*. In the section devoted to Law Reports there was this imaginary report of an imaginary case before the Court of Appeal.

Grenouille v National Union of Seamen

A frog was a person in law and accordingly had the necessary *locus standi* to bring injunction proceedings before the courts, especially where the respondent was a wicked and irresponsible trade union. The Court of Appeal so held in allowing an appeal by Mr. Grenouille, a frog, of Ball's Pond, against a decision by Mr. Justice Woolf refusing to grant an injunction restraining the National Union of Seamen from mounting a picket around the appellant's pond.

Mr. George Carman QC and Mr. Douglas Hogg appeared for the frog. Mr. Peter Taylor QC and Mr. Fenton Bresler for the union.

THE MASTER OF THE ROLLS said that the appeal raised issues of profound importance to the rule of law. No less than the continued existence of the courts to protect citizens from oppression was at stake. The facts were simple. Mr. Grenouille awoke one May morning to find his pond surrounded by pickets belonging to the National Union of Seamen. They were stopping the public from throwing food into the pond. The frog became ill. He was on the way to starvation. The National Association for Freedom, Enterprise, and Self-Reliance took up his case and last week, through counsel, asked a judge to order the union to remove the pickets. The union, in an affidavit to the court, said that the picket was lawful. It was 'in furtherance of a trade dispute', it claimed, the dispute being between Sandanista guerrillas and the Nicaraguan Government over working hours and conditions. The court had no doubt that the union's action did not fall within the criteria laid down for a union to be able to claim immunity from an action in the courts.

But counsel for the union had persuaded the learned judge below that a frog had no legal right to be heard by the courts at all. Lord Denning said that he had no hesitation in adopting the opposite view. It would be a black day indeed for British justice if it were only to be available to brave men such as Mr. John Gouriet and Sir Freddie Laker, and not to humble, law-abiding frogs. No-one, however lowly, was below the law. It was the court's duty to protect the weak against the strong. The decent member of the community – frog or human – who has fallen victim to injustice at the hands of dangerous, unchristian, wicked and irresponsible conglomerations of power, of which trade unions were, together with the Home Office, the main examples, must have the right to seek help from the courts, and the courts must offer a remedy. For them to do otherwise would be to betray those revered men who, so many centuries ago, gathered in that silent meadow at Runnymede. To those who said that frogs were beyond the law, the answer was that if frogs were beyond the law, then the rule of law existed no longer. He was in no doubt that that could not be so, and that frogs, for all legal purposes, were persons able to sue and be sued in the courts of Her Majesty.

It was true, Lord Denning said, that there were six decisions of the House of Lords which appeared to be dead against that proposition. He would pay little heed to them. They seemed to him to have been all wrongly decided, and it was settled law, at any rate in his court, that decisions of the House of Lords were not binding on the Court of Appeal. But even if he were obliged to follow precedent set by that House (and, it was fair to point out, some commentators took that view) he would have no difficulty in distinguishing the facts of the present case. None of the House of Lords decisions relied on by counsel for the union referred specifically to the legal status of frogs. Their Lordships had simply not turned their minds to Ranidae, and it could not be assumed that the principles which governed the legal positions of horses, prawns and budgerigars would necessarily apply to the very different circumstances of the appellant. He could not see how Mr. Grenouille's case could be said to be analagous to the facts in *Red Rum v Marks and Spencer Ltd* [1979] AC 165 where the court had refused to allow Mr. Rum, a horse, to sue for fees owed to him for opening the store's Hampstead branch.

Lord Denning said that he had been conducting some researches and had found a case in point, supporting his view. It was a decision by the deputy magistrate of East Tonga (South Sea Reports, 1931–1958, p. 645) prohibiting the destruction of 5,000 toads for use in a marriage ceremony. With the greatest respect to their noble Lordships, he found their reasoning less persuasive than that of the experienced Tongan magistrate.

LORD JUSTICE LAWTON said that although he had the greatest possible respect for the Master of the Rolls, he disagreed with everything he had said. Nevertheless he agreed that the appeal should be allowed. Trade unions ought to be restrained from actions which would result in anarchy and the inevitable breakdown of parliamentary democracy.

LORD JUSTICE EVELEIGH said that the law was under attack from a number of politically motivated groups.

Solicitors: Goodman Derrick & Co.; Kingsley Napley & Co.

7 Case-law

i *Reports in* The Times

As Master of the Rolls, I owe much to those who report our judgments. Whenever a case is of sufficient interest, a report of it will appear in *The Times* the next morning. *The Times* is the only newspaper which gives authentic reports of law cases – by which I mean reports which are prepared by barristers and will be accepted by the judges as correct. Almost every day counsel quotes to us from *The Times'* reports. Not only do the lawyers profit from them. But many laymen do. Geoffrey Fisher, when he was Archbishop of Canterbury, told me that he always read every day the law reports in *The Times*. These are followed in due course by the regular series of *Law Reports* – which are taken by lawyers in all the English-speaking world.

ii *Boswell on Johnson*

Since I have been Master of the Rolls, Miss Mavis Hill has been to me what James Boswell was to Samuel Johnson. If it were not for Boswell, Samuel Johnson would have been, by now, relegated to obscurity. To me Johnson's prose, his poetry and his philosophy, are turgid and unreadable. It was James Boswell who brought on record for us the humour, wit and sturdy common-sense which appear in Johnson's conversation – and a kindness of heart concealed under a gruff exterior. It was James Boswell who recorded for us Johnson's celebrated dictum:

Depend upon it, Sir, when a man knows he is to be hanged in a fortnight, it concentrates his mind wonderfully.

And his advice to the lawyer (as distinct from the judge):

A lawyer has no business with the justice or injustice of the cause which he undertakes, unless his client asks his opinion, and then he is bound to give it honestly. The justice or injustice of the cause is to be decided by the judge.

iii *Our indebtedness to reporters*

Few judges ever acknowledge their indebtedness to the law reporters. It is to them that we owe the whole of our great body of case-law – the greatest of all collections of law. Far outdoing the *Digests of Roman law* or the *Codes of Napoleon*. Not only do the law reporters correct our grammar and our spelling. They make the unintelligible sentence become intelligible. They summarise facts and law into short head-notes – so that many read no further.

iv The Year Books

Our case-law is built upon precedents: and our precedents are contained in the *Law Reports*. No other country in the world has anything like it. We have the *Year Books* covering the period from 1292 to 1534 – before the days of Caxton – in Norman-French. The writing is so small and the letters so odd that I cannot read it. Only a mediaeval scholar can do so. In the 16th century they were printed but even then almost unintelligible to us moderns. It is recorded that the great Sergeant Maynard

(1602–1690) 'had such a relish of the old *Year Books* that he carried one in his coach to divert him in travel and said he chose it before any comedy'. He was 86 when James II (who had sacked the judges) was expelled: and William Prince of Orange took his place. In 1689 William came to Westminster Hall and, addressing the lawyers, said:

'Mr. Sergeant, you must have survived all the men of law of your time'.

The Sergeant replied:

'Yes, and I would be likely to have outlived the law itself if Your Highness had not come over.'

v *Lord Coke's* Reports

After the *Year Books*, there was the great Lord Coke. His *Reports* cover 40 years of cases in the time of Elizabeth I and James I. They superseded the old *Year Books*. Even Francis Bacon acknowledged that

Had it not been for Sir Edward Coke's *Reports* ... the law by this time had been almost like a ship without ballast, for that the cases of modern experience are fled from those that are adjudged and ruled in former times.

The fame of his *Reports* moved John Milton to say in a sonnet to Coke's grandson Cyriack Skinner (which Francis Palgrave thought worth including in *The Golden Treasury*):

> Cyriack, whose grandsire, on the royal bench
> Of British Themis, with no mean applause
> Pronounced, and in his volumes taught, our laws,
> Which others at their bar so often wrench.

The Bar still do it. They 'wrench' our laws – to suit their arguments.

Coke's *Reports* were so highly esteemed that they were called *'The Reports'* – and a citation from them was the final word without need of any other authority. They are not much used nowadays because as Blackstone says, they are 'not a little infected with the pedantry and quaintness of the times he lived in'.[1]

vi *And others also ran*

After his time there were reporters of varying qualities. Some were bad, such as Espinasse. He was so deaf that it was said that

> He only heard half of what was said
> And reported the other half.

1 *Commentaries on the Laws of England*, Book I, page 72.

Others were good, such as John Campbell, afterwards Lord Campbell. As a young man he sat in Lord Ellenborough's Court and reported his correct decisions – with improvements – and discarded the incorrect ones. Such is the power of a law reporter to make or mar the reputation of a judge!

Afterwards there was Colin Blackburn. He was Eighth Wrangler but he had not much practice at the Bar. He was a reporter of the first quality but so little known that when he was appointed a judge, *The Times* headed its leading article, 'Who is Colin Blackburn?'

vii The Law Reports

The last stage started in 1865 with the setting up of a Council of Law Reporting and the employment of members of the Bar to report regularly the decisions of the Courts. They are – for some – the tools of trade. They are – for others – a haystack. The difficulty is now for anyone to find the needle in the haystack. One lawyer finds one needle. His opponent finds another. The judge spins a coin to decide between them.

viii *In person*

I have told you of my years as Master of the Rolls. I have heard many cases and delivered many judgments. Those of interest to the profession are recorded in the *Law Reports*. But those of no interest to them are not. On Monday mornings ordinary folk come to my Court – without lawyers – and make their applications. From time to time they conduct their own cases. Or rather, shall I say, I conduct them for them. No one should be at a disadvantage by not having a lawyer. I know that litigants in person can be very trying. They can be very wrong-headed. They will not take 'No' for an answer. They would exhaust the patience of Job. Often I tell them: 'I am afraid we cannot help you'. They go away disappointed. They may try my patience but, as I have already said, I try never to lose my temper.

Section Eight

Tom—in other roles

1 Away from the Courts

i *Not in an ivory tower*

Outside the Courts I have done many things. So many that I hardly know where to begin. Some of them connected with the law. Others well away from it. But all of them go to the making of me. It is sometimes thought that a judge should keep himself within an ivory tower away from all experience of life.

> *Et Vigny plus secret,*
> *Comme en sa tour d'ivoire, avant midi rentrait.*[1]
> (And Vigny more reserved,
> Returned ere noon, within his ivory tower).

But to my mind a judge is the better equipped to be a judge – if he has had first-hand experience of life itself. He is a better judge if he knows how meetings are conducted, how finance is negotiated, how goods are bought and sold, how people travel by bus, or underground, and the like. I do not suggest that he should be a poacher turned gamekeeper, or a criminal turned honest man. I do not think that a divorced person should be made a Divorce judge. A judge's experience should never be such as to expose him to reproach. Otherwise the litigant or the accused will point the finger of scorn at him just as the Hebrew did (who smote his fellow Hebrew). He said to Moses (who had smitten the Egyptian): 'Who made thee a prince and a judge over us?'[2] No man is perfect: but a good judge should so conduct himself as to deserve the confidence of all those who come before him. He should be *'sans peur et sans reproche'*.

ii *A formidable list*

My other roles make a formidable list. They are so many and so various. Some go with the very office of Master of the Rolls.

1 Charles-Augustin Sainte-Beuve, *Les Pensées d'Août, à M. Villemain.*
2 *Exodus* 2:14.

Such as the special relationship with the Law Society comprising the Solicitors of England and Wales. The close connection with the records of government departments as Chairman of the Advisory Council. The interest in private collections of papers as Chairman of the Royal Commission on Historical Manuscripts. All these have already been referred to in this book. Others flow from close connection with the City of London. Such as the coming of the Lord Mayor to the Courts; and my association with one of the great Livery Companies – the Drapers. Yet others flow from my interest in education. Such as President of Birkbeck College, London; and of Cumberland Lodge in Windsor Great Park. Still others from legal societies. Such as Chairman of the British Institute of International and Comparative Law; and of the Magistrates' Association. Others from local government. Such as President of the National Association of Parish Councils; and now of Hampshire.

Together with Joan, I have played a part in charities and other good causes. Such as President of the National Marriage Guidance Council; Chairman of the Cheshire Homes for the Sick; and a trustee of Outpost Emmaus (for young lads) which is inspired by our dear friend Josephina de Vasconcellos (Banner).

To add to all this, there are the visits overseas. During the vacations, Joan and I have visited most of the countries of the world. We have friends everywhere.

So many are our roles – and they stretch over so long a period – that I can in this section only make a selection. In the hope that those I omit will realise that it is only for want of time – and of space – that I cannot tell of them.

2 The Great Charter

i *750 years ago*

As Master of the Rolls I am Chairman of the Magna Carta Trust. This was formed by my predecessor Lord Evershed in 1957 – in company with that very influential and distinguished society of US lawyers – the American Bar Association. They put up a memorial on Runnymede. Every three years the Trust arranges for a commemorative service in one of the principal cities associated with Magna Carta. The 750th anniversary was in 1965. I wrote an article which was printed in *The Times*. It has not been published elsewhere. I repeat it here for you to read more of the most important constitutional document we have ever had.

ii *Fount of English Liberty*

Seven centuries and a half ago, in the month of June 1215, the meadow of Runnymede looked much as it does today. The season was early and the commoners of Egham had cut their hay. To this meadow came the King and the Barons. Their parleys culminated in the greatest constitutional document of all time. It is commonly called Magna Carta, or the Great Charter. The proceedings spread over the ten days from June 10 (the Wednesday after Whit Sunday) to June 19 (the Saturday before Trinity Sunday). This year, 750 years later, the occasion is being commemorated over the self-same ten days, June 10 to June 19, and the self-same festivals of the Church.

In 1215 the principal characters were the King, John Lackland; the Arch-bishop of Canterbury, Stephen Langton; the Barons, led by Robert fitz-Walter; with the significant backing of William Hardell, the Mayor of London. Their successors in office are coming to the commemoration this year. The Queen is coming to the City of London on the morning of Thursday, June 10. She will be met at Temple Bar by the Lord Mayor of London. She will go to a service at St. Paul's Cathedral at which will be present all the descendants of the Barons who can be mustered. The address will be given by the Archbishop of Canterbury. The Charter itself will be there, in the form in which it was confirmed by Parliament and became the law of the land.

iii *The King did not sign*

It is usual to picture King John signing Magna Carta, pen in hand. In point of fact he did not sign it at all. It is doubtful if he could even write. There is no evidence that he could. It is probable that he did not even affix his own seal. That would be done for him by his clerks in Chancery. The rest of the story can, however, be pieced together from the records that have survived.

On May 5, 1215, many of the Barons openly rebelled against the King. They renounced their fealty to him. When he read their demands, his retort was: 'Why do not the Barons, with these unjust exactions, ask my kingdom?' On May 12 he ordered their estates to be seized. But the Barons marched towards London which, on May 17, opened its gates to them. This was decisive. The Barons, with the support of London, had the whip-hand. John had to sue for peace. Emissaries went to and fro with safe conduct. At length a truce was arranged from June 10 to June 15. During those days meetings were to be held at Runnymede. The place suited both sides. It lay next the river between Windsor and Staines. The Barons made their base at Staines, where they were protected by the line of the river. The King had his base at his castle at Windsor. In between was the meadow of Runnymede. It was a good camping ground. There they negotiated, suspicious of each other, in reach of their arms.

iv *The Great Seal is affixed*

The first meeting at Runnymede was on June 10, 1215. There were present King John, the Archbishop Stephen Langton, and some baronial envoys. At this meeting the Barons presented their demands and the King submitted to them. According to the historians of today Heads of Agreement were drawn up then and there on June 10. The scribe headed them, *'Ista sunt Capitula que Barones petunt et dominus Rex concedit'* (Here are the demands which the Barons seek and the King concedes). The King caused his Great Seal to be affixed. The baronial envoys took the Heads of Agreement back to their colleagues to show that the King had agreed. Stephen Langton put a copy in his pocket whence it found its way into the archives of the Archbishops of Canterbury.

On June 15 the truce was due to expire. On that day the parties assembled in great numbers at Runnymede and agreement was reached on all points. The King and those present all solemnly swore to abide by the agreement. This day was regarded as so important that, when the Charter was afterwards drawn up, it was given the date, June 15. *'Testibus supradictis et multis aliis. Data per manum nostram in prato quod vocatur Ronimed inter Windlesoram et Stanes, quinto decimo die Junii, anno regni nostri decimo septimo'* (Witness the above-mentioned and many others. Given under our hand in the meadow which is called Runnymede between Windsor and Staines on the fifteenth day of June in the seventeenth year of our reign).

v *The Pope annuls it*

The parties continued to meet at Runnymede: for there was a good deal more to be done before peace could be secure. The Barons had to renew their homage to the King, for by that alone could the war be brought to an end. Twenty-five Barons (with whom was included the Mayor of London) were to be appointed to see the due fulfilment of the Charter. The formal document had to be engrossed and sealed. But by June 19 all was done and John authorised this writ to be issued: *'Sciatis quod firma pax facta est per Dei gratiam inter nos et barones nostros die Veneris proximo post festum Sancte Trinitatis apud Runemed', prope Stanes; ita quod eorum homagia eodem die ibidem cepimus'* (Let it be known that a firm peace has been made, by the Grace of God, between us and our barons on the Friday next after the feast of the Holy Trinity at Runnymede near Staines: on which account we received their homage on that day at that place). Several copies of the Charter were engrossed and sealed and sent round to important strongholds and to the cathedrals. Only four are in existence today. Two of them are in the British Museum, one of which is the copy delivered to the Barons of the Cinque Ports. The other two are in their original places of deposit, the Cathedral Chapters of Lincoln and Salisbury.

The peace did not last long. In a couple of months the parties were again at war. The King looked for aid to Rome. It came. By a Papal Bull dated August 24, 1215, Pope Innocent III purported to annul the Charter. He forbade the King to observe it and he also forbade the Barons to exact its performance. At a Lateran Council he excommunicated the English Barons who had persecuted John, he said, by endeavouring to take from him his kingdom. But John's death on October 12, 1216, at Newark Castle, altered everything. Early in the reign of the young King Henry III the Great Charter was confirmed by his regents. In the year 1225 it was re-issued by the King himself under the Great Seal. Magna Carta then took its final form, word for word, as it stands today as the earliest enactment on the Statute Rolls of England.

vi *The influence of the City*

The Great Charter dealt with grievances of the time in a practical way. It gave legal redress for the wrongs of a feudal age. But it was expressed in language which has had its impact on future generations. It put into words the spirit of individual liberty which has influenced our people ever since.

We can trace the hand of Stephen Langton in the first clause which guarantees the freedom of the English Church: *'In primis concessisse Deo et hac presenti carta nostra confirmasse, pro nobis et heredibus nostris in perpetuum, quod Anglicana ecclesia libera sit, et habeat jura sua integra, et libertates suas illesas'* (We have in the first place granted to God, and by this our present Charter confirmed for us and our heirs forever, That the English Church shall be free and enjoy her rights in their integrity and her liberties untouched).

We can trace the influence of the City of London in the thirteenth clause which ensures the liberties of the City: *'Et civitas Londoniarum habeat omnes antiquas libertates et liberas consuetudines suas, tam per terras quam per aquas'* (The City of London shall have all her ancient liberties and free customs, both by land and water).

vii *The guarantee of freedom*

We find set down in the thirty-ninth clause the guarantee of freedom under the law: *'Nullus liber homo capiatur, vel imprisonetur, aut disseisiatur, aut utlagetur, aut exuletur, aut aliquo modo destruatur, nec super eum ibimus, nec super eum mittemus, nisi per legale judicium parium suorum vel per legem terre'* (No free man shall be taken, imprisoned, disseized, outlawed, banished, or in any way destroyed, nor will we proceed against or prosecute him, except by the lawful judgment of his peers and by the law of the land).

Immediately following, in the fortieth clause, is the guarantee of the impartial administration of justice: *'Nulli vendemus, nulli negabimus aut differemus rectum aut justiciam'* (To no one will we sell, to no one will we deny or delay right or justice).

These words have re-echoed down the centuries. Their influence has been thus assessed by Trevelyan: 'The constant repetition of these brave words in centuries to come, by persons ignorant of the technical meaning they bore to the men who first wrote them down, helped powerfully to form the national character'. The greatest of those who gave currency to the words was Sir Edward Coke, Lord Chief Justice of England. Four hundred years after the meeting at Runnymede he forsook his crabbed learning, threw aside his lawyer's commentary and brought out this little gem: 'Upon this chapter, as out of a roote, many fruitfull branches of the Law of England have sprung....As the gold-finer will not out of the dust, threds, or shreds of gold, let passe the least crum, in respect of the excellency of the metall: so ought not the learned reader to let passe any syllable of this law, in respect of the excellency of the matter'.

viii *'The reeds at Runnymede'*

The constitutional significance of Magna Carta is immense. It was thus measured by Bryce: 'The Charter of 1215 was the starting point of the constitutional history of the English race, the first link in a long chain of constitutional instruments which have moulded men's minds and held to-gether free governments not only in England, but wherever the English race has gone and the English tongue is spoken'. When the colonists crossed the seas from England to countries the world over, they took with them the principles set down in the Great Charter. Those who went to Virginia took its very words. When they renounced their allegiance in 1776, they stated in the Declaration of Rights that 'no man be deprived of his liberty, except by the law of the land or the judgment of his peers'. Thence the provisions of the Charter found their place in the Constitution of the United States. There it is revered as much as here.

Rudyard Kipling has expressed the feeling we have for the Great Charter as the foundation of our liberties:

> 'And still, when mob or monarch lays
> Too rude a hand on English ways,
> A whisper wakes, the shudder plays
> Across the reeds at Runnymede'.

3 The City of London

i *Lord Mayor's Day*

Every year the new Lord Mayor comes to be presented to the Judges. In mediaeval times he went by river to Westminster Hall. Now he comes by road to the Law Courts in the Strand. He comes in his glorious old coach of 1756, weighing nearly 3 tons – with no springs, only leather straps. It is drawn by six shire horses. The Lord Mayor is preceded by a pageant of drums and bands – of sailors and soldiers and airmen – and of laughing tradesmen and craftsmen. The streets are packed with children and their parents. It is London's show day – the Lord Mayor's Show. It used to be on the 9th November in every year. Now it is on the second Saturday in November.

At the Law Courts the Lord Mayor goes first into the Court of the Lord Chief Justice and then comes to mine. We are dressed in our fine gold robes with full-bottomed wig – and on the top a tricorne hat. It is the only occasion on which we wear tricorne hats. They perch uneasily over our wigs – and have been known to topple off – to the amusement of those who are watching. The Aldermen enter the Court in their red robes, lined with fur. We all wait. Then the Usher calls out: 'The Right Honourable The Lord Mayor'. He enters. He doffs his hat three times to us and we doff ours in return. The Recorder makes a speech presenting him to us. I make a reply – always in a light-hearted vein – as it is a gladsome occasion. I take some time to prepare it – because the

Aldermen are mostly the same each year. It is difficult to find something fresh to say. I try to find something appropriate to the City. At the end the Recorder expresses the hope of the Lord Mayor that we will dine at Guildhall. I reply: 'Some of their Lordships will be pleased to attend'. It may be interesting if I tell you some of the historical episodes connected with the City, of which I have spoken – on some of the days.

ii *The trial of William Penn*

8 November 1963 : Sir James Harman

This year I would remind you of a most celebrated way in which the citizens of London maintained their freedom in the City. It is recorded on a memorial in the Great Hall of the Central Criminal Court. You will see it in the north-east corner:

> 'Near this Site WILLIAM PENN and WILLIAM MEAD were tried in 1670 for preaching to an unlawful assembly in Gracechurch Street. This tablet commemorates the courage and endurance of the Jury, Thos. Vere, Edward Bushell and ten others who refused to give a verdict against them, although locked up without food for two nights, and were fined for their final Verdict of Not Guilty. The case of these Jurymen was reviewed on a Writ of Habeas Corpus and Chief Justice Vaughan delivered the opinion of the Court which established "The Right of Juries" to give their Verdict according to their Convictions'.

All that William Penn and William Mead, who were Quakers, had done was to preach in Gracechurch Street in the City of London on a Sunday afternoon in 1670. They were charged with causing an unlawful and tumultuous assembly there. The Recorder directed the jury to find the Quakers guilty, but they refused. The jury said Penn was 'guilty of preaching in Gracechurch Street', but not of an unlawful assembly. The Recorder refused to accept this verdict. He threatened them with all sorts of pains and punishments. He kept them 'all night without meat, drink, fire or other accommodation: they had not so much as a chamber-pot, though desired'. They still refused to find the Quakers guilty of an unlawful assembly. He kept them another night, and still they refused. He then commanded each to answer to his name and give his verdict separately. Each gave his verdict 'Not Guilty'. For this the Recorder fined them 40 marks apiece and cast them in prison until it was paid. One of them, Edward Bushell, thereupon brought his habeas corpus before the Court of King's Bench. It was there held that no Judge had any right to imprison a juryman for finding against his direction in point of law; for the Judge could never direct what the law was without knowing the facts, and of the facts the jury were the sole judges. The jury were thereupon set free. By their conduct they had established the right of a jury to give a general verdict of 'Not Guilty'; and once this is given, the accused man is free. The prosecution cannot appeal from their verdict. It is useless for them to say it was wrong in law. No one in the land – be he statesman or judge – can go behind their decision of 'Not Guilty'....

233

It was the citizens of London who established that precedent which is recited all the world over as an example. They have done more than any other to establish this land of ours as the land of freedom.

William Penn afterwards went to America and founded Pennsylvania.

iii *The Great Fire of 1666*

12 November 1966 : Sir Robert Bellinger

It is our great pleasure to greet you today at the apex of your career, which reminds us not a little of your great predecessor, Sir Richard Whittington, save that you have never looked back and so never had occasion to 'turn again'. And in your splendid show you have demonstrated that the streets of London are paved with gold, albeit invisible. When in the measuring pans the balance of payments turns against us, it is then that the City of London, out of its hidden store, throws into the scales the unseen credits – the product of centuries of accumulated knowledge, experience and integrity – and tips the balance, be it ever so slightly, once more in our favour.

Over the years we are proud to recall the close association between the City of London and the Judges. Vivid pictures still remain with us. Let me go back three hundred years.

September 1666. London. The Great Fire raging through the wooden houses, recently ridden with plague. The citizens salvaging their goods. None insured. The King sends Samuel Pepys with a message to the Lord Mayor, telling him to pull down the houses to stop the spread of the fire. Samuel Pepys thus describes it: 'At last met my Lord Mayor in Canning Street, like a man spent, with a handkercher about his neck. To the King's message, he cried, like a fainting woman, "Lord, what can I do? I am spent. People will not obey me. I have been pulling down houses: but the fire overtakes us faster than we can do it. I've been up all night. I must go and refresh myself". Poor Lord Mayor. He was greatly blamed.

November 1666. This very month three hundred years ago. The Great Fire over. 'A sad night to see how the river looks', said Pepys. 'No house nor church near it, from London Bridge to the Temple where it stopped'. In their plight the Lord Mayor, Sheriffs and Aldermen went in their barges to Westminster Hall to Sir Matthew Hale and his fellow-Judges. They entreated them to get a Bill through Parliament so that the City of London should be rebuilt. The Judges did so. In two months they established the Fire Court. It sat in Cliffords Inn, hard by here. It decided all questions of rebuilding. The restoration of the City was mainly attributed to their care. It was reckoned one of the wonders of the age. The work done, the Court of Aldermen ordered that the portraits of the Judges should be painted by a skilful hand. The portrait of Sir Matthew Hale still hangs in Guildhall: and he received from the Lord Mayor, as his only further recompense, a silver snuff-box.

Over all the centuries the Lord Mayor, Sheriffs and Aldermen have seen well to the Government of this great City. Their principal duty is as magistrates. They are chosen and elected for their fitness for this office: and well and truly have they carried it out. Our old books tell us of one matter which is of consequence today. It is that 'The Aldermen are by their Charter Justices of the Peace within the City and Freedom thereof'. I trust that this ancient privilege will not be taken away.

iv *Samuel Pepys at the play*

11 November 1967 : Sir Gilbert Inglefield

We read, my Lord Mayor, that you hope to return Shakespeare to his own city. He has, we believe, never left it. He himself, you will remember, portrayed a scene like today's when Henry the Fifth came back from Agincourt:

> But now behold
> In the quick forge and working-house of thought
> How London doth pour out her citizens
> The Mayor and all his brethren – in best sort –
> Like to the Senators of the antique Rome.

But when you are building the new Barbican Theatre for his plays, we hope you will see that the audience are not discomfited as was Samuel Pepys, when three hundred years ago he went to see *Henry V*. He says in his Diary that it was well done by the players:

> In most excellent habit, all new vests, being put on for this night. But I sat so high and far off that I missed most of the words, and sat with a wind coming into my back and neck, which did much trouble me.

Samuel Pepys, like you my Lord Mayor, was a man of many parts. He loved music as you do. Listen to the effect of it on him, which we trust will have like effect in the new concert hall you are to build:

> But that which did please me beyond anything in the whole world was the wind-musique when the angel comes down; which is so sweet that it ravished me, and indeed, in a word, did wrap up my soul so that it made me really sick, just as I have been formerly when in love with my wife...and makes me resolve to practise wind-musique and to make my wife do the like.

We do not expect, my Lord Mayor, that either you or the Lady Mayoress will have much time to practise this year.

And with the music, my Lord Mayor, will you not set the people dancing? From the Mansion House, if we judge aught from today's picture in 'The Times':

> All night have the roses heard
> The flute, violin, bassoon;
> All night has the casement jessamine stirr'd
> To the dancers dancing in tune.

The art of painting too you will encourage: and show its value as was once done in these Courts when Whistler was under cross-examination by the Attorney-General one hundred years ago:

'The labour of two days, then, is that for which you ask, two hundred guineas?'

235

'No', said Whistler, 'I ask it for the knowledge of a lifetime'.

Last among the arts, the poetry of words. Most beautifully put by Wordsworth when he was on Westminster Bridge one early morning, looking down the river to the City, a bright morning like today:

> Earth has not anything to show more fair....
> This City now doth, like a garment, wear
> The beauty of the morning; silent, bare,
> Ships, towers, domes, theatres, and temples lie
> Open unto the fields, and to the sky;
> All bright and glittering in the smokeless air....
> Dear God! the very houses seem asleep;
> And all that mighty heart is lying still!

That mighty heart, my Lord Mayor, is in your keeping in this coming year. It beats and throbs with vigour still after centuries of endeavour. Under your leadership the citizens of London will still show the world how to work hard and to play hard, in a gay swinging London.

v *The Lord Mayor retreats out of the Temple*

14 November 1970 : Sir Peter Studd

You are the first printer we remember to have come here: though we know that 500 years ago the first English printer – William Caxton – came: a Mercer – apprenticed to the Lord Mayor of the time. But Caxton printed books. You print money – but not of the inflationary sort.

We know, of course, of your interest in students everywhere: but when you come to visit, as we hope you will, the Inns of Court, we would advise you to study the precedents, as lawyers do. Just over 300 years ago, the Lord Mayor was invited to the Temple. He was, like you, a Merchant Taylor. Samuel Pepys tells us what happened. The Lord Mayor, as a symbol of his authority, endeavoured to carry his sword up – but the students pulled it down and forced him to stay there all day. At length, says Pepys: 'My Lord Mayor did retreat out of the Temple by stealth with his sword up'. This made great heat among the students and the train-bands had to be called to disperse them.

My Lord Mayor, the sword which is borne before you – the sword which stands aloft above the Central Criminal Court – is the Sword of Justice. There is a Bill recently laid before Parliament which seeks to bring our Courts under an all-embracing department of Government. But I am glad to see in it a provision that the Lord Mayor and any Aldermen of the City shall be entitled to sit as Judges of the Court: and I trust, my Lord Mayor, that no one else will sit in your Chair, even though he be a Judge of the High Court. I am glad to see also that the standing and dignity of Mr. Recorder and of the Common Serjeant are to be maintained as hitherto.

I see you chose as your theme 'LONDON CALLING'. The call of London is irresistible. It has long been so. When James Boswell doubted whether he might get tired of London, Samuel Johnson replied:

Why, Sir, you find no man who is at all intellectual, who is ready to leave

London. No, Sir, when a man is tired of London, he is tired of life: for there is in London all that life can afford.

To which he added a piece of advice to those living out of London:

A country gentleman should bring his lady to visit London as soon as he can, that they may have agreeable topics of conversation when they are by themselves.

vi *The welcome on 8 November 1980*

I would like to give you in full the words by which we welcomed the present Lord Mayor, Sir Ronald Gardner-Thorpe. In the middle of it, my tricorne hat fell off.

In this Court we always try to keep the right balance – but today it is more than usually difficult. Our tricorne hats leave us poised with uncertainty between the dignified and the ludicuilt.

On this fine day we have watched with joy a pageant as glorious as any we have ever seen. You must have had a twinkle in your eye when you arranged for the leading cars – all six – to be Rolls – vintage – veterans – like me – still on the road.

Now let me tell you of my brethren who have been to greet you. On my right is Lord Justice Buckley, who presides over the Chancery work. If I were to cast him in a role – and, after all, I am the Master of the Rolls, I would cast him as W. S. Gilbert's Lord Chancellor (with a slight change of wording):

> The constitutional guardian he
> Of pretty rum things in Chancery…
> A pleasant occupation for
> A rather susceptible Lord Justice!

On my left is Lord Justice Brightman – whose name also begins with B – B for Buckley – B for Brightman. I feel a little disconcerted at having these two Bs (Bees) buzzing around my head – or in my bonnet. But, my Lord Mayor, they are not drones. They are worker bees. For this Court is a hive of industry – like your own Central Criminal Court – where the Recorder in your hive presides with such dignity – quite unlike the justice portrayed by Shakespeare:

> The sad-eyed justice, with his surly hum,
> Delivering o'er to executors pale
> The lazy yawning drone.

Turning from my brethren to you, my Lord Mayor, we have this in common: We are both from the County of Hampshire. Born there. At school there. When I was a boy, they used to say:

> Hampshire born and Hampshire bred
> Strong in the arm and weak in the head.

In this coming year you will need to be strong in the head as well – lest all the wine you are offered puts you off balance. At school at Southsea – you and the

Lady Mayoress – what recollections you must have of Spithead and all the ships, recalling the scene when Henry V set off:

> Behold the threaden sails,
> Borne with the invisible and creeping wind,
> Draw the huge bottoms through the furrow'd sea,
> Breasting the lofty surge.

Then the Buffs – and you their Colonel. You will know of Private Moyse – who, one hundred years ago, refused to kowtow to the Chinese – so they knocked him on the head and threw his body on a dunghill. The poet describes him:

> Last night, among his fellow roughs,
> He jested, quaff'd, and swore,
> A drunken private of the Buffs,
> Who never looked before.
> Today, beneath the foeman's frown,
> He stands in Elgin's place,
> Ambassador from Britain's crown,
> And type of all her race.

You, my Lord Mayor, in this coming year will be our Ambassador – proving to all the world the worth of this City and of England.

Stress too, as you have planned to do – the cause of youth – for that very poet goes on to say:

> Vain, mightiest fleets of iron framed;
> Vain, those all-shattering guns;
> Unless proud England keep, untamed,
> The strong heart of her sons.

How pleased we are, too, my Lord Mayor, that you should hope to create during this year an oecumenical atmosphere – drawing together the Churches in unison. For you I would especially recall Sir Thomas More – 'A Man for all Seasons' – who was Under-Sheriff of the City of London for nine years from 1510 to 1519 – and was paid £400 a year – a princely salary, far more comparatively than your Under-Sheriff is paid now. It was he who in 1535, when he was in the Tower of London awaiting execution, exclaimed almost as if looking forward:

I am nearer to heaven in this house than I am in my own home.

For myself, I recall the scene twenty years later in 1555, at the stake at Oxford, Hugh Latimer saying:

Be of good comfort Master Ridley, and play the man. We shall this day light such a candle by God's grace in England, as (I trust) shall never be put out.

Now, 400 years later, those rivalries are gone. The time has come when all must work together – to support true religion and virtue in this City and in our land.

One word more. We thank you greatly for your support of the magistrates. We know you will well fulfil your role as Chief Magistrate of this

City. You sit there – as we do – in a Court of three. But you have this advantage over us – you do not have to give reasons for your decisions. You follow the advice of Lord Mansfield:

> Give your decision, but never give your reasons; for your decision may well be right, but your reasons are almost certain to be wrong.

Under your leadership, my Lord Mayor, we are confident that this great City of London will maintain its high place.

You rightly remind us of the valuable roles still played by the Livery Companies in education and in training. They have over the centuries upheld the integrity and expertise of the City on which its high reputation depends. We wish you well.

4 Cumberland Lodge

i *A dynamic lady*

Inside Windsor Great Park there is Cumberland Lodge. A fine stately house some 250 years old, built for the first Duke of Cumberland. Set in the midst of the Park – with its great oak trees going back to the first Elizabeth. At the end of the Second World War King George VI and Queen Elizabeth decided to devote it to the good of students of the Commonwealth. Sir Walter Moberly – Christian and philosopher – was the first principal. A dynamic lady, Amy Buller, was the first warden. Early in the 1950s Walter Moberly invited me to become Chairman of the Trustees. That led to the students of the four Inns of Court spending weekends there – together with the benchers and barristers of the Inns. They have lectures, discussions, mock trials. They go for walks in the lovely Savill Gardens and Valley Gardens – and in the Great Park. They watch the polo. They visit Windsor Castle. On Sundays they may go to the small Royal Chapel near Royal Lodge, the home of Her Majesty The Queen Mother. Joan and I joined in everything. We found it most rewarding. So do the students. We have been photographed there – with the students – a thousand times. Latterly I became too busy to be Chairman of the Trustees. But I remain the Visitor.

ii *'This royal throne'*

All are grateful for and proud of the interest and support which Her Majesty The Queen Mother takes in Cumberland Lodge. She is the Royal Bencher of the Middle Temple and she comes when the Middle Temple are there. Her Royal Highness The Princess Margaret is the Royal Bencher of Lincoln's Inn. She comes when Lincoln's Inn are there. The Inns value greatly their Royal Benchers, reminding us that England is still:

> This royal throne of Kings, this scepter'd isle,
> This earth of majesty, ...
> This blessed plot, this earth, this realm, this England... .[1]

5 The Cheshire Homes

i *Gamma for jurisprudence*

As I have told you, Geoffrey Cheshire was one of the law dons at Oxford who in 1922 examined me at my *viva*. Years later he showed me my marks. Many Alphas in most subjects. But one Gamma. That was in jurisprudence. Gamma minus. Jurisprudence was too abstract a subject for my liking. All about ideologies, legal norms and basic norms, 'ought' and 'is', realism and behaviourism: and goodness knows what else. The jargon of the philosophers of law has always been beyond me. I like to get down to the practical problems which come up for decision. Contracts, torts, crimes, and the like. So did Geoffrey Cheshire. He became Vinerian Professor of Law at Oxford. He wrote the leading text-books on Contract (with Cecil Fifoot); on Real Property; and on Private International Law.

ii *Up in a balloon*

Geoffrey and his wife Primrose became our greatest friends. In a way he was a typical professor. Quiet, with a keen penetrating sense of humour. But with an extraordinary gift of clear exposition. It showed itself in his lectures and his books. And also in his conversation. You should have heard him tell of the occasion in the First War when he was in balloon service. Two of them went up to observe. The wind changed. They were carried by it from London – across the Midlands – to North Wales. Over hills. Through trees. At a great pace. They came down – at the edge of the Irish Sea. Geoffrey scrambled out. His companion was killed.

---

1 Shakespeare, *Richard II*, Act II, sc. 1.

iii *The pathfinder*

Such courage showed itself in their son, Leonard Cheshire. Twenty years old. The bomber-pilot. The pathfinder. Fearless. Over 100 raids to his credit. Dealing death and destruction to the enemy. Group Captain. Victoria Cross, DSO and two bars. Watching the atom bomb drop on Nagasaki. Awesome in the extreme. It seems to have changed his whole approach to life. He became a Roman Catholic. He had a faith which could remove mountains. And it did remove them – in founding and establishing the Cheshire Homes for the Sick.

iv *Dying of cancer*

After the war, in 1948 Leonard had an old house near Liss in Hampshire. He took in a sick old man who was dying of cancer. He nursed him himself. He decided to do the same for others in need. He determined to found Homes where sick persons could find a place of shelter physically and of encouragement spiritually. He got his father, Geoffrey, to help. And Geoffrey got me – and Joan.

v *The three trustees*

I will not go through the rest of the story. Suffice it to say that we three – the Professor (agnostic) – Leonard (Roman Catholic) – and I (Church of England) – formed an undenominational trust. I was Chairman. Much money was needed. Much was forthcoming. Due, I am sure, to the deep faith of Leonard – and his prayers.

The old house near Liss was pulled down and replaced by a fine new one called 'Le Court'. A lovely house was built opposite St. Michael's Mount in Cornwall, called 'St. Teresa's'. A stately house at Staunton Harold was taken over. And many others were started all over England. Overseas as well – in Nigeria – in India – and many other countries.

We had meetings of the trustees once a month. It meant my going up to London – all day Saturday.

vi *The inspired leader*

Joan and I visited the Homes and talked to the residents. We looked for new Homes and got them. Leonard Cheshire was the inspired leader in everything. Geoffrey and I trailed on behind. New trustees were appointed. The work expanded greatly. This

241

continued all the time from 1948 to 1962. Then I became Master of the Rolls. I had too much else to do. So I retired as Chairman. Geoffrey took it on for a couple of years – to be succeeded by his old pupil – our dear friend, and accomplished lawyer – Lord Edmund-Davies. There are now 72 Homes in the United Kingdom. And many overseas.

How did we find the time to do all this? As well as our judicial work? I can't think how. But we did.

6 Overseas

i *We are travellers*

Joan and I have been to the five continents and to most of the countries in them. I could write a book about our travels. I could tell you of all sorts of adventures. Waylaid by night on the way back from the Kruger National park. Up the Khyber pass to Afghanistan. An elephant charges at us in Central Africa. At peril in a tropical storm. In an observation car across Canada. A typhoon in Japan. Through the Andes by air. Forced return to Hong Kong. Safe conduct to Kota Bharu. Bugged in Warsaw. Taj Mahal by moonlight. Arsenic in New Zealand. And so on and so on. But this is not a travel book. So I will finish with points where we have helped to advance the law.

ii *The Nyali Bridge*

In Kenya there is a pontoon bridge. It connects the island of Mombasa with the mainland. Tolls are payable to cross it. Ought the British soldier to pay the toll or not? That was the question which prompted me to speak of how the common law should be applied in the territories overseas: it was in *Nyali Ltd v Attorney-General*.[1] In my judgment I said the Order in Council provided that

…the common law is to apply 'subject to such qualifications as local circum-stances render necessary'. This wise provision should, I think, be liberally construed. It is a recognition that the common law cannot be applied in a foreign land without considerable qualification. Just as with an English oak, so with the English common law. You cannot transplant it to the African continent and expect it to retain the tough character which it has in England. It will flourish indeed, but it needs careful tending. So with the common law. It has many principles of manifest justice and good sense which can be applied

1. [1956] 1 QB 1, 16.

with advantage to peoples of every race and colour all the world over: but it has also many refinements, subtleties and technicalities which are not suited to other folk. These off-shoots must be cut away. In these far-off lands the people must have a law which they understand and which they will respect. The common law cannot fulfil this role except with considerable qualifications. The task of making these qualifications is entrusted to the judges of these lands. It is a great task which calls for all their wisdom.

iii *The challenge ahead*

In 1959 I was appointed to be Chairman of a Conference on *The Future of Law in Africa*. In a foreword to the Record of the Conference I stated the way ahead:

This year 1960 is for Africa a year of decision. Indeed a year of destiny. One country after another is acquiring independence or looking forward to it. Statesmen and lawyers are meeting together to frame new constitutions. But the well-being of a people depends not only on the form of government they have, but also on the ordinary laws of the land. By ordinary laws, I mean such laws as the criminal law which says that a man must not kill, must not steal, and so on: the law of land-holding which says who is entitled to occupy a piece of land, and who is entitled to sell it or dispose of it; the law of marriage which says how many wives a man may have and prescribes the conditions of marriage; the law of succession which says what happens to a man's property when he dies: and so forth.

On all these matters the laws of Africa are rapidly changing. As people become better educated and are influenced by modern ideas the old laws are being developed so as to meet new conditions. At present the laws are a jumble of pieces, much like a jig-saw or a mosaic: customary law, Islamic law, English law, and so forth. All have to be fitted together to form a single whole, and developed so as to meet modern conditions. How is this best to be done?

Now is the time to think and do. Africa, like some great giant awaking out of centuries of slumber, stretches its limbs, stands up and looks at the dawn. It is the dawn of its own day it is looking at. We in the older civilisations have almost forgotten what that kind of dawn can be. We no longer expect to see the dew on the grass. But Africa sees it now and will soon be on the march. Can we not help it gird on its coat for the journey – it is a coat of many colours – the coat of African Law?

iv *A coat of many colours*

A year later we did help Africa to gird on its coat. I was appointed to be Chairman of a Committee on *Legal Education for Students from Africa*. Joan and I travelled in Africa for six weeks. We went to Nigeria, Kenya, Uganda, and to Tankanyika and Zanzibar (now Tanzania) – a most interesting and rewarding time. Afterwards the Committee had many sittings in London

243

and we made a Report.[1] It had much effect. These are one or two extracts from it:

The great need in most of the territories is to train up Africans to take their proper part in the administration of justice. One territory after another is gaining independence or looking forward to it. On the transfer of power the territories will not only need legislators and administrators. They will also need judges and lawyers. And these should, so far as possible, be fairly representative of the community as a whole.

Until very recently higher legal education has not been available at all in these countries. Students desiring to enter the profession have had to leave Africa and go to England or some other countries of the Commonwealth: for the simple reason that it is only by so doing that they become qualified to practise....

There is a real need in each territory for an institute where basic legal training can be given. Conditions vary from territory to territory so that there may be variations in detail, such as the length and content of the courses and so forth. But the overall pattern is clear, and that is that in every territory there should be an Institute for Legal Training, call it a law school, if you will, where basic legal training can be given.

I am glad to say that our recommendations were for the most part accepted.

v *Sugar in Fiji*

In 1969 there was anxiety in Fiji. There were differences between the millers of sugar (Australian) and the growers (mainly of Indian origin). Many feared that there might be trouble, and even violence, unless a new contract could be agreed. I was asked to arbitrate. Joan and I spent four weeks in Fiji – interrupted by one week in San Francisco. We were commuting across the Pacific. We much enjoyed our time in Fiji – with me sitting in Lautoka – and Joan painting the lovely scenery. One picture is of the quay with the boat alongside. My report shows me in my role of arbitrator. It was received well by the people of Fiji but not by the Australian millers, the Colonial Sugar Refining Company. They issued a broadside against it. This is how my report concludes:

I have settled the terms of such a contract as is, in my opinion, just and equitable and fair. It would be too much to hope that it will give pleasure to all parties. If I have erred at all, I think it will be because I have been too favourable to the growers. So much so that the millers may say that their share does not leave them enough to maintain and modernise the mills and transport system as they ought, or to give a reasonable return upon capital. But I would remind them that they have had a good innings over the last eight

1 Cmnd. 1255.

years. They have played a good innings – a first-rate innings – for the sugar industry in Fiji. But, so far as finance is concerned, they have done well. Events have tipped the scales in their favour. During all these years the costs of the millers have been covered, they have received considerable contributions to their capital improvements and, in addition, they have had good reward. They have not gone short. But the growers have. In settling the terms of the new contract, I have tried to restore the balance. I have tried to give the growers the reasonable remuneration which the Commonwealth Sugar Agreement intended that they should have. I hope this will not deter the millers from continuing their good work for Fiji and for the sugar industry in Fiji. The great public companies of today owe a duty, not only to their shareholders to make a profit, but to the people amongst whom they live and work, to do their best for them. Every responsible shareholder recognises this. If the sugar industry in Fiji is to prosper, the bitterness of the past must be removed. Growers and millers must work together in a spirit of mutual trust and goodwill – as befits partners. Let this new contract be the foundation on which to build.

The report led to the withdrawal of the Australian millers from Fiji and to the nationalisation of the industry. Fiji has since obtained independence. Throughout, the new contract has worked well. The good people of Fiji keep me well informed. They assure us of a good welcome if we ever have the chance to return.

vi *Ambassador-at-large*

These are only a few of the places to which we have been. Much more could I tell of our visits to the universities, the judges and the lawyers, of the United States of America, of Canada and Australia, of India and Pakistan, of New Zealand and Hong Kong, of Jamaica and Trinidad, of Brazil and Guyana, of the Argentine and Chile, of Malaysia and Singapore, of Malta and South Africa, of Belgium and the Netherlands, of Israel, and even of Poland. In all of these countries we have friends with whom we correspond. We have Christmas cards – hundreds of them – every year. Joan tries to answer them. Lord Elwyn-Jones, as Lord Chancellor, sometimes referred to me as an Ambassador-at-large but I hope of a truthful kind, not coming within Sir Henry Wotton's definition: 'An Ambassador is an honest man sent to lie abroad for the good of his country'.

Epilogue

Throughout this last year every item in the press about me has started off 'The 81-year-old' or 'The Octogenarian'. Very often an interviewer puts the question: 'When are you going to retire?' I reply: 'I am going to stay as long as I can do the job'. I repeat the outworn quip about having 'Every Christian virtue except resignation'.

I like to think that I can still do most things reasonably well. I can see to read without glasses – even the small numbers in the telephone directory. I can see long distances – even the time by Big Ben from Waterloo Bridge. My one drawback is walking. Arthritis in my right hip makes me limp. I use a stick. I am slow in getting along. I miss my country walks. But I still walk for my daily paper and to each of the Inns in turn for lunch. I still cut the lawn at home in Whitchurch. The handles of the mower take the weight off my hip.

And I have taken to the air. Last May on BBC radio there was the broadcast of 'Desert Island Discs'. Eight records such as I would choose to have with me if stranded on a desert island. Guided by Roy Plomley they played my favourites. I have no ear for classical music. I chose simple tunes such as please simple folk. The very English *Greensleeves* which Shakespeare commends in *The Merry Wives of Windsor*. *Colonel Bogey* which was played as we entrained for the front in 1918. *To be a pilgrim* which was written by John Bunyan in *The Pilgrim's Progress*. Then, *My soul hath seen the coming of the glory of the Lord* which was used at Norman's memorial service. Next, *Roses are blooming in Picardy* which again recalls the emotions of the First World War. *The King and I* sung by Valerie Hobson – from the show to which we took the children years ago. *The Judge's Song* in *Trial by Jury* with its line 'And a good Judge too'. As the last I chose *Land of Hope and Glory* from Elgar's *Pomp and Circumstance*

249

which reflects the very spirit of England. For a book, the Bible
was forbidden. So was Shakespeare. I chose Palgrave's *Golden
Treasury* which I think is the best of anthologies. For my luxury
on the desert island I chose tea with fresh milk – believing that
fresh milk would be almost unobtainable. I cannot stand
artificial milks. As an alternative, I chose rice pudding. The
newspapers once misquoted Joan as saying, 'He adores rice
pudding!'

After the broadcast I had scores of letters – especially from
people of my own generation – saying they had enjoyed it
greatly. I have a cassette of it – which I can play – on the recorder
which Joan has just given me for Christmas!

In November there was all the excitement of the Richard
Dimbleby Lecture. Mine was the ninth in the series which was
instituted to remember him. I knew Richard Dimbleby well. He
and I served together on the governing body of a college for
speech and drama. He was the most gifted commentator of his
time. In his choice of words, his powers of description – of
occasions great and small – his clear pronunciation and his ease
of manner. He was a great man.

The choice of subject was important. I drew on my
philosophy, spoken of earlier in this book – *Misuse of Power*. I did
it live in the lecture theatre of the Royal Society of Arts – in their
lovely Adam building in the Adelphi. The BBC arranged everything in superb fashion. A specially invited audience – politicians, judges and friends – but not many as it only holds 160.
The showing took nearly 50 minutes. It came on at the peak
hour – immediately after the 9 o'clock news. I was very nervous
– because of the unseen millions. It was hot under the lights. But
we managed. I tried to put in a few light touches: but, as often
happens, one thinks of the best afterwards – when it is too late. I
quoted Mr. Michael Foot as saying 'Denning is an ass'. But I
forgot to add the light touch: 'What fun it would be if we had
him up before us for contempt of court!' I concluded in this way:

There remains the most touchy question of all. May not the Judges themselves sometimes abuse or misuse their power? It is their duty to administer
and apply the law of the land. If they should divert it or depart from it – and
do so knowingly – they themselves would be guilty of a misuse of power. So
we come up against Juvenal's question, '*Sed quis custodiet ipsos custodes?*' (But
who is to guard the guards themselves?) That question was asked in the
United States at the time of President Roosevelt's New Deal in 1935. It may
be asked here again before long. In theory the Judges of the higher echelon are
appointed by Her Majesty The Queen: but in practice by the Prime Minister,
who in turn looks to the Lord Chancellor. Suppose a future Prime Minister

should seek to pack the Bench with Judges of his own extreme political colour. Would they be tools in his hand? To that I answer 'No'. Every Judge on his appointment discards all politics and all prejudices. You need have no fear. The Judges of England have always in the past – and always will – be vigilant in guarding our freedoms. Someone must be trusted. Let it be the Judges.

To return to whence I started: 'Power tends to corrupt'. This I have shown you. That is why in civilised society there should be a system of checks and balances – to restrain the abuse of power. It is why in times past we stood firm against the oppression of King John, and set store by our Magna Carta. It is why we rebelled against the divine right of kings and enacted our Bill of Rights. It is why we resist today the conferring of absolute power on any person or body, or any section of the community. There is, as far as I know, only one restraint on which we can rely. It is the restraint afforded by the law. We have to respect all that Parliament has done, and may do, in the granting of powers – and of rights and immunities – but let us build up a body of law to see that these powers are not misused or abused. Combined with upright Judges to enforce the law. It is a task which I commend to all. If we achieve it, we shall be able to say with Milton:

> Oh how comely it is and how reviving,
> To the spirits of just men long oppressed!
> When God into the hands of their deliverer
> Puts invincible might.... .

The might of the law itself.

In this very month of January 1981 I have helped with another broadcast programme. It is called 'With Great Pleasure', produced by Brian Patten. It was for me to choose my favourite pieces of prose and poetry. I made a varied selection. Gay and grave. Light and heavy. Alternating. We recorded the programme in Whitchurch in a hall packed to capacity with our friends. We had a delightful party for it. Paul Rogers, the actor, read magnificently. Jill Balcon, the actress, read beautifully. My part was to introduce the items. You may remember what Shakespeare said:

> As in a theatre, the eyes of men,
> After a well-grac'd actor leaves the stage,
> Are idly bent on him that enters next,
> Thinking his prattle to be tedious;
> Even so ...[1]
> They idly bent on me.

The programme gave great pleasure to our good Whitchurch folk.

Remembrance Day has come and gone once more. Our

---

1 *Richard II*, Act V, sc. 2.

church was full with the families of Whitchurch. On no other day is it so full. The old soldiers came wearing their medals of many campaigns. The standard-bearers marched with their colours up the nave. Scouts and Guides, Cubs and Brownies with their colours too. These were placed on the altar. I read the names. A long list of those killed in the First World War. All from our little town. Jack and Gordon among them. Most of them were boys with me. A shorter list of the Second World War but far too many. I wonder how long this Service of Remembrance will continue. I hope for ever. It is to those men that we owe our freedom.

The survivors of the two Wars get fewer each year. When I go out – on the occasions when decorations are worn – only one or two have the medals of the First World War. A good few more of the Second World War. But many have no war medals at all. For it is over 35 years now since that war ended. No one under 55 will have had experience of it. Yet if it comes to another war, they will, I am sure, do just as we did. Fight for freedom.

Reg and I, as I have told you, are the only ones now left of us five brothers. Marjorie is in a nursing home and approaching 90 years of age. Physically weak, but mentally good. She still plays bridge. Reg is 86 and still getting about. As alert in mind as ever. Also his wife Eileen at 80. I am 81 and Joan 80 but we still carry on – much the same as ever. We still walk up the 62 steps to our flat in Lincoln's Inn – without a pause. We take a delight in our grandchildren – who now number 11. We enjoy our home and garden – and spend as much time in it as we can afford – though we still have much to do. We are not yet retired.

Here I finish the Family Story. It is 'a round unvarnish'd tale'[1] – but it is a true tale. So far as it goes. I have left much unsaid. And you will know that a tale can mislead by what is left unsaid – as well as by what is said. Memory also may play us false: just as it does a witness who reconstructs an event as he wishes it had occurred – not as it did occur.

Much of it, too, is a self-portrait. As such, it must be suspect. If we could only see ourselves as others see us, it would, as Robert Burns said, 'frae mony a blunder free us, And foolish notion'.

A lot of it, too, is quotation from others – *Other Men's Flowers* as Lord Wavell put it – but overgrown, I fear, with docks and

---

1 Shakespeare, *Othello*, Act I, sc. 3.

thistles of my own. In the Preface I started off with Shake-speare's stage and pictured myself as playing the seven ages. Or, shall I say, six of them. Perhaps you will quote against me that other passage of his and say of me:

> A poor player,
> That struts and frets his hour upon the stage,
> And then is heard no more; it is a tale
> Told by an idiot, full of sound and fury,
> Signifying nothing.[1]

If such be your verdict, I pray you give me a light sentence: for please remember that it is the Family of whom I wished to tell you. Just to record what we have done in our time.

1 *Macbeth*, Act V, sc. 1.

Index

Notes: References in the index entries to 'D', except where preceded by a Christian name, are to Lord Denning.

To assist users of the index members of the Denning family are indexed under the names by which they are generally referred to in the text of the book. As a further aid relationships are indicated in parentheses following the name entry.

NON-FICTION

GENERAL
- [ ] Truly Murderous — John Dunning — 95p
- [ ] Shocktrauma — Jon Franklin & Alan Doelp — £1.25
- [ ] The War Machine — James Avery Joyce — £1.50
- [ ] The Fugu Plan — Tokayer & Swartz — £1.75

BIOGRAPHY/AUTOBIOGRAPHY
- [ ] Go-Boy — Roger Caron — £1.25
- [ ] The Queen Mother Herself — Helen Cathcart — £1.25
- [ ] Clues to the Unknown — Robert Cracknell — £1.50
- [ ] George Stephenson — Hunter Davies — £1.50
- [ ] The Borgias — Harry Edgington — £1.50
- [ ] The Admiral's Daughter — Victoria Fyodorova — £1.50
- [ ] Rachman — Shirley Green — £1.50
- [ ] 50 Years with Mountbatten — Charles Smith — £1.25
- [ ] Kiss — John Swenson — 95p

HEALTH/SELF-HELP
- [ ] The Hamlyn Family First Aid Book — Dr Robert Andrew — £1.50
- [ ] Girl! — Brandenburger & Curry — £1.25
- [ ] The Good Health Guide for Women — Cooke & Dworkin — £2.95
- [ ] The Babysitter Book — Curry & Cunningham — £1.25
- [ ] Pulling Your Own Strings — Dr Wayne W. Dyer — 95p
- [ ] The Pick of Woman's Own Diets — Jo Foley — 95p
- [ ] Woman X Two — Mary Kenny — £1.10
- [ ] Cystitis: A Complete Self-help Guide — Angela Kilmartin — £1.00
- [ ] Fit for Life — Donald Norfolk — £1.35
- [ ] The Stress Factor — Donald Norfolk — £1.25
- [ ] Fat is a Feminist Issue — Susie Orbach — 95p
- [ ] Living With Your New Baby — Rakowitz & Rubin — £1.50
- [ ] Related to Sex — Claire Rayner — £1.25
- [ ] The Working Woman's Body Book — Rowen with Winkler — 95p
- [ ] Natural Sex — Mary Shivanandan — £1.25
- [ ] Woman's Own Birth Control — Dr Michael Smith — £1.25
- [ ] Overcoming Depression — Dr Andrew Stanway — £1.50

POCKET HEALTH GUIDES
- [ ] Migraine — Dr Finlay Campbell — 65p
- [ ] Pre-menstrual Tension — June Clark — 65p
- [ ] Back Pain — Dr Paul Dudley — 65p
- [ ] Allergies — Robert Eagle — 65p
- [ ] Arthritis & Rheumatism — Dr Luke Fernandes — 65p
- [ ] Skin Troubles — Deanna Wilson — 65p

TRAVEL
- [ ] Guide to the Channel Islands — Anderson & Swinglehurst — 90p
- [ ] The Complete Traveller — Joan Bakewell — £1.95
- [ ] Time Out London Shopping Guide — Lindsey Bareham — £1.50
- [ ] A Walk Around the Lakes — Hunter Davies — £1.50
- [ ] England by Bus — Elizabeth Gundrey — £1.25
- [ ] Britain at Your Feet — Wickers & Pedersen — £1.75

HUMOUR
- [ ] Ireland Strikes Back! — Seamus B. Gorrah — 85p
- [ ] Pun Fun — Paul Jennings — 95p
- [ ] 1001 Logical Laws — John Peers — 95p
- [ ] The Devil's Bedside Book — Leonard Rossiter — 85p

REFERENCE

- ☐ The Sunday Times Guide to
  Movies on Television   Angela & Elkan Allan   £1.50
- ☐ The Cheiro Book of Fate and Fortune   £1.50
- ☐ Hunter Davies's Book of British Lists   £1.25
- ☐ What's Wrong With Your Pet?   Hugo Kerr   95p
- ☐ Caring for Cats and Kittens   John Montgomery   95p
- ☐ The Drinker's Companion   Derek Nimmo   £1.25
- ☐ The Complete Book of Cleaning   Barty Phillips   £1.50
- ☐ The Oscar Movies from A-Z   Roy Pickard   £1.25
- ☐ Collecting For Profit   Sam Richards   £1.25
- ☐ Questions of Motoring Law   John Spencer   £1.25
- ☐ Questions of Law   Bill Thomas   £1.25
- ☐ It's A Fact 1, 2, 3, 4   85p

GAMES AND PASTIMES

- ☐ The Hamlyn Book of Brainteasers
  and Mindbenders   Ben Hamilton   85p
- ☐ The Hamlyn Book of Crosswords 2   60p
- ☐ The Hamlyn Book of Crosswords 3   60p
- ☐ The Hamlyn Book of Wordways 1   75p
- ☐ The Hamlyn Family Quiz Book   85p

WAR

- ☐ World War 3   Edited by Shelford Bidwell   £1.50
- ☐ The Black Angels   Rupert Butler   £1.35
- ☐ Gestapo   Rupert Butler   £1.50
- ☐ Hand of Steel   Rupert Butler   £1.35
- ☐ The Flight of the Mew Gull   Alex Henshaw   £1.75
- ☐ Sigh for a Merlin   Alex Henshaw   £1.50
- ☐ Hitler's Secret Life   Glenn B. Infield   £1.25
- ☐ Wing Leader   'Johnnie' Johnson   £1.25

GARDENING/HOBBIES

- ☐ 'Jock' Davidson's House Plant Book   £1.25
- ☐ A Vegetable Plot for Two — or More   D. B. Clay Jones   £1.00
- ☐ Salads the Year Round   Joy Larkcom   £1.25
- ☐ Sunday Telegraph Patio Gardening   Robert Pearson   £1.00
- ☐ Greenhouse Gardening   Sue Phillips   £1.25

COOKERY

- ☐ A-Z of Health Foods   Carol Bowen   £1.50
- ☐ The Giant Sandwich Book   Carol Bowen   £1.50
- ☐ Vegetarian Cookbook   Dave Dutton   £1.50
- ☐ Know Your Onions   Kate Hastrop   95p
- ☐ Indian Cooking   Attia Hosain and Sita Pasricha   £1.50
- ☐ Home Preserving and Bottling   Gladys Mann   80p
- ☐ Home Baked Breads & Cakes   Mary Norwak   75p
- ☐ Easy Icing   Marguerite Patten   85p
- ☐ Wine Making At Home   Francis Pinnegar   80p
- ☐ Cooking for Christmas   Shona Crawford Poole   £1.25
- ☐ Mixer and Blender Cookbook   Myra Street   80p
- ☐ Pasta Cookbook   Myra Street   75p
- ☐ Diabetic Cookbook   Elisabeth Russell Taylor   £1.50
- ☐ The Hamlyn Pressure Cookbook   Jane Todd   85p

FICTION

SAPPHIRE ROMANCE LIBRARY

☐ Whisper to the Waves	Helen Beaumont	75p
☐ The Clouded Mirror	Judith Bordill	75p
☐ A Little Loving	Jill Eckersley	75p
☐ The Sweet Bells of Utrecht	Denise Emery	75p
☐ Before the Darkness Falls	Maynah Lewis	75p
☐ Love Has Two Faces	Maynah Lewis	75p
☐ Never Forget Me	Jill Sanderson	75p
☐ Suntrap	Gabrielle Shaw	75p
☐ Journey's End	Anna Stanton	75p
☐ Escape to Hong Kong	Jean Stewart	75p
☐ The Takamaka Tree	Alexandra Thomas	75p
☐ The Weeping Desert	Alexandra Thomas	75p

MOONSHADOW ROMANCE LIBRARY

☐ Jacob's Well	Aileen Armitage	£1.10
☐ The Dark Palazzo	Virginia Coffman	£1.10
☐ Night at Sea Abbey	Virginia Coffman	
☐ Skeleton Key	Daoma Winston	95p
☐ Yesterday's Child	Barbara Wood	£1.25

HAMLYN WHODUNNITS

☐ Some Die Eloquent	Catherine Aird	£1.25
☐ The Case of the Abominable Snowman	Nicholas Blake	£1.10
☐ The Worm of Death	Nicholas Blake	95p
☐ Thou Shell of Death	Nicholas Blake	£1.25
☐ Tour de Force	Christianna Brand	£1.10
☐ A Lonely Place to Die	Wessel Ebersohn	£1.10
☐ Gold From Gemini	Jonathan Gash	£1.10
☐ The Grail Tree	Jonathan Gash	£1.25
☐ The Judas Pair	Jonathan Gash	95p
☐ Blood and Judgment	Michael Gilbert	£1.10
☐ Close Quarters	Michael Gilbert	£1.10
☐ Hare Sitting Up	Michael Innes	£1.10
☐ Silence Observed	Michael Innes	£1.25
☐ The Weight of the Evidence	Michael Innes	£1.10
☐ There Came Both Mist and Snow	Michael Innes	95p
☐ The Howard Hughes Affair	Stuart Kaminsky	£1.10
☐ Inspector Ghote Draws a Line	H. R. F. Keating	£1.10
☐ Inspector Ghote Plays a Joker	H. R. F. Keating	£1.25
☐ The Murder of the Maharajah	H. R. F. Keating	£1.25
☐ The Perfect Murder	H. R. F. Keating	£1.10
☐ A Fine and Private Place	Ellery Queen	£1.25
☐ The French Powder Mystery	Ellery Queen	£1.25
☐ The Siamese Twin Mystery	Ellery Queen	95p
☐ The Spanish Cape Mystery	Ellery Queen	£1.10

FICTION

GENERAL

☐ **Chains**	Justin Adams	£1.25
☐ **Secrets**	F. Lee Bailey	£1.25
☐ **Skyship**	John Brosnan	£1.65
☐ **The Memoirs of Maria Brown**	John Cleland	£1.25
☐ **The Last Liberator**	John Clive	£1.25
☐ **A Forgotten Season**	Kathleen Conlon	£1.10
☐ **My Father's House**	Kathleen Conlon	£1.25
☐ **Wyndward Fury**	Norman Daniels	£1.50
☐ **Ladies in Waiting**	Gwen Davis	£1.50
☐ **The Money Wolves**	Paul Erikson	£1.50
☐ **Rich Little Poor Girl**	Terence Feely	£1.50
☐ **Fever Pitch**	Betty Ferm	£1.50
☐ **Abingdon's**	Michael French	£1.50
☐ **Rhythms**	Michael French	£1.50
☐ **A Sea Change**	Lois Gould	80p
☐ **Forced Feedings**	Maxine Herman	£1.50
☐ **Love Among the Mashed Potatoes**	Gregory Mcdonald	£1.10
☐ **Gossip**	Marc Olden	£1.25
☐ **The Red Raven**	Lilli Palmer	£1.25
☐ **Summer Lightning**	Judith Richards	£1.25
☐ **The Hamptons**	Charles Rigdon	£1.35
☐ **The Dream Makers**	John Sherlock	£1.50
☐ **The Affair of Nina B.**	Simmel	95p
☐ **The Berlin Connection**	Simmel	£1.50
☐ **The Cain Conspiracy**	Simmel	£1.20
☐ **Double Agent — Triple Cross**	Simmel	£1.35
☐ **Celestial Navigation**	Anne Tyler	£1.00
☐ **Earthly Possessions**	Anne Tyler	95p
☐ **Searching for Caleb**	Anne Tyler	£1.00

NAME ....

ADDRESS ....

....

Write to Hamlyn Paperbacks Cash Sales, PO Box 11, Falmouth, Cornwall TR10 9EN.

Please indicate order and enclose remittance to the value of the cover price plus:

U.K.: Please allow 45p for the first book plus 20p for the second book and 14p for each additional book ordered, to a maximum charge of £1.63.

B.F.P.O. & EIRE: Please allow 45p for the first book plus 20p for the second book and 14p per copy for the next 7 books, thereafter 8p per book.

OVERSEAS: Please allow 75p for the first book and 21p per copy for each additional book.

Whilst every effort is made to keep prices low it is sometimes necessary to increase cover prices and also postage and packing rates at short notice. Hamlyn Paperbacks reserve the right to show new retail prices on covers which may differ from those previously advertised in the text or elsewhere.